T0304350

LOVE the foods that love the planet

Recipes to Cool the Climate and Excite the Senses

Cathy Katin-Grazzini
photography by Giordano Katin-Grazzini

Health Communications, Inc.
Boca Raton, Florida
www.hcibooks.com

Climate footprint data for every recipe is provided with permission from CarbonCloud@carboncloud.com.

Library of Congress Cataloging-in-Publication Data
is available through the Library of Congress

Publisher: Health Communications, Inc.
     301 Crawford Boulevard, Suite 200
     Boca Raton, FL 33432-3762

Photography by Giordano Katin-Grazzini
Cover, interior design, and formatting by Larissa Hise Henoch

THE GREATEST THREAT
TO OUR PLANET IS THE BELIEF THAT
SOMEONE ELSE WILL SAVE IT.

ROBERT SWAN

CONTENTS

STARTERS AND SMALL BITES | 65

SOUPS, SALADS, AND SANDWICHES | 109

BREADS, CRACKERS, AND CRÊPES | 157

SIDES | 205

MAINS | 263

CELEBRATIONS | 317

SWEETS | 359

INTRODUCTION

My passion is food. Nothing excites me more than coming across a sumptuous new dish from a faraway land or playing with some heady new spice. I love exploring culinary traditions and how inventive home cooks make delicious use of simple, humble foods. But as heat waves, droughts, wildfires, and floods upend so many lives and livelihoods in every corner of the world, I wondered and worried about what could be done.

So, a few years back I embarked on a journey to learn more about how food and climate change interconnect. What I discovered, frankly, shocked me. Who knew that after energy, food systems generated the most greenhouse gas emissions (GHG) worldwide? Who knew that buying local or organic or free-range made hardly a blip on emissions while land use, farming practices, and food loss and waste were all-important? Who could have guessed that of all the things I could do to lower my individual climate footprint, changing what I put in my mouth was by far the most impactful move I could make?

If you have found your way to this cookbook, then climate is on your radar. You may wonder if one person can make any difference or be curious about what you can do to help. As it turns out, every person can . . . and by a lot!

—Cathy

THE CLIMATE: HOW BAD IS IT?

First, let's briefly recap where we are in the climate crisis in 2024. Despite progress on the energy front in recent years with large investments in renewables and the shift away from coal, global GHG emissions continue to rise, causing steep increases in land and ocean temperatures, evidenced even more dramatically in the Arctic. The last nine years, from 2015 through 2023, were the hottest years on record; 2024 may be hotter still, according to the World Meteorological Organization.

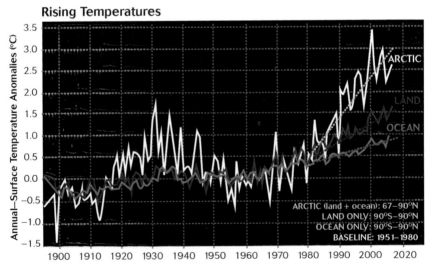

Rising Temperatures

Annual mean surface air temperature anomalies for the Arctic (67–90°N; white line), the global average over land areas (90°S–90°N; red line), and the global average over ocean areas (90°S–90°N; blue line) from 1900 to 2023. Linear trend lined (dotted) are also shown over the 1990 to 2023 period.

Source: "Rising Temperatures" by Zachary M. Labe, PhD (https://zacklabe.com/). Adapted from NOAA /ESRL Physical Sciences Division (https://www.esrl.noaa.gov/psd/cgi-bin/data/testdap/timeseries.pl) and used with permission by Zachary M. Labe under CC by 4.0 (https://creativecommons.org/licenses/by/4.0/).

Remember the UN Paris Climate Agreement of 2015? To thwart the most extreme and catastrophic effects of climate change on ecosystems and biodiversity—heat, drought, extreme weather—196 parties pledged to limit the rise in global temperatures to 1.5°C above preindustrial levels, each setting targets to reduce national emissions with the goal of reaching net zero by 2050. Scientists now think global warming may be accelerating faster than anyone thought possible.[1] According to James Hansen, the former NASA scientist who first sounded the alarm about climate change in the 1980s, "We are not moving into a 1.5C world, we are briefly passing through it in 2024. We will pass through the 2C (3.6F) world in the 2030s unless we take purposeful actions to affect the planet's energy balance."[2]

Tipping Points: How Worried Should We Be?

With the global temperature increase approaching 1.5°C, multiple climate "tipping points" are likely to be breached this decade through the 2030s. Tipping points are critical ecological thresholds—like the collapse of the ice sheets on Greenland and Antarctica, the weakening of the North Atlantic Ocean currents, the demise of the world's coral reefs, and the dieback of the Amazon rainforest. When tipping points are exceeded, climate systems shift from one state into a profoundly different state. Such major ecological shifts are believed to be unstoppable and irreversible, no matter what actions follow, even if global temperatures should drop. Grave concern over tipping points is why the goal of the Paris Climate Agreement is to limit warming to 1.5°C. Unfortunately, according to Professor Johan Rockström, director of the Potsdam Institute for Climate Impact Research, the world is currently on track to hit between 2 to 3°C in global warming.[3]

Scientists are concerned that hitting any tipping points is likely to aggravate climate change and might trigger additional tipping points, which would have even more dramatic, devastating effects.[4] For example, the collapse of the Greenland and Antarctic Sea ice sheets and thawing of the northern permafrost are expected to cause sea level rise reaching 2 meters by 2100. This will accelerate the melting of glaciers, exacerbate the slowing of ocean currents, and spur the release of greenhouse gases into the atmosphere. These changes pose substantial risks of flooding to numerous coastal and island communities. They are also likely to alter weather and rainfall patterns significantly, threatening agriculture, food and water supplies, and human health, security, and survival worldwide.

Time is of the essence to do what we can while we still can to lower GHG emissions that drive climate change and risk actuating any tipping points. There's a lot we can do.

Climate Tipping Elements and Their Sensitivity to Global Warming

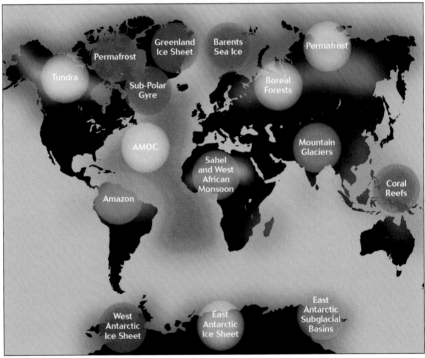

Tipping threshold   ● < 2°C   ● 2–4°C   ○ > 4°C

Tipping elements are categorized as cryosphere (blue), biosphere (green), or circulation (purple). Colors of labels denote temperature thresholds categorized into three levels of global warming above pre-industrial (key above), with darker red indicating lower temperature thresholds (greater urgency). Permafrost appears twice as some parts are prone to abrupt thaw (at lower temperatures) and some (organic-rich Yedoma) to self-propelling collapse (at higher temperatures).

Source: "Climate Tipping Elements and Their Sensitivity to Global Warming" by T. M. Lenton, J. F. Abrams, A. Bartsch, et al. Adapted from Nature Communications (https://doi.org/10.1038/s41467-023-44609-w) and used with permission under CC BY 4.0 (https://creativecommons.org/licenses/by/4.0/).

What's Food Got to Do with It?

As it turns out, food is a huge piece of the climate puzzle. Starting with land use and extending all the way to cooking and food waste, food systems account for a massive 17.9 billion metric tons or 34% of total GHG emissions worldwide.[5]

It also turns out that what we eat specifically matters a great deal. Counter to conventional wisdom (and to my surprise), transportation (in red in the following chart) barely makes a dent in GHG emissions, though eating local is an admirable way to support our local farmers. On the other hand, land use, like the destruction of forests and wetlands for farmland (in green); agriculture practices, including the use of fertilizers, pesticides, soil amendments, and irrigation (in tan); and the considerable loss and waste of food all along the supply chain (in light gray) are the key drivers of GHG emissions in the food system.

Which foods generate the most GHG emissions? They sit at the top of the chart on the following page—beef and other land and sea animals, chocolate and coffee, processed oils. By contrast, emissions from whole grains, legumes, vegetables, nuts, and fruits fall toward the bottom.

After fossil fuels, animal agriculture is the next largest contributor to global emissions, and a key driver as well of deforestation, water and air pollution, and the loss of biodiversity.[6]

Weaning the world off fossil fuels is beginning to happen. There are lots of exciting decarbonization projects, and many dedicated people are working their hardest to get us there. The demand for coal worldwide is dropping precipitously, which is certainly encouraging. At the same time, however, global oil demand is up, with production poised to hit record highs in 2024.[7] Today, the United States has the dubious distinction of leading the world in oil production, pumping out more oil than any other country in history.[8]

The demand for liquified natural gas (LNG) is rising too, with the United States exporting more LNG than any other nation.[9]

Food: Greenhouse Gas Emissions across the Supply Chain

Greenhouse gas emissions[1] are measured in kilograms of carbon dioxide-equivalents (CO_2eq)[2] per kilogram of food.

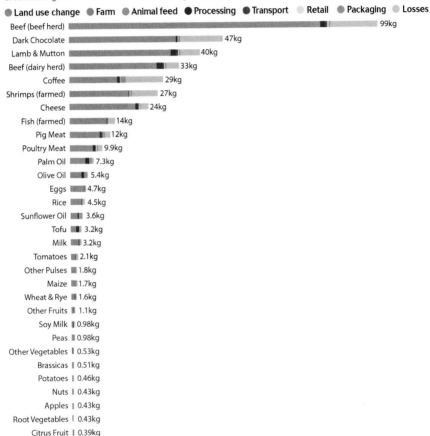

● Land use change ● Farm ● Animal feed ● Processing ● Transport ○ Retail ● Packaging ● Losses

Beef (beef herd)	99kg
Dark Chocolate	47kg
Lamb & Mutton	40kg
Beef (dairy herd)	33kg
Coffee	29kg
Shrimps (farmed)	27kg
Cheese	24kg
Fish (farmed)	14kg
Pig Meat	12kg
Poultry Meat	9.9kg
Palm Oil	7.3kg
Olive Oil	5.4kg
Eggs	4.7kg
Rice	4.5kg
Sunflower Oil	3.6kg
Tofu	3.2kg
Milk	3.2kg
Tomatoes	2.1kg
Other Pulses	1.8kg
Maize	1.7kg
Wheat & Rye	1.6kg
Other Fruits	1.1kg
Soy Milk	0.98kg
Peas	0.98kg
Other Vegetables	0.53kg
Brassicas	0.51kg
Potatoes	0.46kg
Nuts	0.43kg
Apples	0.43kg
Root Vegetables	0.43kg
Citrus Fruit	0.39kg

1. Greenhouse gas emissions: A greenhouse gas (GHG) Is a gas that causes the atmosphere to warm by absorbing and emitting radiant energy. Greenhouse gases absorb radiation that is radiated by Earth, preventing this heat from escaping to space. Carbon dioxide (CO_2) is the most well-known greenhouse gas, but there are others including methane, nitrous oxide, and in fact, water vapor. Human-made emissions of greenhouse gases from fossil fuels, industry, and agriculture are the leading cause of global climate change. Greenhouse gas emissions measures the total amount of all greenhouse gases that are emitted. These are often qualified in carbon dioxide equivalents (CO_2eq), which take account of the amount of warming that each molecule of different gases creates.

2. Carbon dioxide equivalents (CO_2eq): Carbon dioxide is the most important of greenhouse gas, but not the only one. To capture all greenhouse gas emissions, researchers express them in "carbon dioxide equivalents" (CO_2eq). This takes all greenhouse gases into account, not just CO_2. To express all greenhouse gases in carbon dioxide equivalents (CO_2eq), each one is weighted by its global warming potential (GWP) value. GWP measures the amount of warming a gas creates compared to CO_2. CO_2. is given a GWP value of one. If a gas had a GWP of 10 then one kilogram of that gas would generate ten times the warming effect as one kilogram of CO_2. Carbon dioxide equivalents are calculated for each gas by multiplying the mass of emissions of a specific greenhouse gas by its GWP factor. This warming can be stated over different timescales. To calculate CO_2eq over 100 years, we'd multiply each gas by its GWP over a 100-year timescale (GWP100). Total greenhouse gas emissions—measured in CO_2eq—are then calculated by summing each gas' CO_2eq value.

Source: "Food: greenhouse gas emissions across the supply chain" by Joseph Poore and Thomas Nemecek. Adapted from Our World in Data (https://ourworldindata.org/grapher/food-emissions-supply-chain) and used with permission under CC by 4.0 (https://creativecommons.org/licenses/by/4.0/).

Despite their ambitions, the many worthy green investments and advances in new technologies are not enough to outpace fossil fuel growth, let alone thwart the rapid rise in global temperature.

Why Individual Involvement Matters

While one hundred corporations account for 71% of GHG emissions in fossil fuel and cement production, these sectors only produce 12% of direct emissions; the remaining 88% come from our consumption of products.[10] What we do as individuals matters. Each one of us influences our friends, families, and communities. Ultimately, our collective consumer demand determines what producers produce.

In our race against climate change we are falling behind, and we are running out of time. Given all that is at stake, we can't afford to look only to technological advances and our political leadership to save us. Pressuring leaders to make wise climate-supportive choices is vitally important but not sufficient. Therefore, we must look to our own behaviors too, and each of us must do our bit. In fact, without the involvement of every one of us, we are unlikely to succeed.

Lightening Our Climate Footprints

In a 2023 webinar, Dr. Joseph Poore, director of the University of Oxford Martin Program on Sustainability and one of the world's leading environmental scientists, outlined the ways we each can lower our personal climate footprints. As you see as follows, he found that swapping plants for animals in our diets is the most powerful way to lower GHG emissions as individuals, though of course the other ways to lower our emissions help too. Dr. Poore's research found if we embraced eating plants to the max, that is, if we went fully plant-based, our personal climate footprint would contract by a whopping 73%.[11]

Greenhouse Gas Emissions Saved Per Person (tons CO₂eq, Europe)

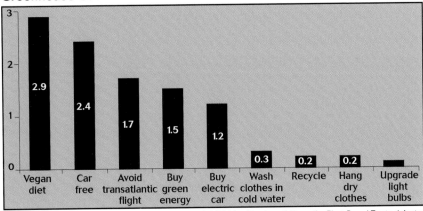

Source: "Reducing the Environmental Impact from Food: A Webinar" by Joseph Poore for Plant Based Treaty. Adapted and used with permission by Joseph Poore.

Today, half of the world's habitable land is used for agriculture. Over three-quarters of those agricultural lands are used to raise and feed livestock. Animal agriculture is a very inefficient use of our resources, however: Meat and dairy provide just 18% of global calories (82% come from plants) and only 37% of global protein supply (63% come from plants).[12]

Animal agriculture accelerates the environmental degradation of our air and waterways. It is responsible for the destruction of wildlife habitats and spurs biodiversity loss. As regards human health, animal agriculture is also problematic: It is the cause of infectious zoonotic diseases,[13] like MERS, SARS, and COVID-19. Food-producing animals are the major source of food-borne pathogens, like E. coli, listeria, campylobacter, salmonella.[14] Consumption of animals significantly increases our risks of developing "chronic diseases, like cardiovascular disease, cancer, diabetes, obesity, and other disorders."[15]

Let's think big for a moment: If everyone were to stop eating animal foods, how big a difference could that make? Seventy-five percent of current agricultural land would become available to help restore forests, grasslands, and natural habitats. Rewilding these landscapes would sequester carbon. Both GHG emissions and eutrophication (ocean hypoxia from fertilizer runoff that leads to ocean dead zones) would drop by 50%.[16] In fact, phasing out animal agriculture worldwide in favor of plant nutrition could halt the rise in GHG emissions for thirty years, which would give the world time it so desperately needs, especially now, to complete its shift away from fossil fuels and reach net zero or even negative emissions.[17]

Don't Worry

If you find yourself overwhelmed by the enormity and gravity of climate change and the catastrophic havoc it portends, you are not alone.[18] According to the World Health Organization, 3.6 billion of us are already "highly susceptible" to the ravages of the climate. From 2030 to 2050 climate change is projected to take the lives of 250,000 more people every single year, directly or indirectly.[19] That realization should frighten all of us. But take heart: The most effective antidote to climate anxiety is action. Changing what you eat and how you cook are the most personally impactful ways to help, as previously noted. Realizing that you are not alone and joining with others to work toward shared goals is another powerful remedy for anxiety. See pages 404–5 for resources, ideas, and groups to connect you with others, to amplify your voice, and to make a material difference, on local, national, and global levels. Together, we will succeed!

To quote botanist Robin Wall Kimmerer, "So much of what we think about in environmentalism is finger-wagging and gloom-and-doom, . . . [but] where people are taking things into their hands, they're joyful. It's . . . good to feel your own agency."[20]

Eating to Cool Our Feverish Planet

To sum things up, as the writer Jonathan Safar Foer remarked, "Changing how we eat will not be enough, on its own, to save the planet, but we cannot save the planet without changing how we eat."[21] *Love the Foods That Love the Planet* gives you a rich road map of exciting low-emissions dishes from all over the world. They are sourced and prepared in the healthiest of ways, and because they are so high in fiber and low in fat, you may find you drop a few pounds even with second helpings. Your taste buds will thank you, as these dishes are richly flavored to excite and stimulate all the senses. Start with a dish or two for the first week and steadily add more. Have fun finding greener versions of old favorites and new ones that delight you.

SHOPPING AND STOCKING

ove the Foods That Love the Planet will comfort you with climate-friendly, healthy remakes of traditional American classics: You'll find burgers, chilies, tostadas, Sloppy Joes, omelets, cornbread, and pastries. It also will transport you to faraway lands, from Peru to Persia, Italy to India, West Bengal to West Africa—and beyond—with dishes that are distinctive, satisfying, and very kind to the planet.

We'll be eating low on the food chain with an emphasis on whole, unprocessed ingredients. I will show you how to build robust flavor and excitement in your cooking without relying on oils, refined sugars, or salt. We will take full advantage of herbs, spices, mushrooms, and chilies. They may be tiny, and we may use them judiciously, but these potent flavor boosters are also nutritional powerhouses. You will find that eating for the planet also confers multiple health benefits because plant foods are so nutrient rich and calorie light.[22–28]

While most of the ingredients in this cookbook will be very familiar, some of them may be used in surprising ways. You may learn some new cooking techniques. You may discover ingredients you've never worked with before. Don't be daunted! Just think of it as adding colors to your culinary palette. Have fun and see it as going on adventures from the comfort of your own kitchen. It will feel good to stretch your culinary wings.

Sourcing Ingredients

If you live in a large metropolis, you will be blessed with many small mom-and-pop markets featuring foods from their country or region of origin. In smaller cities and suburban towns, depending on which immigrant communities reside nearby, you may also find ethnic markets where you will find native foods, often sold in bulk and at affordable prices. It is educational to explore these venues and be rewarded by their rich offerings.

For example, in Latino groceries you are likely to find a wide variety of dried and canned beans, dried and fresh chilies, hominy, cornmeal, masa harina, fresh produce, dried herbs, and an amazing diversity of frozen vegetables.

South Asian markets are packed with many types of dried peas, lentils, and beans, fresh and frozen produce, whole grains, fresh herbs and chilies, nuts, lotus seeds, and huge array of whole spices. In the spring, some will sell you fresh curry tree (*B. koenigii*) seedlings, if you inquire, to grow at home and reward you with a continual source of aromatic curry leaves, a mainstay in South Indian dishes. In local markets the cinnamon sold is cheaper cassia, not true (Ceylon) cinnamon, which has a beautiful floral character. Find it online.

If you are near Middle Eastern groceries, you may find other dried legumes, like fava beans, Mediterranean chickpeas, and lupine beans, dried herbs, culinary flowers and spices, rose and orange blossom water, pomegranate and date molasses, dried fruits, and varieties of olives from the Levant in barrels. Lightly fermented dried Persian limes can flavor a stew or soup and then be discarded or be ground into a seasoning powder.

If you are lucky enough to live in a major metro area with an H-Mart, have fun exploring its extraordinarily large selections, including fruits, vegetables, fresh and dried mushrooms, sea vegetables, tofu varieties and miso pastes, fresh and dried soba noodles, Korean *dangmyeon* (sweet potato starch) noodles, varieties of rice and dried beans, and condiments from throughout the

Far East and even from Latin America and the Caribbean (at least in my area). I have found fresh chickpeas and fresh fava beans, when in season.

Japanese groceries tend to be more expensive, but they offer additional products you won't find elsewhere, like the delightful whole spice blend *shichimi togarashi*, natto, fresh yuba and *okara*, wonderful tea selections, small batch koji-fermented tamari, and other koji-fermented condiments. East Asian markets, however, only sell Shaoxing rice wine that is salted. Instead, order drinking-quality Shaoxing wine online or at a liquor store.

Increasingly, national supermarkets stock more produce varieties than ever to cater to their local clientele. Don't overlook the ethnic aisles either for legumes, whole grains, flax seeds, polenta, cornmeal, masa, seeds, spices, herbs, and other minimally processed ingredients.

Local natural food stores are another option for buying whole grains and legumes in bulk or in small packages. Some shops offer discounts if you order quantities of 20 to 50 pounds, saving you from having to pay considerable transportation costs for large bulk online deliveries. Plant-based milks, tofu, sea vegetables, miso pastes, nuts, and seeds are also found in these shops, and usually a small selection of fresh local and regional produce.

Don't overlook local farms in your vicinity for fresh locally grown and seasonal produce, mushrooms, and fruits. Many have vegetable stands or participate in weekly farmers markets. Some offer community supported agriculture arrangements for pickup or delivery. By getting to know your local growers, you can learn of their growing practices and spraying policies for different crops.

If you live near farming communities, you might be able to pick up bulk quantities of whole grains, flours, and dried beans directly from farms or farmer collectives, which would be the most affordable option. If you reside elsewhere, consider Azure Standard, an online cooperative for bulk organic dry goods and other household items, delivered to specific local zones across the United States monthly.

Finally, even if you do not live near ethnic markets or farms, you can still find just about every dried food and spice online.

Stocking Up

To keep emissions low and to maximize flavor and nutritional potency:

- Don't forget to stock your freezer with frozen fruits and vegetables. They generally are picked and frozen at peak ripeness for optimal flavor and nutritional potency. Moreover, frozen foods often have a lower climate footprint than fresh foods because they reduce loss and waste that can accrue along the supply chain.

- Buy whole grains, dried beans, spices, dried chilies, and dried mushrooms whole and in bulk. Stored in tightly lidded containers in a dark, cool, dry cupboard, they will last for years without spoiling or losing nutritional potency.

- With a grain mill you can mill small quantities at a time of whole grains, legumes, and dent and flint corn (not popcorn) into flours, polenta, and cornmeal.

- With an inexpensive coffee or spice grinder you can pulverize spices, dried herbs, dried chilies, dried mushrooms, even dehydrated fruits, vegetables, and miso pastes, into potent seasoning powders.

- You would not believe the difference in flavor of freshly milled flours, cornmeal, and seasonings compared to those that have languished in warehouses and on grocery shelves for who knows how long. Moreover, buying whole products instead of pre-ground, you can avoid any adulterated products, which dilute a spice with cheap and sometimes harmful additives.[29]

- Save a bundle. The markup on tiny jars of processed spices and spice blends can be considerable. In medieval times the price of spices was driven by how far they traveled, and later by trading monopolies with prices padded by layers of middlemen. Today, the main reasons spices are so expensive are their high production costs and the destruction of crops from extreme weather. Some spices, like saffron and vanilla, require manual labor to pollinate and harvest, making them particularly expensive. If you buy jars of ground spices at boutique venues, you are also paying for fancy packaging, marketing, and shelf space.[30]

Purchasing whole spices in bulk at ethnic local groceries is fine for common spices with low climate footprints. For others that are often grown unsustainably and unethically, look online to purchase directly from single-origin, sustainable growers to eliminate costs of middlemen. Developing direct ties with growers helps ensure higher product quality and encourages sustainable farming, fair-trade, and ethical (child-free) labor practices.[31]

TOOLS OF THE TRADE AND COOKING HINTS

A Good Knife and a Board

There are some tools that any well-equipped kitchen should have, starting with a good chef knife that fits your grip, and sharpening whetstones to maintain its razor edge. Most kitchen mishaps happen when a knife is blunt, so a sharp knife is your best defense. A large wooden or bamboo cutting board is best to preserve a knife's edge, and preferable to plastic from an environmental perspective.

Also consider an Italian mezzaluna, a curved, two-handled blade specifically designed to quickly and precisely mince herbs, garlic, ginger, and other vegetables with great control and no risk of crushing or mashing delicate ingredients or fingers.

Cookware

There are a vast number of cookware options available at every price point. As a rule, titanium is the highest quality. It tolerates very high temperatures, is the most durable, and is nonreactive to acidic foods. However, it is also very costly. Borosilicate glass cookware matches titanium in safety and is less expensive. Stovetop borosilicate pots are only available in smaller sizes, however. They can be used on gas and electric cooktops but not induction.

Pyrex, made today of soda-lime glass, is more subject to thermal shock than borosilicate glass, though both are vulnerable to breakage if dropped or hit.

Multi-clad stainless steel cookware is a very safe, economical choice. Stainless steel is durable, cooks and bakes evenly, and comes in a range of prices. You can find excellent professional, high-quality stainless steel cookware and bakeware if you keep an eye out for those on sale. Avoid aluminum cookware, bakeware, and foils, however, as data suggests it may be linked to neurodegenerative diseases like Parkinson's disease, Alzheimer's disease, and breast cancer.[32]

Cast-iron cookware is very durable. Uncoated is more affordable but must be seasoned with oil regularly to avoid rusting. Acidic foods and frying will leach heme iron, a risk for hemochromatosis patients, and for most people seeking to avoid high iron blood levels. High heme iron is associated with increased risks for cancers, diabetes, and heart disease.[33] Enameled cast iron is a safe option but may be pricey. Older red and orange enamel cookware may contain lead, a particular concern since over time, and with wear, the enameled interior can chip and flake into foods.

Nonstick Cookware

Safer alternatives to Teflon are available with titanium, diamond, ceramic, and an array of new non-poly-fluoroalkyl chemical (PFA, PFOA, PTFE) surfaces. PFAs are "forever chemicals" that don't degrade over time in the environment or in our bodies and are linked to cancers, thyroid disease, high cholesterol, lower vaccine responses in children, and more.[34] According to *Consumer Reports*, not all nonstick manufacturers' nontoxic claims hold up on testing,[35] so consumer caution is warranted. Moreover, all nonstick cookware, so far, is more vulnerable and shorter lived than standard cookware. Some good rules are:

- Use nonstick pans lightly, reserving them for oil-free pancakes, crêpes, and similar griddle cakes and flatbreads.
- When cooking oil-free on a nonstick pan, the pan must be heated adequately before adding batters to prevent sticking. However, do not exceed the manufacturer's temperature limits for their cookware.

Overheating risks damaging the pan. Invest in a small infrared laser thermometer gun to stay below your limits for stovetop and oven cooking.

- Avoid metal utensils that can scratch their surfaces.
- Store them carefully and without placing other objects on top of them.
- Replace them if their surfaces develop deep scratches, signs of wear, or if food begins to adhere to their surfaces when used properly.

Small Kitchen Hand Tools

A good vegetable peeler, a citrus zester, and a manual citrus juicer all come in handy. A simple manual pepper mill is a must, and if you love nutmeg as much as I do, consider a nutmeg rasp, grater, or mill.

For baking bread you will need a digital scale and spray bottle to spritz water to ensure a crispy dough crust. A large baking stone isn't essential, but for pizzas, flatbreads, and crackers, it creates a crispier crust.

A mandolin slices raw and lightly cooked vegetables and fruits precisely and uniformly in no time at all. It's a great asset when making *Tian* (see page 258), and slicing fruit for Pretty Apple Packets (see page 397).

Small Appliances

Stone mortar and pestles will crush seeds and nuts with some persistence. Personally, I prefer the precision and ease of a small, inexpensive coffee grinder to grind spices, dried chilies, dried mushrooms, and small quantities of dehydrated fruits or vegetables to make seasoning powders, and to purée fresh garlic, ginger, and green chilies into pastes.

I strongly encourage you to make your own seasonings from whole spices. It takes only minutes. The intense aromas and flavors from freshly ground spices will elevate your cooking to a higher level.

Mexicans swear by their larger igneous molcajetes to grind spices and vegetables into moles, guacamole, and salsas. For such tasks and to make sauces, lightly chunky or silky smooth, and dried fruit pastes, you can't beat high-speed blenders. They do an expeditious job of chopping to puréeing ingredients but only if there is sufficient liquid in the mixture. When blending hot soups and sauces, it is safer and more convenient to use a simple immersion blender in the pot.

Food processors come with many attachments to break down produce in myriad ways very efficiently. You can shred vegetables for slaws, julienne them for salads, and mince them for sauces like *Sugo Senza Carne* (see page 60), and chunky sauces like Salsa Verde (see page 58). Food processors efficiently blend thicker mixtures like Three Bean Party Dips (see page 99) and are a huge time-saver when whipping up Beety Burgers (see page 270). I also use food processors to mix unleavened doughs for layered tortes like Eggplant-Zucchini Torte (see page 335). In just a minute or two a food processor can mix, knead, and gather these doughs into a tidy, supple ball, ready for rolling out.

A pressure cooker will reduce cooking times for whole grains, legumes, and vegetables too, while preserving their nutrients very well. Many prefer an instant pot, which combines the functions of a pressure cooker and slow cooker.

If you decide you would like to make homemade soy yogurt, you can incubate it in a yogurt maker, an instant pot, an oven if it has a very low bread-proofing temperature setting, or a warming drawer that can maintain a steady temperature between 90 and 110°F.

A dehydrator is a convection oven that works at low temperatures only. I often incubate soy yogurt in a dehydrator, which I also use to dry miso paste into powder for *Parmigiano Perfetto* (see page 56) and citrus slices for Citrus Powders (see page 41). You can dehydrate many fruits, vegetables, even mushrooms to make snackable dried fruit, fruit leathers, vegetable jerkies, and dried foods that can be ground as needed into nutritious and brightly colored seasoning powders.

If you have a good convection oven, particularly one with a double fan, you may not need a tabletop air fryer. With the traits of a dehydrator at high heat, air fryers give potatoes and battered vegetables a delightful crispy crunchiness.

Lastly, for those of you who love to bake, consider a manual or electric grain mill. As mentioned above, a grain mill will enable you to create flours out of whole grains and legumes, make polenta out of flint corn, and corn-meal and grits out of dent corn. For rustic breads you can choose coarser grinds, and finer settings to make flour for sweets and pastry.

One could go on and on, as there is a surfeit of kitchen gadgetry available today. Depending on your storage capacity and pocketbook, and on the types of dishes you care to make, consider adding some of these devices and tools to enhance your pleasure and save you time in the kitchen.

A Few General Cooking Hints

- Always read a recipe to the end, measure out all seasonings, and prep ingredients *before* beginning to cook a dish.
- To make a fruit paste, cover the dried fruit with water and heat for 2 minutes in a microwave or on a stovetop to rehydrate. Cool and blend in a high-speed blender, adding just enough of the soaking liquid to facilitate blending. Store fruit pastes in the fridge for two weeks or freeze for up to three months.
- When baking bread, use a small digital scale to weigh ingredients instead of measuring by volume. The results will be far more accurate and consistent.
- When fermenting, culturing, or baking yeasted or sourdough breads, only use untreated or spring water. Water treatment chemicals like chloride and fluoride will damage baker's yeast, and the beneficial wild yeasts and bacteria in a sourdough ferment.
- As a rule, when cooking with spice blends and chili powders, to avoid overseasoning, add them slowly, tasting as you go, and adjust their levels toward the end of cooking.
- No time to wait for A Better Buttermilk (see page 27) to culture? You will sacrifice its luscious, creamy mouthfeel and sweet flavor, but you can still activate baking soda in your baking by acidulating soy (or another plant-based milk) with an acid like vinegar or lemon juice, using the ratio of 1 tablespoon acid to 1 cup milk.

CLIMATE DATA IN
THE RECIPES

n some of the recipes to follow, I summarize the major climate challenges facing the country where that dish originated. In others I review that government's actions in response to the crisis. Elsewhere, the impact of extreme weather and climactic changes on crop yield and viability are discussed, or how specific farming practices or types of food processing affect greenhouse gas (GHG) emissions.

Every recipe also includes climate footprint information about one or more key ingredients in that dish. This information is a snapshot in time from the database of the Swedish climate intelligence platform Carbon-Cloud.[36] CarbonCloud helps food businesses improve the sustainability of their products by calculating climate footprint data in real time for individual foods and beverages at every stage along the food supply chain. Its proprietary software is based on inputs from participating companies from all over the world. For more information see carboncloud.com.

Each food's climate footprint is described in kilograms per CO_2 equivalents per kilogram (kg CO_2eq per kg), a standard for combining emissions from key greenhouse gases like carbon dioxide CO_2, nitrous oxide (N_2O), and methane (CH_4) into a single climate footprint value.

For GHG emissions at the farm, every climate footprint is then apportioned by different land use practices, so you can see what factors may be driving that food's farm emissions. For example:

- "Fertilizer production" refers to the energy used and GHG gases produced when synthetic fertilizers are manufactured.

- "In-field bacteria" are direct N_2O emissions produced when fertilizers and field waste left in the field postharvest are digested by soil microbes. Crop residues and stubble are the organic matter commonly left in the field to improve soil quality and water retention.

- "Off-field bacteria" are indirect N_2O emissions carried by harvested crops after they have left the farm.

- "Farming on drained wetlands" destroys marshes, swamps, peatlands, mangroves, and deltas, causing high emissions that accrue over decades. Wetlands are among the largest carbon stores that exist. They filter pollutants from surface water sources and modulate the impact of floods and coastal surges. When drained, the decomposing plants and animals release considerable quantities of CO_2 and N_2O. Destroying wetlands creates other environmental harms as well: lowering the water table, disrupting flow to other waterways, and reducing the capacity of groundwater aquifers to recharge. About 40% of all species rely on wetlands. Their destruction destroys wildlife habitats, contributing to biodiversity losses.[37]

- "Deforestation," or the practice of cutting down swaths of virgin forest and jungle to convert to crop and pastureland or to clear the land for urban infrastructure, housing, and roads, releases CO_2 into the atmosphere and eliminates the capacity of those trees to capture carbon from the air and store it. Nearly 95% of deforestation today occurs in tropical regions of South America and Southeast Asia. In addition to the risk this poses for global warming, it endangers ecosystems where most of the world's biodiversity is concentrated. Forest degradation, where forestland is lost to wildfires or trees are thinned by plantation logging, also contributes to global forest loss. Both deforestation and forest degradation today are driven by the demands for livestock and their feed crops, palm oil, rubber, and fuel in tropical zones, and lumber and paper products in temperate regions.[38]

"Limestone and urea" are examples of soil amendments used in farming to decrease or increase soil pH and to promote plant growth. Both contain CO_2 that is released when these amendments are applied.

"Pesticide production" refers to the energy used when herbicides and insecticides are manufactured for farm use to manage weed and insect infestations.

"Farm machinery" refers to the energy used by all the power tools and vehicles typically used on farms for activities like sowing, fertilizer/soil amendment/pesticide application, harvesting.

"Irrigation" is the diesel, gas, or electric energy required to pump water onto fields to water the crops.

"Drying" is the power used to heat air to dry certain crops like grains and legumes before they leave the farm.

"Flooding rice fields" is a practice unique to rice cultivation, where fields are flooded with water to promote growth and hamper weeds. Bacteria in flooded rice paddies release significant amounts of methane, which is twenty-eight times as potent as carbon dioxide when it comes to trapping heat in the air.[39]

And now, let's see what's cooking!

SEASONINGS
and
SAUCES

A BETTER BUTTERMILK

In the era before dairy products were processed and mass-produced, buttermilk was the liquid left over when cultured cream was churned into butter. Modern commercial producers typically culture pasteurized milk, adding salt and thickeners. This plant-based buttermilk inoculates minimally processed soy milk with live cultures, rich in lactobacilli and other beneficial bacteria. The result is heavenly: thick, rich, and creamy and without any additives, thickeners, or salt.

Enjoy this better buttermilk in salad dressings (Green Goddess Buttermilk Dressing on page 46), in fritters (Okra Fritters on page 86), in batters, biscuits, and any baked desserts that require an acid to activate baking soda as a leavening.

The climate footprint of soy milk sold in U.S. groceries is 0.6 kg CO_2eq per kg, with 32% of GHG (greenhouse gas) emissions attributable to agriculture, 13% to transport, 22% to processing, 26% to packaging, with 7% uncategorized. Dairy buttermilk, sold in U.S. shops, is 3⅓ times higher at 2 kg CO_2eq per kg, 89% due to agricultural emissions, 4% to transport, and 7% to packaging.

Prep time 5 minutes   Culture time about 4 hours   Makes 1 cup

1 cup minimally processed or homemade soy milk, containing only organic soybeans and water

2 capsules ultra-strength, broad spectrum probiotics, each with a minimum of 40 billion colony forming units (CFUs) per capsule

1. Pour the soy milk into a jar. Open the probiotic capsules and stir into the soy milk. Cover tightly and shake for a minute to disperse and dissolve the cultures into the milk. Set in a warm corner or shaded spot outdoors where the ambient temperature can be maintained at a steady 85 to 100°F. Note: Heating beyond this temperature risks killing the microorganisms.

2. Check at 3 hours. Shake the jar and open it to test its thickness and taste. It may require another hour or more, depending on the ambient temperature. The buttermilk is ready when it develops a viscosity that is thicker than whipping cream but thinner than yogurt with a flavor that is rich and barely tangy.

3. Refrigerate until use. A Better Buttermilk will keep in the refrigerator for 2 to 3 weeks.

ADVIEH BERENJ

Persian dishes are full of aromatic, floral notes from spices, fruits, fresh herbs, nuts, and flowers. Here is one variation of *advieh berenj* used to season Persian-inspired rice dishes, like *Tahchin* (see page 354). It can jazz up other whole grains and pilafs too, like Fragrant Millet Pilaf (see page 224). Climate friendly and anti-inflammatory, its aroma is simply heavenly.

While climate footprint data for spices from Iran is not available, the benchmark for commercial spice mixes is 2.0 kg CO_2eq per kg at Swedish stores.

Iran and Energy

Iran is rapidly urbanizing. Tehran alone has 9 million residents. According to the United Nations Development Programme, Iran is among the top ten carbon-emitting countries. It consumes 2.5 to 4% more energy than the global mean. Seventy-five percent of its population is urban and 70% of its energy is required by municipal buildings but is burned very inefficiently with 60% of that energy lost. With economic stress, high inflation, and the impact of COVID-19 lingering, Iran's economy remains fragile. Its investments in renewable energy for now remain limited, according to the Climate Action Tracker. For more on Iran and its environmental challenges, see page 201.

Prep time 10 minutes   Makes about ⅓ cup

1½ tablespoons food-grade rose petals

1 tablespoon Ceylon (true) cinnamon from one 7-inch quill

2 teaspoons coriander seeds

1 teaspoon cumin seeds

½ teaspoon green cardamom seeds

½ teaspoon nutmeg, freshly grated

¼ teaspoon cloves

¼ teaspoon white peppercorns

1. Combine the petals and spices in the bowl of a coffee grinder and grind into a powder, grinding in batches if necessary.

2. If you have leftover *Advieh Berenj*, try to use it up soon afterward while storing the blend in a tightly lidded spice jar in the fridge or a cool, dark cupboard.

ARUGULA PESTO

If you are a fan of arugula like I am, you will delight in this delicious pesto variation. Lively and creamy, this piquant sauce with its mild peppery bite can enhance dishes like Eggplant-Zucchini Torte (see page 335), gnocchi, pasta, potatoes, whole grains, whipped beans, and steamed vegetables. It's also terrific when spread on canapes and sandwiches for a flavorful accent. Arugula is packed with phytonutrients like nitrates that relax our arteries and cancer-fighting polyphenols like sulforaphane and erucin.

In U.S. groceries, arugula has a climate footprint of 0.6 kg CO_2eq per kg, with 24% of emissions coming from agriculture, 18% from transport, 3% from processing, and 55% from the greenhouse gases produced from packaging materials.

Prep time 30 minutes to roast garlic, plus 15 minutes   Makes 1½ cups

1 head garlic, roasted

3 cups packed baby arugula leaves

⅓ cup *Parmigiano Perfetto* (see page 56)

½ teaspoon lemon juice (optional) to preserve the bright color

1 teaspoon shiro (mild, white) miso paste

¼ cup pine nuts

Freshly ground black pepper, to taste

1. Preheat oven to 375°F. To roast the garlic head, peel off the papery exterior garlic skins and roast for 30 minutes. Separate the cloves and peel them.

2. Combine the arugula, *Parmigiano Perfetto*, garlic cloves, lemon juice, shiro miso paste, and pine nuts with ⅔ cup water in a high-speed blender. Run until smooth, about 30 seconds. Add 1 to 2 teaspoons of water as needed to blend into a dense sauce for canapes. If using the sauce to drizzle over pasta or polenta, thin with a little more water.

3. Season, to taste, with black pepper and, if required, a little more miso.

Allspice
Whole

BAHARAT

This spice blend is savored throughout North Africa, Southern Europe, and the Middle East, with each region putting its own spin on this fabulous mix of toasted spices and chilies. In this Tunisian-inspired *Baharat* we use mild chilies, but if you prefer more heat, just mix in or substitute with hotter varieties. Use *Baharat* in sauces and stews like *M'nazaleh* (page 348) and your dishes will spring to life. Find dried Kashmiri and Aleppo peppers online or at Middle Eastern groceries. Tunisian *Baklouti* peppers may be harder to find; they are so delicious, if you have the opportunity, consider growing a few plants in your garden or on your windowsill to enjoy fresh or dried.

Green chilies and peppers grown on Tunisian farms have a climate footprint of 0–0.1 kg CO_2eq per kg, with 36% of emissions caused by fertilizer production, 41% from N_2O released by in-field bacteria, 14% by off-field bacteria, 7% due to soil amendments to adjust the soil pH, and 2% from irrigation. Dried Tunisian chilies have a climate footprint of 0.64 kg CO_2eq per kg, 24% of which are generated by fertilizer production, 27% by in-field bacteria, 9% by off-field bacteria, 6% from deforestation, 5% from soil amendments, 11% from the use of farm machinery, and 17% from irrigation.

Tunisia and Climate Change

With its arid climate and topography, Tunisia is extremely vulnerable to the adverse impacts of a warming planet. According to the World Bank, Tunisia is expected to experience rising temperatures, increasing aridity, reduced rainfall, and sea level rise, all of which will threaten its limited water resources, agriculture, healthcare, and tourism sectors. A 2022 European Investment Bank survey stated that 84% of Tunisians say climate change and the environmental damage left in its wake has impacted them daily, 52% of those surveyed reported that climate disasters and extreme weather events caused a loss to their income or cost them their job, and 83% of Tunisians urged their leaders to prioritize renewable energy investments.

Prep time 15 minutes   Makes about $2/3$ cup

4 to 6 mild dried *Baklouti,* Kashmiri, or Aleppo peppers

1 teaspoon black peppercorns

2 teaspoons cumin seeds

2 teaspoons coriander seeds

½ teaspoon cloves

½ teaspoon green cardamom seeds

1 large Ceylon cinnamon stick, broken in 1-inch pieces

¼ teaspoon allspice berries

Large pinch saffron filaments

1 teaspoon dried mint

½ teaspoon food-grade rose petals

1½ tablespoons sweet or smoked paprika

½ teaspoon ground dried ginger

1 teaspoon nutmeg, freshly grated

1. Heat a medium skillet on medium for 3 minutes. Add the chilies, peppercorns, cumin seeds, coriander seeds, cloves, cardamom seeds, cinnamon stick, and allspice.

2. Stir the spices and peppers as they roast for barely a minute, with your nose poised above the pan. Once they become fragrant and before there is any hint of smoking, remove the pan from the heat and immediately pour the contents onto a plate to halt cooking. Burned spices are acrid and bitter so take care not to over-roast them.

3. Place the saffron in the hot skillet, but off direct heat, and toast it briefly, about 30 seconds.

4. Cool for a minute, then pour the roasted spices and chilies into a coffee grinder. You can grind in two batches if necessary. Add the toasted saffron, dried mint leaves, and rose petals. Grind into a powder and transfer to a bowl.

5. Add paprika and dried ginger powder. Use a nutmeg rasp to grate nutmeg into the bowl. Stir well to combine. Store *Baharat* in a tightly lidded jar in the fridge for up to a month or freeze for up to 3 months.

CHEESY WHITE SAUCE

Here is a delectably rich, cheesy sauce that will add luscious creaminess to your cooking. It whips up in no time. Enjoy it on your climate-friendly burgers and in tortes, casseroles, crêpes, eggless omelets, and blended soups. In other words, everywhere.

For more indulgent uses on special occasions, include a few soaked cashews for a more velvety texture and richer flavor. And for those dishes that call for a funkier cheese flavor, season with a pinch of intensely flavored Indian spice asafoetida (hing), a resin, grinding it right before use.

The climate footprint of soy milk produced in Canadian factories is 0.14 kg CO_2eq per kg, with 30% of greenhouse gas emissions produced from agriculture, 4% from transportation, and 66% from processing. Cashew trees grow in tropical climes, where their climate footprints range from 1.3 kg CO_2eq per kg in Africa to 2.6 kg CO_2eq per kg in East Asia. In U.S. shops GHG emissions for cashews rise to 4 kg CO_2eq per kg, with 62% of emissions driven by agriculture, 5% by transport, 25% by processing, and 8% from packaging.

Prep time 4 hours to soak cashews, if using, plus 5 minutes
Cook for 5 to 10 minutes   Makes 2 cups

⅓ cup cashews, soaked (optional)

Pinch whole asafoetida (hing) resin, freshly ground (optional)

2 cups unsweetened soy milk

⅓ cup silken tofu, drained

⅓ cup *Parmigiano Perfetto* (see page 56)

½ teaspoon granulated garlic

½ teaspoon granulated onion

2 tablespoons arrowroot for a pourable sauce, 3 tablespoons for a thicker sauce for toppings

1 teaspoon shiro (mild, white) miso paste

1. If using cashews, soak them in water for 4 hours. Drain.
2. If using asafoetida, put a small amount of hing resin in a coffee grinder, and process into a fine powder. Store any excess in a tight-lidded spice jar in the fridge.
3. Place all ingredients in a high-speed blender. Run on high for a minute until smooth. Taste and adjust any seasonings now.
4. Transfer the liquid to a saucepan. Cook it over medium heat, whisking constantly, until it thickens, about 5 minutes.
5. The sauce will continue to thicken as it cools but thins again upon reheating. Cheesy White Sauce can be kept in the fridge for about 5 days.

HINTS

• *Decide how thick you'd like the sauce to be at the get-go, adding the proper amount of arrowroot during blending, not during cooking, since arrowroot dissolves best in a cold liquid.*

• *Arrowroot activates at a low temperature, about 140°F. After it thickens, turn off the heat. Its thickening quality will break down in high heat over time.*

CHESAPEAKE OLD BAY SPICE BLEND

This is a salt-free version of classic Maryland Old Bay seasoning, created by Gustav Brunn who escaped Nazi Germany and opened his spice shop in Maryland in the 1930s. I love to use this blend in Chesapeake Crabless Salad Sandwich (see page 122), *Causa Rellena* (see page 66), Split Pea Eggless Omelets (see page 300), Okra Fritters (see page 86), in chowders and mocktails, and wherever and whenever a bland dish calls for some livening up.

Spices are a wide and diverse category with climate footprints varying depending on their country or region of origin. In the United States, greenhouse gas emissions for spices average 0.40 kg CO_2eq per kg on farms, but by the time they are processed and sold at retail, emissions range but rise as high as 30 kg CO_2eq per kg for curry powder, seasoned salt, sazón caliente, and many others. Buying spices whole and in bulk and grinding them in small quantities may be far less impactful to the climate than commercial products.

Seeking Sustainable Spices

The lucrative trade in exotic, fragrant seeds, bark, flowers, roots, and dried fruits dates back as early as 2000 BC to the Silk Road and other spice routes. The Portuguese dominated the spice trade in the fifteenth and sixteenth centuries, later to be surpassed by the Dutch, and then by other European powers as they colonized peoples in the global South and the New World in a global struggle for economic and military advantage. Today's $37 billion spice market is still colored by its exploitative history with a very convoluted, expensive supply chain with many intermediaries. Smallholder farmers are often underpaid and rely on environmentally damaging farming practices. Lack of quality control, fraud, contamination, child labor, and deforestation are all too prevalent in the spice trade. Seek single-origin spices, sourced directly from growers, to ensure that your spices are unadulterated, and fairly and ethically traded, and to encourage sustainable growing practices.[40]

Prep time 30 minutes to dry celery leaves, plus 15 minutes
Makes about ⅓ cup

⅓ cup packed celery leaves, chopped, oven-dried, and ground

¼ teaspoon from 1 to 2 dried red chilies, like Hungarian *csipős*, cayenne, or similarly hot chilies, stem removed and ground

¼ teaspoon nutmeg

¼ teaspoon Ceylon (true) cinnamon from ½ a quill

⅛ teaspoon whole mace blades preferably, or ground mace powder

½ of a dried bay leaf, stem removed, crumbled with your fingers, then ground

1 teaspoon black peppercorns, freshly ground

1 teaspoon yellow mustard seeds preferably, or pre-ground yellow mustard powder

⅛ teaspoon green cardamom seeds

3 allspice berries

3 cloves

2 teaspoons sweet paprika

¼ teaspoon dried ginger powder

1. Preheat oven to 175°F. Bake the fresh celery leaves, if using, on a square of parchment for about 30 minutes or until they crumble easily.

2. Using a coffee or spice grinder, grind the dried chili, including its seeds, into fine flakes.

3. Use a nutmeg rasp to grate the whole nutmeg seed.

4. Combine the ground chilies, baked celery leaves, Ceylon cinnamon, mace blades (if using), crumbled bay leaf, black peppercorns, mustard seeds, cardamom seeds, allspice berries, and cloves in a coffee grinder and process them into a powder. While mace blades would need to be ground in Step 4 with the other whole spices, mace powder would not and would be added with the other powders in Step 5.

5. Transfer the mix to a bowl and add mace blades (if using), grated nutmeg, paprika, ginger powder, and mustard powder (if using). Stir well. Taste and adjust the seasonings as you like.

6. Store Chesapeake Old Bay Spice Blend in a tightly lidded spice bottle or jar in a dark, cool cupboard for up to 3 months, or in the fridge for up to 6 months.

CITRUS POWDERS

Citrus fruits are extremely low emitters of greenhouse gas emissions, which is great because they are superb at building flavor, allowing us to dial down on cooking oils, sugar, and salt. The acidity in orange, lemon, and lime juice sharpens and brightens a dish. Citrus zests add color, scent, and antioxidants with powerful anti-inflammatory heft. I use citrus powders for their fantastic flavor and floral aromas to punch up flavor, finish dishes, and to provide a colorful floral garnish. Add them at the very end of cooking, ideally when plating. All you need is a dehydrator and a little coffee grinder.

Lemons and limes grown on U.S. farms generate 0.12 kg CO_2eq per kg, with 21% of greenhouse gases produced by agriculture, 20% from in-field bacteria, 6% from off-field bacteria, 5% from draining wetlands for farming, 13% from the production of pesticides used, 26% from the use of farm machinery, and 8% from irrigation.

Citrus Production in a Changing Climate

According to a 2021 study from the University of Valencia, the impacts of rising temperatures, increased solar radiation, flooding, and unseasonal frost events have threatened citriculture around the world. Citrus production in Florida has been blighted by greening disease and has suffered significant losses from recent hurricanes. California is now the major citrus-producing state in the United States, with rising imports of lemons and limes from Argentina, Chile, and Mexico.

Prep time 10 minutes   Dehydration time 40 hours   Oven bake time 10 hours
Makes 2 to 3 ounces, depending on the size of the fruit

1 organic lemon, lime, orange, or blood orange, sliced ⅛ inch thick, seeds removed

1. Wash and dry the fruit. Slice uniformly and remove the seeds, which are bitter.

2. Arrange the sliced fruit on a dehydrator tray, spacing them ½ inch apart.

3. Set the dehydrator to 105 to 110°F, but no higher, for 40 hours, flipping them over at 20 hours.

4. If using an oven, preheat to 150°F and bake for about 10 hours, flipping them at 5 hours. Placing the slices on a metal drying rack set over a cookie sheet allows the heat to circulate and dry the fruit more evenly.

5. The fruit is ready for grinding when it is dry, brittle, and has no interior stickiness when pinched.

6. Grind in small batches into a fine powder with a coffee grinder. Store in a tightly lidded bottle in the refrigerator for up to 3 months or in the freezer for up to 6 months.

GARAM MASALA

This beautiful Indian spice blend originated in Northern India but today is widely enjoyed throughout India and around the world. Garam Masala is a heady combination of warm spices, savory seeds, and herbs, with a hit of anise flavor and oftentimes chili. Enjoy it in Three Bean Party Dips (see page 99) and Creamy Tomato Korma (see page 285). If you add it towards the end of cooking or even as a finishing spice, its aroma and flavor will have their strongest effect. There are as many variations of Garam Masala as there are families, each putting a unique spin on the blend's choice and quantity of spices. You will not believe the depth of flavor you achieve by dry roasting and grinding spices yourself. Because the volatile oils in these ingredients oxidize and degrade quickly, it is best to make Garam Masala in small batches like this and often.

The climate footprint on Indian farms for the general category of spices is 0.52 kg CO_2eq per kg, with 13% of emissions from fertilizer production, 14% from in-field bacteria, 5% from off-field bacteria, 14% from deforestation, 40% from running farm machinery, and 9% from irrigation.

India's Climate Record

According to the Climate Action Tracker, India's overall climate rating is "highly insufficient." Although India has made admirable strides installing renewable energy, like solar and green hydrogen, its reliance on fossil fuels, like coal power and liquified natural gas imports, continue to rise as well.

Prep time 15 minutes   Cook time under 5 minutes   Makes ⅓ cup

1 7-inch Ceylon cinnamon quill, broken into smaller pieces

½ teaspoon black peppercorns

2 teaspoons coriander seeds

1 teaspoon cumin seeds

½ teaspoon green cardamom seeds

2 black cardamom pods

½ teaspoon cloves

½ teaspoon fennel seeds

3 dried mild Kashmiri chilies, or for much greater heat 1 dried Indian red chili (*desi laal Mirch*)

2 Indian bay leaves

2 star anises

¼ teaspoon fenugreek seeds

½ teaspoon freshly grated nutmeg

½ teaspoon whole mace blades preferably, or ground mace

1. Heat a medium skillet over a medium-low flame for 5 minutes. Put in all the spices and chilies, but save the nutmeg and ground mace, if using.

2. Stirring constantly and with your nose poised over the pan, dry roast for just a few minutes or until the aroma of the spices reaches your nose. Remove from heat immediately and pour the contents onto a plate to cool. Do not allow the spices to smoke or burn or they will be bitter and ruin the spice blend. Cool.

3. Grind the roasted spices and chili in a coffee grinder into a powder. Pour in a bowl. Use a nutmeg rasp to grate in the nutmeg. If using ground mace, stir it in well.

4. Store Garam Masala in a glass, tightly lidded jar in a dark, cool cupboard or in the refrigerator and use it often.

GREEN CHUTNEY

This simple herby chutney has it all: a little lemony tang, a little heat from green chilies and ginger, bright grassy notes of cilantro and mint, and smoky earthy notes from roasted cumin. It pairs beautifully with soy yogurt and *Rajgira* Roti (see page 186), but you will find loads of ways to enjoy this tasty condiment for its cheery color and lively flavor as a garnish for soups, on canapes, and as a spread on crisps and crackers.

In open Canadian fields, the climate footprint for fresh herbs like cilantro and mint is low at 0.11 kg CO_2eq per kg.

The Environmental Value of Herbs and Medicinal Plants

The strong aroma and flavor of herbs make them repellent to many insects and mammals, so herbs are an environmentally friendly way to enhance home gardens and landscapes, attracting and supporting pollinators. Grown in their native locales, herbs are well adapted and usually require less water than non-native plants, making them not only healthy and delicious enhancements for home cooking but sustainable choices for landscaping.[41] Medicinal plants, like herbs, are essential in regions where pharmaceuticals are unavailable. Rising global temperatures and changes in precipitation patterns have raised concerns among scientists that the quality and potency of these plants may suffer, and that unsustainable harvesting of medicinal plants may push some of these valuable specimens to extinction.[42]

Prep time 15 minutes   Makes about 1 cup

1 teaspoon cumin seed, lightly roasted and ground

2 cups cilantro

2 cups fresh mint, leaves only

2 green Indian chilies, cut into small pieces

2 cloves garlic, cut into small pieces

½ inch ginger root, peeled and cut into small pieces

1½ tablespoons lemon juice from ½ medium lemon

1 teaspoon shiro (mild, white) miso paste

1. Heat a small skillet on medium low for 2 minutes. Put in the cumin seeds, stirring constantly. Roast briefly until your nose perceives the aroma of the seeds and before it begins to smoke or burn. Burned cumin seeds are bitter, so start over if you over-roast them.

2. Cool the roasted cumin seeds and, using a coffee grinder, grind them into a powder, for about 30 seconds.

3. Place the cilantro and mint leaves, the chopped chili, garlic, ginger, lemon juice, roasted cumin powder, and shiro miso in a high-speed blender. Run on high to create a smooth but dense sauce, adding a spoonful or two of water as needed to facilitate blending.

GREEN GODDESS BUTTERMILK DRESSING

It's a cinch to make a creamy, fragrant Green Goddess Dressing. Scented with tarragon and chives, the secret to this delicious, pretty pastel Green Goddess is to start with A Better Buttermilk (see page 27). Its active live cultures lend a luscious flavor, velvety texture, and probiotic benefits. This Green Goddess is a colorful alternative to mayo on sandwiches like Tempeh BLT (see page 152) and salads like Newfoundland Tricolor Salad (see page 144). The beautiful thing about the culinary herbs used here and throughout this cookbook is that they are so compact, they can be grown in tiny apartment spaces, in window boxes, or in gardens. Not only do they add excitement to one's dishes, herbs are potent sources of anti-inflammatory polyphenols, which are powerful antioxidants.

Climate footprint data for fresh herbs in the United States is unavailable. At nearby Canadian factories fresh field-grown herbs generate a very low 0.11 kg CO_2eq per kg in greenhouse gas emissions. For more on how culinary herbs support the environment, see page 45.

Prep time 5 minutes   Makes 1 cup

½ teaspoon dried wakame fronds, ground, or to taste

1 cup A Better Buttermilk (see page 27)

2 teaspoons fresh tarragon leaves, stems removed, cut in small pieces

3 teaspoons fresh chive leaves, cut in small pieces

2 teaspoons fresh parsley, thick stems removed, cut in small pieces

1 small clove garlic, smashed

1½ teaspoons white wine vinegar

2 scallions, whites and greens, cut in a medium dice

⅛ teaspoon white pepper

2 teaspoons shiro (mild, white) miso paste, or to taste

1. To create the wakame powder, put the seaweed in a coffee grinder and run for 30 seconds or until the dried fronds are reduced to a fine powder.

2. Combine all ingredients in a high-speed blender. Run at high speed for a minute. Scrape down the sides of the bowl and repeat.

3. Taste and adjust any seasonings as you like.

HARISSA

Harissa, a lively, flavorful chili paste out of Tunisia, is beloved throughout the expansive Maghreb region of North Africa and the Levant. This condiment is so delicious, it is recognized by UNESCO as unique to and part of Tunisia's cultural heritage. Harissa's gentle, smoky heat wakes up tagines, stews, soups, and spice rubs. It makes a terrific addition to marinades, sauces, dips, and dressings too. In other words, look to Harissa whenever a bland dish calls for more flavor and some jazzy heat. This Harissa is mouth-warming, not hair-raising; if you prefer a bolder level of heat, feel free to substitute hotter chilies for some of those included here.

Dried Tunisian chilies have a climate footprint of 0.64 kg CO_2eq per kg, 24% of which are generated by fertilizer production, 27% by in-field bacteria, 9% by off-field bacteria, 6% from deforestation, 5% from soil amendments, 11% from the use of farm machinery, and 17% from irrigation. Spices grown in Tunisian soils emit 0.59 kg CO_2eq per kg, with 26% of those emissions stemming from fertilizer production, 29% by in-field bacteria and 10% by off-field bacteria, 5% from deforestation, 5% from the generation of soil amendments, 12% from running farm equipment, and 12% from diesel or electric energy required for irrigation. For more information on how climate change is affecting Tunisia, see page 34.

Prep time 15 minutes   Makes ⅓ cup

12 dried Tunisian *Baklouti* or 4 Aleppo plus 8 Kashmiri peppers

1 teaspoon coriander seeds, freshly ground

1 teaspoon caraway seeds, freshly ground

½ teaspoon cumin seed, freshly ground

3 large cloves garlic, minced

2 teaspoons aka (red) miso paste

1. Heat a cast-iron skillet or comal on medium for 3 minutes or until a flick of water dances across the surface of the pan.

2. Put in the dried chilies, pressing them down with a spatula to roast and darken them here and there. Toasting the chilies will add smokier flavor notes to the chili paste.

3. Transfer the chilies to a bowl and cover with very hot water, using a weight or bowl to keep them submerged.

4. Soak the roasted chilies for 30 minutes or until they soften. Alternatively, microwave the bowl for 2 minutes and allow the chilies to soak for 15 minutes so they rehydrate and soften. Drain, retaining the soaking water.

5. Reheat the skillet or comal over medium-low heat for 3 minutes. Put in the coriander, caraway, and cumin seeds, stirring constantly. Roast the spices for less than a minute—just until the air directly above the pan becomes aromatic. Transfer the seeds immediately from the hot skillet to a bowl to cool. If the spices smoke or burn, they may taste bitter and ruin the Harissa.

6. When the roasted spices are cool, grind them into a powder in a coffee grinder.

7. Combine the drained soft chilies, toasted spice powder, minced garlic, and aka miso paste in a food processor. Process to create a thick sauce, adding a spoonful or two of the chili soaking water if needed to achieve this texture.

8. Harissa can be refrigerated for a week or frozen for 3 months.

JADE MAYO

A mayonnaise without oil or eggs? This herby oil- and nut-free mayo makes a luscious dip for vegetables for an appetizer or light supper. Like any mayonnaise, it also works well as a creamy spread for sandwiches, like Tempeh BLT (see page 152), and on canapés. If you thin it with a dash of unsweetened soy milk, you have a tasty dressing for salads like Newfoundland Tricolor Salad too (see page 144).

Blanched and uncooked seasonal vegetables and raw fruits love to take a dip in Jade Mayo. Peas, radishes, asparagus, and baby artichokes work well with baby strawberries in spring. Summer broccolini and flowering Asian cauliflower complement radicchio, endive, and cherry plums. For fall, why not try beets, baby Brussels sprouts, edamame, and pears? And in winter, golden and red beets, Chinese broccoli, delicata squash, and blood oranges make a delicious ensemble. The possibilities are practically infinite.

The benchmark climate footprint for tofu is 1.4 kg CO_2eq per kg at UK groceries, with 31% of emissions driven by agriculture, 11% by transport, 34% from processing, and 24% from packaging.

The United States Climate Performance

The Climate Action Tracker rates the United States' "Nationally Determined Contribution" (NDC), that is, its commitments to reduce national emissions and to adapt to climate change, as "insufficient." Despite the enactment of the 2022 Inflation Reduction Act with major investments in clean energy, the United States has yet to shift from its increasing reliance on fossil fuels, and its global sales of oil and natural gas worldwide are increasing. The Climate Action Tracker also judged U.S. climate targets, its current actions, and its financing of climate projects as "insufficient."

Prep time 15 minutes   Makes about 2 cups

1 (14-ounce) block silken tofu

1 tablespoon granulated garlic

2 tablespoons nutritional yeast

2 tablespoons granulated onion

1½ tablespoons unseasoned rice vinegar

1½ tablespoons Dijon mustard

2 teaspoons shiro (mild, white) miso paste

3½ teaspoons lemon juice from ½ lemon

¼ teaspoon ground white pepper

1 cup packed mixed chopped dill, baby arugula, and baby watercress

1. Combine all ingredients in a high-speed blender and process for 1 to 2 minutes until very smooth.

2. Taste to adjust seasonings as needed. The mayo will thicken slightly as it cools in the fridge. Refrigerated Jade Mayo will last 5 to 6 days.

MANGO SALSA

Bright and sassy, I love Mango Salsa's combo of ginger and red chili with lime and tomatoes in this sweet-spicy condiment. It is a perfect topping on Mexican dishes like Black and Red Bean Chili and Chips (see page 273) and ¡Tostadas *Estupendas*! (see page 313), on Beety Burgers (see page 270), to serve with *Rajgira* Roti (see page 186), and to embellish canapes. With its sunny flavor and cheery colors, this salsa will enliven any dish. Mangos contain over twenty different vitamins and minerals, are rich in vitamin C, folate, and copper, and are a good source of fiber, vitamin A, and vitamin B_6.

Mangos date back at least 4,000 years on the Indian subcontinent and today are the fifth most cultivated fruit in the world. About 86% of this tropical fruit sold in U.S. groceries are imported from Mexico. On Mexican farms mangos emit 0.45 kg CO2eq per kg in greenhouse gases, 8% due to fertilizer production, 10% to in-field bacteria, 3% to off-field bacteria, 2% due to pesticide production, 72% from the running of farm machinery, and 3% due to irrigation.

Prep time 15 minutes   Makes about 3 cups

2 (12-ounce) packages frozen mango, defrosted and cut in a small dice

1 cup cherry tomatoes, cut in a small dice

2 tablespoons grated fresh ginger

3 tablespoons finely diced red onion

Juice from ½ lime, about 1 tablespoon

1 small fresh red Indian or Thai chili, cut in a small dice

¼ cup chopped cilantro leaves

1. In a medium bowl, combine all the ingredients.
2. Taste and adjust the flavors, adding more ginger, onion, lime juice, chili, or cilantro, as you like.
3. Set aside at room temp for a few hours to allow all the flavors to meld.
4. Cover and refrigerate until use.

PANCH PHORON

Popular in Nepal, parts of Northern India, Bangladesh, and West Bengal, *Panch Phoron* combines five spices that are used to flavor many types of sabzi and dals. Unlike other spice blends, *Panch Phoron* is a mix of whole seeds, not ground spices. Because *Panch Phoron's* seeds are intact, you can store it for indefinite periods without it becoming rancid or losing flavor and nutritional potency. You will find it used in Cauliflower with Yogurt Sauce (see page 216) and *Mashur* Dal (see page 238).

Spices cultivated on Nepalese farms have a climate footprint of 0.52 kg CO_2eq per kg, with 10% of emissions coming from fertilizer production, 15% from in-field bacteria, 5% from off-field bacteria, 21% from the energy required to drain wetlands for farming, 3% from deforestation, 40% from running farm equipment, and 4% from the diesel or electric pumping of water to irrigate fields.

Climate Action in Nepal

According to the Climate Action Tracker, Nepal's climate performance is "almost sufficient." Its electricity generation has come entirely from renewable sources since 2015. In 2022, it initiated electric vehicle policies offering financial incentives. Having released a long-term strategy to address climate change, Nepal aims to reach its net zero emissions target by 2045 or sooner with negative emissions by 2050, a goal the Climate Action Tracker rated as "average." Once its forests and land use served as a carbon sink but no longer. Since 2010 its GHG emissions have been rising with over half its emissions from methane produced from agriculture. Despite its worthy climate mitigation projects, under its current policies Nepal will fall short of its 2030 climate target. As a least-developed country, it relies on international support. More stringent climate action is required with international financial backing for Nepal to achieve its climate ambitions.

Prep time 5 minutes   Makes about ¼ cup

1 tablespoon cumin seeds

1 tablespoon brown mustard seeds

1 tablespoon nigella seeds

1 tablespoon fennel seeds

1½ teaspoons fenugreek seeds

1. Mix the seeds together in a bowl.

2. Transfer to a tightly lidded spice jar and store *Panch Phoron* in a cool, dark cupboard.

PARMIGIANO PERFETTO

If you have a dehydrator, you can make a grated parmesan-like seasoning that is bursting with umami flavors. My Florentine husband swears it is an amazing proxy for dairy *parmigiano*—but with a far, far lower climate footprint and much healthier profile! All it takes is two ingredients and time in the dehydrator. Enjoy *Parmigiano Perfetto* on any dish that traditionally calls for grated cheese, such as soups, stews, pasta, and polenta, and as a garnish whenever sauces like Arugula Pesto (see page 31), Cheesy White Sauce (see page 36), and *Sugo Senza Carne* (see page 60) are used.

In Japanese factories miso paste emits 0.57 kg CO_2eq per kg, with 75% of those emissions coming from agriculture, 9% from transportation, and 14% from packaging. The climate footprint of nutritional yeast at EU factories is 3.2 CO_2eq per kg, with 23% coming from agriculture, 5% from transport, and 70% from processing. To put this in perspective, dairy parmesan cheese produced in Northern European factories generates 18 kg CO_2eq per kg, all of which are attributable to agriculture. Climate emissions data for various types of salts sold in different markets vary widely, but for example, iodized salt, garlic salt, and Himalayan pink salt, all sold at U.S. retail, each generate high levels of GHG emissions at 28 kg CO_2eq per kg.

Prep time 30 minutes to spread the miso, plus 40 hours to dehydrate   Makes about 3$1/3$ cups

1 (16-ounce) tub shiro (mild, white) miso paste

About 1½ cups non-fortified nutritional yeast

1. Cut six 14-inch-square pieces of thin parchment paper to line 15-inch-square dehydrator trays. Thin parchment paper releases dehydrated miso paste much more easily and without waste, unlike silicone sheets.

2. Use an offset spatula to spread miso paste as thinly and evenly as you can on each parchment sheet, leaving a 1-inch border on all sides.

3. After spreading the miso, place the sheets on the dehydrator trays and insert them in the dehydrator.

4. Set the temperature to 108°F and the timer for 40 hours. Your ambient temperature and humidity may dry the paste more quickly or slowly, so check at 30 hours for readiness.

5. When the miso is extremely dry and flakes off into shards when you bend the parchment, it is ready.

6. Remove each sheet. Position each one in turn over a large bowl and bend the parchment paper back and forth to separate the dried miso from the paper. Continue until every bit of dried miso falls into the bowl.

7. Pour the miso shards into the bowl of a high-speed blender. Run on low to break them up, and then increase the speed to pulverize the miso into a fine powder.

8. Use a measuring cup to determine your final quantity, about 1½ cups, possibly a little more.

9. Transfer the miso powder back into the mixing bowl.

10. Measure the same quantity of nutritional yeast as your miso powder. Add about three-quarters of it to the bowl and mix well. Taste and adjust by adding more nutritional yeast, to taste. I like a 1:1 ratio myself, but you can decide what ratio tastes best to you.

11. Store *Parmigiano Perfetto* in a tightly lidded container in the refrigerator.

SALSA VERDE

Who doesn't adore the citrusy, spicy zip of Salsa Verde? This variation roasts the tomatillos and sautés the aromatics to intensify their flavors. Use Salsa Verde as a dip for baked chips and chili in Black and Red Bean Chili and Chips (see page 273), on ¡Tostadas *Estupendas*! (see page 313), and on your favorite burritos, enchiladas, and empanadas. This salsa gives you a medium-spicy buzz. For more heat, add additional or larger green chilis, and for milder heat, add fewer.

Jarred tomatillos sold in American groceries have a footprint of 0.9 kg CO_2eq per kg, with 17% of emissions related to agriculture, 12% to transport, 21% to processing, and 50% to packaging. While data for fresh tomatillos on the farm or at retail is not available, field tomatoes farmed in the United States have a climate footprint of 0 to 0.1 kg CO_2eq per kg. Tomatoes, however, are particularly delicate and require special handling and temperature controls during transport and storage, which increases their climate impact. Tomatillos' husks and tougher skins protect the fruit and avoid these special requirements.

Prep time 15 minutes   Cook time 30 minutes   Makes 2½ to 3 cups

1 pound of tomatillos, papery skins removed and washed well

1 medium white onion, cut in a large dice

A small splash of unsalted vegetable broth to deglaze pan

2 large cloves garlic, minced

2 tablespoons dried yerba buena leaves or 4 tablespoons fresh spearmint leaves

1 jalapeño pepper, seeded

4 serrano peppers, seeded, or 1 green Thai chili, cut in a small dice

1 bunch scallion or 1 large spring onion, greens and whites, cut in ¼-inch slices

1 cup packed cilantro leaves, roughly chopped or torn

Zest and juice from 1 pesticide-free lime

1 teaspoon shiro (mild, white) miso paste (optional)

Cilantro leaves and thinly sliced scallion, to garnish

1. Place the cleaned tomatillos on a cookie sheet lined with parchment and broil them for 5 to 7 minutes or until they are browned on top. Use a spatula to gently flip the tomatillos over and broil them for another 5 to 7 minutes or until they are well roasted, and their pulp has softened and begun to collapse. Allow them to cool. Reserve any juices released by the tomatillos.

2. Heat a large skillet or sauté pan for 3 minutes on medium low. Put in the diced onions and dry sauté, stirring occasionally, until they have caramelized and begun to darken and adhere to the pan.

3. Deglaze the pan with a minimal amount of broth, scraping up the onion sugars with a wooden spoon. Add minced garlic and yerba buena and continue to sauté for a few minutes, stirring.

4. Add the chilies and sliced scallion. Cook for 5 minutes or until all the vegetables are soft and fragrant. Cool slightly.

5. Transfer the sautéed mix to the bowl of a food processor. Add the roasted tomatillos, the roasting juices, and the chopped cilantro. Pulse to your desired consistency, not too chunky but not homogenized. Add lime zest and lime juice. Season, to taste, with shiro miso, if using. Taste and adjust all seasonings as you like.

6. Salsa Verde is best when it is eaten fresh and served at room temp.

7. Garnish with additional fresh cilantro leaves and thinly sliced scallion, if you like. It will keep for about a week in the fridge.

SUGO SENZA CARNE

Sugo di carne is the classic meaty Tuscan ragù used to sauce polenta and pastas. Traditionally, *sugo* is cooked with lard or pancetta, butter, and a few aromatic vegetables over which lean cuts of beef are slowly stewed and then ground. This is far too injurious to the climate and too high in saturated fats and cholesterol for me, so instead I played up the aromatics and looked to fungi for umami-yum and texture to create this *Sugo Senza Carne.* Enjoy it wherever a hearty red sauce is called for.

Mushrooms farmed in the United States emit 0.15 kg CO_2eq per kg in greenhouse gases, with 22% generated by the manufacture of fertilizers, 39% by in-field bacteria, 10% by off-field bacteria, 3% from draining wetlands for farming, and 22% from the use of farm machinery.

Climate Impacts in Tuscany and Beyond

In July 2022, Tuscany declared a state of emergency in response to its extreme heat and drought. The Climate Research Unit at the U.K.'s University of East Anglia estimates that Tuscany's maximum temperatures will continue to increase in half-degree centigrade increments with each passing decade, leading to more erratic and extreme weather conditions. The warming clime and water stress are adversely affecting Tuscan agriculture and wine production, and are also felt throughout Italy's entire agricultural sector: In 2022, the country's grape harvest was down by 10%, fruit and dairy dropped by 15 to 20%, wheat and rice by 30%, and corn and animal crops by 45%.

Prep time 10 minutes   Cook time about 30 minutes   Makes about 3 cups

1 teaspoon porcini powder from ¼ cup dried porcini slices, or to taste

1 large red onion, cut in large pieces

3 cups baby shiitake mushrooms, caps and stems, or larger shiitake mushrooms, caps only

2 stalks celery

2 medium carrots

Small splash of Chianti or dry vermouth, to deglaze pan

2 cloves garlic, minced with a fistful of fresh parsley leaves

About 1½ cups chopped or diced San Marzano tomatoes from a (26-ounce) carton or jar

4 whole cloves

A few grinds of black pepper

About ⅓ cup red (aka) miso paste, or to taste

Dusting of *Parmigiano Perfetto* (see page 56), to garnish

1. Use a coffee grinder to reduce the porcini slices to a fine powder. Measure out a teaspoon and store any excess in a tight-lidded spice jar placed in a cool, dark cupboard.

2. Place the red onion, shiitakes, celery, and carrots in a food processor. Pulse up to ten times to create a fine uniform mix that retains some texture.

3. Heat a 4-quart saucepan on medium for 3 minutes. Put in the pulsed ingredients, lower the heat, cover, and cook, stirring frequently for about 10 minutes. During this time the aromatics and fungi will release their water and soften. If the mix becomes dry or begins to adhere to the pan, add a splash of deglazing liquid, and scrape up any caramelized sugars that may have darkened the pan.

4. Use a mezzaluna to mince the garlic and parsley. Add them to the saucepan and cook for an additional two minutes.

5. Add 1 cup chopped tomatoes initially and observe. This sauce should not be tomato heavy like a *pomarola*; tomatoes are just a fellow choir member here, adding flavor and color but not dominating. The color of the sauce should be a warm orange, not a deep red. Maintain at a simmer.

6. Add the cloves and stir in porcini powder and black pepper, to taste.

7. As the *sugo* cooks, it will become denser. Add water to thin to a dense but pourable sauce consistency.

8. Cover and continue to simmer for a minimum of 20 minutes, adding a bit of water as needed. The flavor, aroma, and texture will mellow and improve the longer it cooks.

9. When you are satisfied, turn off the heat and season with aka miso. Taste to adjust seasonings.

10. Serve *Sugo Senza Carne* hot over your favorite pastas and polenta, and dust the dish with *Parmigiano Perfetto*.

WORCESTERSHIRE SAUCE

I love this sauce for its complex blend of flavors—sweet, sour, smoky, umami, plus a little heat. It engages all your tastebuds. Use it in mocktails, salads, and marinades, and to add zip to dishes like Chesapeake Crabless Salad Sandwich (see page 122), Tempeh BLT (see page 152), and *Okonomiyaki* (see page 350). When you make your own spice blends and condiments, not only can you tweak them more to your liking, but you'll find the flavor will taste much more alive and exciting than commercial brands and come at a fraction of the cost.

Commercial traditional brands of Worcestershire sauce include fermented fish, cooked at high temperatures. A 1988 study in the *Journal of Environmental and Molecular Mutagenesis* found carcinogenic heterocyclic amines in every brand they tested. Happily, our Worcestershire Sauce, which includes no fish, avoids this risk.

While the climate footprint data for the individual components are not available, commercially made Lea & Perrins Worcestershire sauce generates 4 kg CO_2eq per kg, with 76% of emissions attributable to agriculture, 7% to transport, 5% to processing, and 12% to packaging.

Prep time 20 minutes | Makes about ½ cup

2 tablespoons date paste from 1 cup pitted dried dates

1 teaspoon red balsamic vinegar reduction from ½ cup red balsamic vinegar

1 teaspoon dried wakame, freshly ground

⅔ teaspoon cloves, freshly ground

¼ teaspoon dried *pasilla* chili, freshly ground

½ teaspoon sumac berries, freshly ground

½ cup apple cider vinegar

2 tablespoons black strap molasses

1 tablespoon small batch fermented tamari

1 teaspoon tamarind concentrate

1 teaspoon granulated onion

½ teaspoon granulated garlic

¼ teaspoon smoked paprika

1. To make date paste, place the dates in a small bowl and cover with water. Microwave on high for 2 minutes and allow to cool. Alternatively, place the dates in a small pot, cover with water, and simmer for 5 minutes, then cool.

2. Using a high-speed blender, purée the softened dates with just enough of their soaking water to create a soft, smooth paste. Any excess date paste will keep in the fridge for about 2 weeks or can be frozen for up to 3 months.

3. If you can't find a good red balsamic vinegar reduction without added starches and thickeners, it's easy to make your own. Use ventilation as the fumes from boiling vinegar are strong. Simmer ½ cup of vinegar over low heat for about 5 minutes or until half the liquid has evaporated. The reduction should be dense enough to coat the back of a teaspoon. Store any remaining balsamic vinegar reduction in the fridge, where it will keep for several weeks.

4. Use a coffee grinder to grind separately the wakame seaweed, cloves, *pasilla* chili, and sumac berries.

5. Place all the Worcestershire Sauce ingredients in a high-speed blender. Run it at its highest setting for 1 minute. I use the sauce as is, but if you desire a perfectly smooth sauce, feel free to strain it through a fine sieve. Store in the fridge in a bottle with a tight-fitting lid for up to 3 months.

STARTERS
and
SMALL BITES

CAUSA RELLENA

The origin of Peru's popular *Causa Rellena* was 1879 when Peru and Bolivia were at war with Chile. To support the army, Peruvian women gathered potatoes from the fields and fashioned a cold potato layered casserole for their boys, in support of "la causa" (the cause). Today, *Causa Rellena*'s potatoes are mashed, seasoned with ají *amarillo* (a mild, bright yellow chili), lime, and typically layered with tuna salad. Instead of tuna, for a climate-friendly, healthier remake, we will use tasty Chesapeake Crabless Salad (see page 122). Be sure to choose sustainably grown hearts of palm that are multi-stemmed. Nutritionally speaking, chilled potato salads like *Causa Rellena* are a great source of resistant starch, a boon to our friendly gut microbes. *Causa Rellena* makes a stunning appetizer or elegant entrée and is a delicious way to celebrate the flavors of Peru.

Potatoes cultivated at Peruvian farms have a climate footprint of 0.52 kg CO_2eq per kg, with 3% of emissions coming from fertilizer production, 4% from in-field bacteria, 74% from deforestation, and 14% from the use of farm machinery.

Potatoes and the Climate

Potatoes were first cultivated in South America 10,000 years ago. For highest production yields, potatoes prefer a cool 68°F. A rising temperature is problematic for potatoes, because it reduces yields and encourages pathogens, fungal diseases, and insect predation. It also weakens potatoes' immune responses to these threats. Moreover, modern potato varieties have shallow root systems that have low tolerance to drought.[43] Growers are forced to irrigate more frequently, which increases GHG emissions and puts pressure on aquifers. The exhaustion of groundwater reserves is a growing global problem. Violent storms pose another threat to potato crops, rotting roots and delaying fall harvests. Delayed harvests expose potatoes to early frosts that can ruin the crop. To help mitigate all these climate risks, farmers with government support are improving drainage and monitoring weather and water more precisely. Plant scientists are exploring new varieties and hybrids with traits that are better able to withstand the evolving climatic conditions.[44] For Peru's climate challenges, see page 231.

Prep time 60 minutes, plus 3 hours to chill | Cook time 35 minutes | Makes 6 *Causa Rellenas*
Equipment: Potato ricer and six 3-inch ring molds

1 teaspoon freshly ground dried aji *amarillo*, or to taste

2 red bell peppers or long sweet peppers, seeded

2½ pounds unpeeled yellow potatoes

⅛ teaspoon freshly ground white pepper

1 teaspoon Lime Citrus Powder (see page 41), preferably, or 2 tablespoons freshly squeezed lime juice, or to taste

3 tablespoons shiro (mild, white) miso paste, or to taste

1 avocado, thinly sliced

2½ cups Chesapeake Crabless Salad (see page 122)

Garnish ideas:

2 tomatoes, sliced and roasted

1 small red onion, thinly sliced

A small dollop of mayonnaise used to make Chesapeake Crabless Salad (see page 122)

A fresh herb sprig

1. Remove the stem and grind the dried ají *amarillo* in a coffee grinder into a powder. Use 1 teaspoon for this recipe and store any excess in a small spice jar placed in a cool, dark cupboard, where it will remain potent for about 2 months.

2. Heat the oven to 400°F.

3. Core the peppers. Leave whole if using long, sweet varieties; quarter them if using bell peppers. Place on a parchment-lined baking sheet, together with the sliced tomatoes if you plan to use tomatoes as a garnish. Roast the peppers for 20 to 25 minutes, 30 to 35 minutes for the tomatoes, or until the peppers have collapsed and the peppers and tomato slices are lightly toasted on their edges.

4. Toss the roasted peppers in a paper bag, tightly closed, and steam for 15 minutes. The peels should come off very easily.

5. Place the unpeeled potatoes in a medium pot, cover with cold water, and bring to a boil. Lower to a simmer and cook for 15 to 18 minutes, depending on the size of the potatoes. Drain as soon as a knife can penetrate them without resistance; do not overcook or the potatoes will be soggy.

6. Return the potatoes to the pot and set the heat on medium to dry them out, gently turning each potato to encourage evaporation.

7. Remove the potatoes from the pot. Peel and rice each potato back into the pot. Season with ground ají *amarillo*, white pepper, and lime powder. Using the powders helps keep the mix dry. Add the miso paste. Taste and adjust all seasonings. Stir minimally—just enough to combine the ingredients. Over-stirring potatoes can turn their texture gluey and unsuitable for the layered stacking in this dish.

8. To compose a *Causa Rellena*, set a ring mold on a flat surface, ideally the plate you plan to serve it on. Stuff the bottom with the riced, seasoned potatoes, creating a layer about ¾ of an inch thick.

9. Next add a layer of thinly sliced avocado. Follow with an inch layer of Chesapeake Crabless Salad, followed by a slice of the peeled roasted pepper, cut to fit the circular shape of the mold.

10. Finally, top off the ring mold with more potato mix. Use the tamper that comes with the ring molds to compact the layers and to eliminate air pockets. Repeat with the remaining five ring molds.

11. Chill the filled ring molds in the refrigerator for 3 to 4 hours.

12. To serve, use the tamper to hold the *Causa Rellena* firmly in place as you lift the mold up and off. Repeat for the remaining five.

13. Garnish with a slice of roasted tomato, encircled by an onion ring and topped with a thin slice of raw red onion. Add a dollop of mayonnaise that you used to make Chesapeake Crabless Salad and top with a small sprig of fresh herbs. Serve cold.

HINTS

* *Choose potatoes of equal size for even cooking.*

* *The whole trick to a successful* Causa Rellena *is to make a stiff potato mash and to drain your fillings as much as possible. Otherwise, you will have trouble keeping the stacked layers from sliding.*

* *Stir the potatoes as little as possible to keep their consistency dry and compactible.*

CORNY CROSTINI WITH MUSHROOMS

If you have corn grits on hand you can make very tasty crostini. Personally, I like to use the coarsest grits I can find for their flavor and texture, so I made these crostini with deliciously rustic *xerém* grits, popular throughout the Portuguese colonial diaspora from Brazil to the Cape Verdes Islands. But instant polenta works too. Toast the crostini briefly on a grill or griddle, then top with a delicious mushroom sauté and you've got a crowd-pleasing appetizer. These crostini have a crispy exterior and a soft interior. The woodsy umami flavors from the mushrooms complement the corn nicely. *Xerém* corn is nixtamalized (treated with an alkali like lime), unlike polenta, making the niacin it contains bioavailable. Every element of this dish is fiber rich, low in fat, and climate friendly.

Mushrooms cultivated in U.S. soils have a low climate footprint of 0.15 kg CO_2eq per kg, with 22% of emissions coming from synthetic fertilizer production, 39% generated by in-field bacteria, 10% by off-field bacteria, and 22% from the use of farm machinery.

Mushrooms and Climate Change

A 2023 study by the University of Stirling found that growing edible mushrooms around trees not only provides a nutritious source of food, rich in protein, but it is an excellent way to mitigate climate change: Mushrooms capture carbon, reduce deforestation, and incentivize tree planting. Mushrooms are also an excellent option for urban farming, as they require little water, can be grown in small spaces year-round, and have fewer requirements for fertilizers or pesticides compared with most other crops. China leads the world in mushroom production, followed by the United States American mushroom production has risen 1% per year over the past decade and is projected to rise considerably in the coming decade.

Prep time 45 minutes, plus 1 hour for cooling | Cook time 30 minutes
Makes about 12 crostini, depending on size

1 teaspoon porcini powder from 2 teaspoons dried porcini mushrooms

⅓ cup aka (red) miso paste, or to taste

1 cup *xerém* hominy grits or instant polenta

3 cups fresh mushrooms, mixed varieties

½ teaspoon dried thyme leaves

Coarse grinds of black pepper

Up to 2 tablespoons arrowroot

¾ teaspoon granulated onion

¾ teaspoon granulated garlic

Fresh herb leaves, to garnish

1. Grind the dried porcini in a coffee grinder to make porcini powder.

2. In a medium pot, bring 3 cups of water to a boil. Dissolve 2 to 3 tablespoons of aka miso in the water, tasting it to ensure it is mildly flavored but not overly saline. If using *xerém* grits, pour in the corn, stirring constantly. *Xerém* is not precooked like instant polenta, so it will need to rehydrate before cooking. Allow it to boil for 2 minutes, then turn off the heat and cover. Wait about 30 minutes for the corn to soften before proceeding.

3. When the *xerém* grits have softened, bring the pot to a simmer and cook for about 15 minutes, stirring frequently to prevent sticking to the pot. The grits will thicken into a dense porridge.

4. If using instant polenta, no soaking is required. Pour polenta slowly into the simmering water, stirring constantly to prevent lumping. Stir for 6 to 8 minutes or until dense.

5. Pour the cooked corn onto a large wooden board. With an offset spatula spread it into a rectangle ½ inch thick to cool most quickly. Use the spatula to square the corn's edges as best you can. Set it aside for an hour to cool and solidify as you prep and cook the mushrooms.

6. Cut off any mushroom roots and brush off any grit. Use your hands to pull the stems apart for clump mushroom varieties.

7. Place the mushrooms in a large skillet. Add dried thyme, stir in 2 tablespoons of the aka miso, and grinds of black pepper. Stir in 2 cups of water. Cover the pan and bring to a simmer.

8. Cook the mushrooms for 15 minutes and test for doneness. When the mushrooms are uniformly

tender, remove them with a slotted spoon to a bowl, reserving the mushroom juices in the pan. When the mushrooms are cool enough to handle, transfer them to a food processor. Pulse once or twice to cut them into small, similarly sized pieces but do not overprocess.

9. You should have about a cup or slightly more of mushroom juices in the pan. Use a small whisk to mix in a tablespoon of arrowroot. Bring to a simmer and cook until the liquid has thickened into a smooth sauce, thin enough to slowly drip off a spoon. If it is too watery, add more arrowroot. If it is too dense, add a little water. When the sauce is ready, stir in the chopped mushrooms. Season to taste with the porcini powder, granulated onion, and granulated garlic. Adjust any seasonings as you like. Cover to keep warm and turn off the heat.

10. Now fire up a grill on medium. Alternatively, you can heat a good-quality nonstick griddle or skillet on medium for 4 minutes before toasting crostini.

11. Cut the solidified *xerém* or polenta into rectangles about 1½-by-3 inches. The crostini will shrink slightly with heat. Grill or pan toast for a few minutes on each side until you see light grill marks or darkening on their edges. Flip and repeat.

12. To serve, spoon the mushroom mix on each crostino and top with a few fresh aromatic herb leaves. Serve them warm. If you make crostini in advance, reheat them for 30 seconds in the microwave before serving.

HINTS

- *Xerém grits are found at any Latino grocery or online. If using instant polenta, choose one with a coarser grit, like Bob's Red Mill.*

- *Both* xerém *grits and polenta need to cool and solidify for at least one hour before being cut into crostini, so manage your time accordingly.*

FERMENTED *FARINATA*

Farinata, also called *socca*, has long been a crowd favorite all along Italy and France's Mediterranean coastlines and as far away as Argentina. I fermented the batter longer than the few hours usually called for to develop its flavor, texture, and nutrient bioavailability. The result is a fluffier, tastier *Farinata*! Typically baked in a puddle of oil, this *Farinata* is oil free, making it kinder to the climate and our waistlines. I dressed it up with slices of artichoke heart and shallot and seasoned it with rosemary, shiro (mild, white) miso, and generous grinds of black pepper. Serve it very hot, right out of the oven, with virgin aperitifs and a few good olives on a mezze table with other small bites, or as an accompaniment to a hearty soup or salad.

Chickpea flour climate data is not available by country, but at EU factories, it has a climate footprint of 1.2 kg CO_2eq per kg, 86% of those emissions coming from farming, 3% from transportation, and 11% from processing.

The EU's Climate Actions

According to the European Environmental Agency, climate change is increasing the frequency and intensity of floods, droughts, and heat waves throughout the continent. Extreme weather caused the deaths of up to 145,000 Europeans over the past forty years, resulting in about one-half trillion Euros in economic losses over that period. Despite European agriculture being one of the vulnerable and worst-affected sectors, farmers across the continent are protesting against EU's climate regulations. In response, the EU has weakened some of its rules to improve biodiversity and to cut GHG agricultural emissions.[45]

According to the Climate Action Tracker, the EU has made significant progress in adopting policies to reduce its greenhouse gas emissions after Russia's invasion of Ukraine. However, it also continued to invest in new fossil fuel infrastructure, which is slowing its efforts to decarbonize Europe's economy. The EU's NDC (Nationally Determined Contribution) target, its plan to cut emissions in order to meet its 2030 goals, and its climate financing are both rated "insufficient" by the Climate Action Tracker.

Prep time up to 2 days to ferment batter, plus 10 minutes   Bake time 15 minutes
Makes four or five 7- to 9-inch *Farinate*

400 grams (about 3½ cups) chickpea flour

1300 milliliters spring water (about 5 cups)

Up to 5 tablespoons shiro (mild, white) miso paste, or to taste

1 (12-ounce) jar of oil-free artichoke hearts or 7 to 9 frozen artichoke hearts, defrosted, and cut in ¼-inch slices

1 shallot, peeled and thinly sliced

Rosemary needles from a few sprigs of fresh rosemary

Several fresh grinds of black pepper

1. Place the chickpea flour and water in a high-speed blender. Run it for a minute to create a very smooth, thin batter.

2. Transfer the batter to a medium-large bowl, mark the level of the batter in the bowl with a piece of tape, and cover loosely.

3. Set the bowl in a warm corner, ideally a proofing box or oven with a proofing setting. The batter will expand and thicken as it ferments. Whisk it 3 or 4 times per day. The batter will be optimally fermented when it rises about ½ inch or more up the walls of the bowl, develops a velvety texture, and tastes slightly tangy. It is best to make the *Farinata* now.

4. Preheat the oven to 500°F and set a shelf on one of the lower oven racks.

5. Insert a baking sheet or nonstick skillet rated for 500°F in the oven to preheat.

6. Right before baking, season the batter to taste with miso, dissolving it well.

7. Carefully remove the heated baking sheet or skillet from the oven. If using a baking sheet, line it with parchment.

8. Pour two ladles of batter over the parchment or directly on the nonstick pan. *Farinata* should be thin, not more than ¼ inch high. Decorate the batter with artichokes and shallot slices, rosemary needles, and several grinds of black pepper.

9. Return the baking sheet or skillet to the oven. Bake for 10 minutes and check. When the *Farinata* has set and the perimeter has lightly darkened, switch the oven from bake to broil.

10. Once the broiler ignites, broil for just a minute or two, just until the top is lightly browned overall. Transfer the *Farinata* to a cooling rack. The parchment should peel off easily once the *Farinata* has cooled a little.

11. Cut into wedges and serve immediately.

12. Reset the oven to 550°F and return the baking sheet or skillet to the oven.

13. Repeat Steps 8 through 10 for the remaining batter, serving each *Farinata* as soon as it is ready.

GRILLED PEPPERS

Whenever you fire up your grill, it's a good time to grill bell peppers. Served simply, their natural sweetness and light smokiness shine. Here they are, topped simply with tofu crumbles, aromatic lemon zest, and slivers of fresh mint, and very lightly dressed with a drizzle of white balsamic vinegar reduction and lemon. Together they sing with flavor and are so easy to make. Don't save this dish just for sunny, dry days in summer, however: The peppers can be roasted in the oven just as easily for year-round enjoyment.

In Italy white balsamic vinegar is made from white *Trebbiano di Castelvetro* grapes. Pressed and boiled, the crushed grape "must" is fermented in wooden barrels typically for a year for inexpensive commercial products. Traditional balsamic vinegars that carry the *Denominazione di Origine Protetta* authentification, however, are aged far longer—from twelve to twenty-five years. During this lengthy fermentation, their flavors mellow, become sweeter and complex tasting, and more viscous.

Balsamic vinegars made in Italian factories have a climate footprint of 1.8 kg CO_2eq per kg, with emissions coming entirely from agriculture. By the time cheaper, mass-produced Italian balsamic vinegars arrive in U.S. stores, however, their GHG emissions rise to 5 CO_2eq per kg, with 65% of emissions from agriculture, 5% from transport, 23% from processing, and 8% from packaging.

Prep time 15 minutes   Cook time 15 minutes   Makes 16 dressed peppers

⅓ (14-ounce) package of firm tofu, drained and lightly pressed

About 6 tablespoons reduction from ¾ cup white balsamic vinegar

Up to 6 tablespoons lemon juice

4 red, orange, and yellow bell peppers, quartered and seeded

Zest from 1 organic lemon

A handful of fresh mint leaves, cut in a chiffonade (rolled and sliced in thin ribbons)

1. Drain the tofu, wrap in sheets of paper towel, and place on a absorbent towel, folded in quarters on a rimmed tray. Place a small heavy skillet on top to help it release more liquid. Pour off the liquid as it accumulates and press for 30 minutes.

2. Place the tofu in a bowl and, using clean fingers, crumble it into teaspoon-sized clumps.

3. To make white balsamic vinegar reduction, pour the vinegar in a small saucepan. Using ventilation to reduce fumes from the evaporating vinegar, bring to a simmer and reduce the liquid by about half. The reduction is ready when it coats the back of a spoon. The reduction will continue to thicken as it cools.

4. Mix lemon juice with the vinegar reduction, tasting it as you go. Tailor the proportion of juice to vinegar to suit your taste. Transfer the dressing to a squeeze bottle for easy application.

5. Grill the peppers over medium heat until softened and lightly charred, turning them regularly, for about 15 minutes. Alternatively, roast them in a preheated 375°F oven for about 30 minutes, roasting them cut side up. Cool and rub off most of any charred skin, which will be more pronounced with grilling than oven roasting.

6. On a platter or on individual plates, arrange the grilled peppers, cut side up. Top each grilled pepper with a spoonful of crumbled tofu, lemon zest, and plenty of mint. Drizzle the dressing over the tofu very lightly so as not to obscure the natural sweetness of the grilled peppers.

LIMA BEAN PURÉE

This tasty, buttery lima bean spread celebrates the flavors of Peru: Limas are smashed and seasoned with Peru's fruity yellow chilies (ají *amarillo*), lime, cilantro, and cumin. Simple to make, this creamy, mildly spicy purée is high in fiber and protein, and bright with flavor. Spread it on Potato, Corn, and Amaranth Crisps (see page 182), mound it on salad greens, dip crudité in it, and spread it on bread for a hearty, nutritious lunch.

Generally speaking, cultivating dried beans like lima beans produces low levels of greenhouse gas emissions in most countries. For example, beans grown in U.S. soils generate 0.46 kg CO2eq per kg in greenhouse gas emissions, with 3% due to fertilizer production, 16% from in-field bacteria, 25% from draining wetlands for farming, 7% from using soil amendments like limestone or urea, 19% from the use of farm machinery, 10% from the energy required to irrigate fields, and 13% from drying the crop prior to transport.

Farming beans like lima beans in Peru, however, is more injurious to the climate. Bean production in Peru has a climate footprint of 4.4 kg CO2eq per kg, almost entirely driven by deforestation at 93%, with 1% of emissions caused by fertilizer production, 2% from using farm machinery, and 1% from drying the crop. For Peru and its climate challenges, see page 231.

Prep time overnight soak of lima beans   Cook time 1 hour   Makes about 3 cups

3 cups cooked lima beans from ½ cup dried lima beans or 1½ (15-ounce) cans unsalted lima or butter beans

3 cloves garlic

2 bay leaves

1 head garlic, dry roasted

5 to 6 teaspoons puréed *amarillo* chilies from ½ cup frozen ají *amarillos*, defrosted and blended, or to taste

1½ teaspoons cumin seeds, freshly ground

2 teaspoons granulated onion

1 tablespoon shiro (mild, white) miso paste, or to taste

Juice of 1 lime

Several grinds of black pepper

1 cup cilantro leaves, chopped

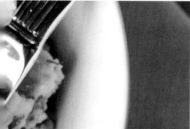

1. Rinse dried lima beans, transfer to a pot, cover with a few inches of water, and soak overnight or for about 8 hours.

2. Drain and refill the pot with the soaked lima beans. Toss in garlic cloves and bay leaves and cook on a low simmer for up to an hour, or until the lima beans are soft in the center but intact. Older beans may take a little longer. Lima beans are delicate and will disintegrate if cooked over high heat, so cook them gently.

3. Drain and discard the garlic cloves and bay leaves.

4. Preheat the oven or a toaster oven to 375°F.

5. To roast the garlic head, remove the loose outer garlic skins. Roast the garlic head whole and without oil in the oven for 30 minutes. Cool and peel cloves.

6. To make ají *amarillo* purée, toss the defrosted chilies in a high-speed blender and run on high, blending the chilies into a sweet, fruity, moderately hot, soft paste.

7. Grind the cumin seeds in a coffee grinder.

8. Combine the cooked lima beans, roasted garlic cloves, ají *amarillo* purée, ground cumin, granulated onion, shiro miso, lime juice, and black pepper in a food processor. Run for a minute, scrape down the sides of the bowl, and run for another minute. Taste and adjust seasonings to your taste. Transfer to a bowl and stir in chopped cilantro.

9. Serve Lima Bean Purée at room temperature or warmed.

OKRA FRITTERS

Okra is one of the oldest cultivated crops. It is an integral ingredient in Cajun gumbos and stews throughout the U.S. South, West Africa, and South Asia. In stews okra melts into a dish as it thickens and flavors it. However, okra is also fantastic crunchy, crispy, and scarcely cooked at all. Just take fresh, young okra, dunk them whole in a flavorful A Better Buttermilk (see page 27) cornmeal batter, and flash bake them in a super-hot oven or air fryer for a delicious, low-emissions appetizer or entrée. When I want Okra Fritters spicy, I dip them in hot sauce or tomato paste spiked with Tabasco and serve them with cultured soy yogurt to cool things back down. Any way you season them, okra is so rich in vitamins C, A, B6, K1, fiber, magnesium, and calcium that it's a vegetable worth getting to know.

Growing okra in most countries has a low climate footprint. On U.S. farms it produces 0.14 kg CO_2eq per kg, with 13% of emissions coming from the production of synthetic fertilizer, 22% from in-field bacteria, 6% from off-field bacteria, 22% from energy used to drain wetlands for farming, 6% from soil amendments, and 28% from the use of farm machinery.

Improving Okra's Climate Resilience

Okra is a tropical/subtropical vegetable and contains 80 to 90% water. It is therefore very sensitive to frost, drought, flooding, salt, and temperature swings—all conditions that are becoming more prevalent and extreme with climate change. The Utopian Seed Project Plant in Asheville, North Carolina, and plant scientists worldwide, are trying to develop okra hybrids and variants to better withstand the environmental stresses that climate change is inflicting on okra and other crops.[46]

Prep time 15 minutes   Bake time 10 to 15 minutes   Serves 3 to 4

⅔ cup yellow cornmeal, medium grind

⅔ cup oat flour

1 teaspoon Chesapeake Old Bay Spice Blend (see page 38)

½ teaspoon sodium-free baking soda

1¼ cups A Better Buttermilk (see page 27) or unsweetened soy milk mixed with 2 teaspoons lemon juice

2 teaspoons shiro (mild, white) miso paste

1 pound small, fresh young okra

Corn starch for dredging

1. Preheat oven to 475°F/450°F for convection ovens and air fryers.

2. In a high-speed blender put in cornmeal, oat flour, Chesapeake Old Bay Spice Blend, and baking soda. Pulse to combine. Now add A Better Buttermilk, or the clabbered soy milk, and shiro miso. Run on high for a minute to create your batter. The batter should be dense like a pancake batter. However, in a few minutes the baking soda will lighten but thicken the batter. If it becomes too thick, it won't coat the okra well and can crack and break off when baking. Thin the batter with a spoonful or two of soy milk, if needed.

3. Transfer the batter to a deep plate or wide bowl.

4. Wash the okra and dry them well. Roll each okra in corn starch. Then dip each one in the buttermilk batter, coating them thoroughly.

5. If you are baking in a conventional oven, transfer each battered okra to a parchment paper–lined baking sheet, spacing them apart and using a second baking sheet to avoid crowding. If you are using an air fryer, place the battered okra directly on the wire basket, but bake in batches to avoid overcrowding them.

6. Bake for 5 to 6 minutes in an air fryer or convection oven or until the batter is firm, golden, and toasted. Add 1 to 2 minutes for baking in a conventional oven. Flip them over and bake for an equal amount of time but keep a close eye on them.

7. The okra fritters are ready when they are crisp and golden with darkened edges. Their interiors should be crunchy. Don't overbake. Okra Fritters are best served on warmed plates, piping hot right out of the oven, so if you plan to dip your frittered okra, have your dipping sauce ready.

HINT

If you have batter left over, don't let it go to waste! Heat a good quality nonstick skillet for a few minutes over medium heat. Then use the batter to make corny pancakes. They're delicious hot out of the pan, especially topped with a spoonful of unsweetened applesauce.

ROASTED LOTUS SEEDS AND PEANUTS

This tasty finger food comes from good friends Parneeta and Haresh, who love to cook as much as I do! They shared this wonderfully healthful Indian snack of roasted puffed lotus seeds (*makhuna* or fox nuts) and peanuts, seasoned with curry leaves, spices, and chilies. All flavors are perfectly balanced to engage every taste bud. Low-fat lotus seeds are packed with vitamins, calcium, magnesium, and antioxidants; peanuts are an excellent source of all twenty amino acids, fiber, vitamins, minerals, polyphenols, and antioxidants. A greener and healthier alternative to humdrum supermarket chips, popcorn, and Chex mix, they make a delicious nibble before dinner with mocktails and at parties.

On U.S. farms, groundnuts like peanuts have a climate footprint of 0.43 kg CO_2eq per kg, with only 2% from fertilizer production, 20% from in-field bacteria, 13% from draining wetlands for farming, 3% from the application of soil amendments, 5% from applying pesticides, 45% from the use of farm machinery, and 5% from irrigation. The only available emissions data for lotus comes from Chinese factories at 0.41 kg CO_2eq per kg, with 94% of GHG emissions attributable to agriculture, 4% to transport, and 1% to processing.

Peanuts and the Climate

Peanuts need an environmental sweet spot to thrive: They like a clime that is warm but not too hot, with enough but not too much water. Extreme heat and intensifying storms pose a threat to peanut yields in India, Africa, and the southeastern United States. If fields become too dry too soon in peanuts' growing cycle, the risk of afla-toxin, a toxic mold caused by soil fungi, increases. Efforts are being made worldwide to conserve and protect local and heirloom peanut varieties. Plant breeders are experimenting with these and developing new hybrids that can best resist the growing climate threats to peanut cultivation.[47]

Prep time 15 minutes   Bake time 45 minutes   Makes about 7 cups

ROASTED LOTUS SEEDS

2 tablespoons almond milk

1 teaspoon nutritional yeast

½ teaspoon ground turmeric

½ teaspoon *amchur* (sour mango powder)

⅛ to ¼ teaspoon ground cayenne

2 teaspoons date sugar

2 teaspoons *Parmigiano Perfetto* (see page 56)

½ (7-ounce package), puffed lotus seeds (*phool makhuna*)

ROASTED PEANUTS

1 tablespoon almond milk

2 Indian green chilies, cut into ¼-inch pieces

2 large sprigs fresh curry leaves, cut into ¼-inch pieces

1 teaspoon nutritional yeast

⅛ to ¼ teaspoon ground cayenne

¼ teaspoon ground turmeric

½ teaspoon *amchur*

2 teaspoons date sugar

2 teaspoons *Parmigiano Perfetto* (see page 56)

²⁄₃ cup raw peanuts

1. Preheat the oven to 250°F.

2. Pour the almond milk in a bowl. Stir in the nutritional yeast, turmeric, *amchur*, cayenne, date sugar, and *Parmigiano Perfetto*.

3. Spread the puffed lotus seeds on a baking sheet, lined with parchment paper. Sprinkle the spiced almond milk over the lotus seeds, using clean hands to lightly coat the lotus seeds.

4. Bake the lotus seeds for about 15 minutes or until they are golden and fragrant. Stir them every 5 minutes to roast evenly. Remove the baking sheet from the oven.

5. Raise the oven temperature to 300°F.

6. In another bowl mix almond milk with chopped chilies, chopped curry leaves, nutritional yeast, cayenne, turmeric, *amchur*, date sugar, and *Parmigiano Perfetto*. This paste will be thicker.

7. Pour the peanuts into the bowl and, with a spoon, coat them evenly with the paste.

8. Spread the coated peanuts on a second baking tray, lined with parchment paper, and bake for 20 to 25 minutes. After 10 minutes stir and separate them for even roasting. Begin testing for doneness at 18 minutes. Remove the tray when the peanuts are dry, a little crispy, and fragrant. Allow the peanuts to cool.

9. Add the spiced roasted peanuts to the lotus seed tray, mixing them together.

10. Serve at room temperature. The lotus seeds and peanuts will become crispier as they cool.

11. Store any leftover mix in an airtight container. If the mix softens a little over time, reheat it in a 250°F oven for 5 to 10 minutes to restore crispness, stirring once.

SAUCY LENTIL MEATBALLS

For centuries home cooks throughout Europe, Central Asia, India, and the Middle East have fashioned tasty balls out of meat, potatoes, legumes, and vegetables. Some are pan-fried, some stewed, some float in soups. This recipe draws from Italian *polpette* (meatballs) but uses lentils and whole barley instead of meat. They are tender with a slightly chewy bite and are cooked in a simple, flavorful, hearty tomato sauce. Enjoy these saucy bites as an appetizer, an entrée, or to sauce whole-grain or bean pastas. This low-fat dish is packed with protein, folate, iron, fiber, potassium, phosphorus, magnesium, and B vitamins with a low glycemic load.

Lentils farmed on U.S. soils have a climate footprint of 0.79 kg CO_2eq per kg, with 2% of emissions driven by fertilizer production, 15% from in-field bacteria, 26% from draining wetlands for farming, 7% from the use of soil amendments like limestone and urea, 38% from using farm machinery, and 4% from the energy required to dry the crop. At U.S. retail, green lentils have a footprint of 1 kg CO_2eq per kg, with 34% of emissions coming from agriculture, 9% from transportation, 17% from processing, and 39% from packaging. By comparison, chopped beef's climate footprint ranges from 17 to 37 kg CO_2eq per kg in most markets.

Prep time 1 hour | Cook time 20 minutes | Makes a dozen *polpette* for 4 appetizers or 2 entrées

HEARTY TOMATO SAUCE

1 red onion, cut in 1-inch pieces

1 medium carrot, cut in 1-inch pieces

1 stalk of celery, cut in 1-inch pieces

Unsalted vegetable broth

1 (24-ounce) carton strained tomatoes

3 tablespoon aka (red) miso, or to taste

Several grinds of black pepper

2 tablespoons nutritional yeast

1 fistful of parsley, minced

LENTIL MEATBALLS

½ cup cooked barley from ¼ cup raw hull-less (whole) barley

2 bay leaves

4 cloves garlic, peeled, 2 left whole, 2 minced

1 cup cooked lentils from ½ cup dried green lentils

1 teaspoon dried porcini mushrooms, freshly ground

½ medium yellow onion, grated

½ cup 100% whole-grain artisanal bread, crusts removed, cut into ⅛-inch cubes

A small handful fresh parsley, leaves and stems, plus more for garnish

A pinch sodium-free baking soda

2 teaspoons nutritional yeast, plus more for garnish

6 grinds black pepper

2 tablespoons aka (red) miso paste, or to taste

About ¾ cup white whole wheat flour

Minced parsley leaves and *Parmigiano Perfetto* (see page 56), to garnish

MAKE HEARTY TOMATO SAUCE

1. Combine the red onion, carrot, and celery in a food processor bowl fitted with S-shaped blade. Pulse until all the aromatics are uniformly small. Heat a medium-sized pot on medium for 2 minutes. Put in the minced aromatics, lower heat, and gently sweat the vegetables until they release their water and soften, about 5 minutes.

2. If they begin to brown or adhere, lower heat, and deglaze with a tablespoon or two of broth.

3. Add the strained tomatoes, cover, and cook on a low simmer for 10 minutes. Season with aka miso, black pepper, and nutritional yeast, to taste. As the sauce thickens, thin it with ¼ cup of water. Stir in a few tablespoons of minced parsley. Cook for at least 10 minutes. If you can afford more time, the *sugo* will only improve in taste and texture.

PREPARE LENTIL MEATBALLS

1. Fill a small pot with water and bring to a boil. Rinse the hull-less barley and transfer to the pot together with a bay leaf and a clove of garlic. Cook until the barley is chewy and just tender, about 40 minutes, but begin testing at 30 minutes to avoid overcooking.

2. Drain the cooked barley, discard the bay leaf, and retain the garlic clove.

3. Transfer ½ cup of the cooked barley to a large board. Use a mezzaluna or chef knife to chop the grains roughly in half. Move the chopped barley with the reserved cooked garlic clove to a small bowl for now.

4. Rinse the lentils and transfer to a medium-sized pot. Fill the pot with water, covering the lentils by 2 inches. Toss in the second whole garlic clove and bay leaf. Bring to a boil and lower to a simmer.

5. Gently simmer the lentils until tender but intact, about 20 minutes. Begin testing them in 15 minutes.

6. Drain the lentils, discarding the bay leaf but retaining the garlic clove.

7. To make porcini powder, simply grind dried porcini slices in a coffee grinder to create a uniform powder. Measure out a teaspoon. Transfer any excess to a small glass jar, and store in a cool, dark cupboard for up to a month.

8. Use a box grater to grate the onion. Scrape the onion into a mixing bowl. Add cubed whole-grain bread and use clean hands to mix them well to moisten the cubes and infuse them with the onion.

9. Using a mezzaluna or chef knife, mince together the parsley and remaining 2 raw cloves of garlic. Stir this mix into the bowl with the bread cubes.

10. Add the cooked lentils, chopped and cooked whole barley, both reserved boiled garlic cloves, a pinch of baking soda, nutritional yeast, and porcini powder. Season to taste with black pepper and aka miso. Taste the mix and adjust the seasonings as you like.

11. Use your hand to knead the *polpette* mix well. Add only enough white whole wheat flour to create a coherent, moderately stiff mixture, about ¾ cup. If the mix is too wet, the *polpette* will be mushy; if it is too dry, the *polpette* texture will be dry and hard. Squeeze and knead for 5 minutes to ensure the ingredients are well mixed and will hold together when you roll them into balls. Cover and rest the *polpette* mix.

12. In a 6-quart saucepan heat the Hearty Tomato Sauce and maintain it at a simmer.

13. Break off pieces of the *polpette* mix and roll them with your hands into 1-inch balls. Drop each into the pot, spooning sauce over each to cover. When all the *polpette* are in the saucepot, cover and cook on a low simmer until the *polpette* have swelled slightly and are cooked thoroughly, about 20 minutes. Taste for doneness and adjust seasonings as you like.

14. Garnish with a sprinkle of nutritional yeast and minced parsley.

15. Serve *polpette* as an appetizer, as an entrée with mashed potatoes, or over whole pasta.

SÜZME

Straining fresh yogurt is an age-old tradition to make yogurt cheese, called by many names and beloved throughout the Middle East and Asia Minor. Start with a batch of cultured, unsweetened soy yogurt, a delicious probiotic food in its own right. Depending on how long you strain it, you can create luscious crème fraîche or cream cheese. Strained overnight it becomes denser for *Süzme*. Shaped into balls or oblongs, the soft cheese is rolled in herbs, nuts, or spices. Served on a thin slice of whole-grain bread or bread crisps, *Süzme* makes a delicious, healthy addition to your meze or tapas tables of small bites.

Soy yogurt's climate footprint data, available for Dutch retailers, is 0.81 kg CO_2eq per kg, with 14% of those emissions coming from agriculture, 28% from transportation, 43% from processing, and 15% from packaging. By comparison, dairy yogurt's GHG emissions average about 3 kg CO_2eq per kg in most markets.

Prep passive time to strain yogurt for 10 hours, plus 15 minutes
Makes 1 cup for 8 to 12 *Süzme*, depending on size

2 cups cultured soy yogurt

Possible toppings: Aleppo pepper flakes; za'atar spice blend; chopped, unsalted pine nuts, pistachio nuts, or walnuts; ground sumac; fresh dill leaves; chopped chives; chopped fresh mint leaves; or toasted sesame seeds

1. Spread a 2-foot square of unbleached muslin over a large bowl and spoon in the soy yogurt.

2. Use a stretch of string to tie up the ends of the cloth into a bag. Hang the bag over the sink or over the bowl for 1 to 2 hours for crème fraîche, 3 to 4 hours for cream cheese.

3. To make *Süzme*, after hanging for 2 hours place the yogurt bag in a strainer and move to the refrigerator for an additional 8 hours of straining. During this time, the yogurt cheese's flavor will continue to ripen, and its texture will continue to firm up, making it easier to handle and roll.

4. Lay the yogurt bag on a board. Open the bag and scrape the yogurt cheese from the cloth into a bowl.

5. Use clean hands to shape into balls or small oblongs. Roll them in your chosen herbs, spices, or nuts.

6. Transfer them to a serving plate, lightly cover with plastic wrap, and refrigerate until serving.

THREE BEAN PARTY DIPS

Whenever friends pop over, this is one of my favorite appetizers. Bean purées generate few GHG emissions and are delicious and nutrient dense: They are full of flavor and packed with fiber, protein, vitamins, and minerals, and are low-fat. Served here as dips for a gorgeous platter of crudité, they also are superb on bread or crackers, in salads, or alongside lightly steamed vegetables. Each dip is seasoned differently with aromatics, citrus, herbs, and spices. Freshly ground chilies add pizzazz. If you have the time, use dried beans instead of canned, so you can infuse them with flavorful garlic and herbs as they cook. Bean purées will keep in the fridge for 5 to 6 days or they can be frozen for up to 3 months. If a bean purée dries out over time, stir in a spoonful of water.

On U.S. farms the climate footprint for dried beans is 0.46 kg CO_2eq per kg, with 3% of emissions from fertilizer, 16% from in-field bacteria, 25% from draining wetlands for farming, 7% from adding soil amendments, 19% from using farm machinery, 10% from irrigation, and 13% from the energy used to dry the crop. At retail in the United States, the climate footprint for black beans, for example, is 1 kg CO_2eq per kg, with 34% of emissions related to agriculture, 9% to transportation, 17% to processing, and 39% to packaging.

The Beauty of Beans

Per 100 grams of protein, beans emit 90% lower greenhouse gas emissions than beef. Far more water efficient, 1 kilogram of beans requires 50 liters of water per year, compared to 13,000 liters required to produce 1 kilo of beef. Like all legumes, beans fix nitrogen in soil, reducing the need for organic or synthetic fertilizers. Wherever beans are cultivated, biodiversity increases and ecosystems become more disease resistant and resilient. These genetically diverse, ancient crops are environmentally resilient and able to cope in higher-temperature/lower-precipitation landscapes.[48] If the United States were to substitute beans for beef, it could reclaim 42% of its current cropland to rewild and to capture carbon.[49]

Prep time 20 to 60 minutes to cook lentils or dried beans and to roast garlic, plus 15 minutes
Makes about 2½ to 3 cups of each variety

MEXICAN BLACK BEAN PURÉE

1 cup dried black beans or 2 (15-oz) unsalted cans, rinsed

2 tablespoons dried *epazote*

2 cloves garlic

½ head garlic, roasted, cloves peeled

½ jalapeno pepper or ½ teaspoon freshly ground dried chipotle chilies

⅓ teaspoon freshly ground cumin seeds

½ teaspoon Mexican oregano

Juice and zest of ½ organic lime

Small handful of cilantro leaves and stems

Up to 2 teaspoons aka (red) miso paste

Chili flakes, lime zest, and/or sliced scallion, to garnish

1. To cook the dried beans, rinse and put in a saucepan. Cover with water by 2 inches and boil for 2 minutes, then turn off the heat, cover, and steep the beans. When all the beans have swelled and sunk in the pot, typically after 30 minutes but the time will depend on the age of the beans, drain the liquid.
2. Refill the pot with water, put in *epazote* and garlic cloves, and simmer until the beans are tender but intact, for 20 to 30 minutes, typically. Drain and reserve the cooking water.
3. If using canned beans, simply rinse and drain them.
4. To roast the garlic head, remove the loose, papery outer layers, leaving the head intact, and roast for 30 minutes in a 375°F oven. When cool enough to handle after roasting, separate the cloves and peel them.
5. Use a coffee grinder to separately grind cumin seed and a chipotle chili, if using.
6. Combine all ingredients in a food processor and run. Add only enough of the cooking water to facilitate blending and to create a smooth, dense dip. Taste and adjust seasonings as you like.
7. Serve warm and garnish.

INDIAN RED LENTIL PURÉE

1 cup red lentils or *masoor* dal, rinsed

1 Indian bay leaf

1 clove garlic, peeled

½ head garlic, roasted, cloves peeled

Pinch of saffron threads

1 tablespoon Garam Masala (see page 42)

Juice and zest of ½ organic lemon

Pinch of ground white pepper

½ red Indian chili or a dash of cayenne

2 teaspoons shiro (mild, white) miso paste

Lemon zest, toasted curry leaves, or chopped cilantro, to garnish

1. To cook the lentils, rinse and add to a saucepan. Cover with water by 1 inch, toss in Indian bay leaf and peeled garlic clove.
2. Gently simmer until the lentils begin to dissolve, about 20 minutes. Pour off but reserve the cooking liquid.

3. To roast the garlic head, remove the loose, papery outer layers, leaving the head intact, and roast for 30 minutes in a 375°F oven. When cool enough to handle after roasting, separate the cloves and peel them.

4. Place the saffron in a small bowl and add 1 teaspoon of very hot water. Steep for 10 minutes before combining the saffron "tea" with the other ingredients.

5. Combine all ingredients in a food processor and run. If they require more moisture to blend, add a little of the reserved cooking water. The puréed lentils should be dense and smooth. Taste and adjust seasonings as desired.

6. To toast fresh curry leaves for a garnish, heat a small skillet, put in a sprig of curry leaves, and press down with a spatula to lightly toast and crisp them, about 2 minutes. Remove from the heat and when they are cool, grind them into flakes in a coffee grinder.

7. Garnish and serve warm.

ITALIAN WHITE BEAN PURÉE

1 cup white beans, canary beans, or chickpeas or two (15-oz) unsalted cans, rinsed

Sprigs of fresh rosemary and sage

2 cloves garlic, peeled

½ head garlic, roasted, cloves peeled

2 to 3 tablespoons fresh rosemary, sage, thyme, leaves only, finely chopped, or 1 to 1½ teaspoons dried Italian herb blend or *herbes de Provence*

Several fresh grinds of black or white peppercorns

2 teaspoons shiro (mild, white) miso paste

2 to 3 tablespoons nutritional yeast

A sprinkling of chopped chives or fresh thyme leaves, for garnish

1. To cook dried beans, rinse and place in a medium saucepan. Cover with water by 2 inches and boil for 2 minutes. Remove the pot from the heat, cover, and let the beans steep until they swell and sink, typically after 30 minutes, depending on the age of the beans.

2. Drain the liquid and refill the pot with water. Tie the fresh herb sprigs in cheesecloth and toss it with the 2 garlic cloves into the pot.

3. Simmer on very low for 30 to 60 minutes until the beans are tender but intact. Drain the beans and reserve their cooking liquid.

4. If using canned beans, rinse them and drain.

5. Place all the ingredients, except for the garnishes, in a food processor. Blend until smooth, adding only as much cooking water as required to blend into a smooth but dense purée. Taste and adjust seasonings as you like.

6. Garnish with chopped chives or thyme leaves and serve warm.

YOGURT WITH CHARD, LEEKS, AND GARLIC

This luscious dish is inspired by the many delectable ways Persians enjoy yogurt. It pairs nicely with Artichoke *Khoresh* with Saffron Rice (see page 319) but also makes a flavorful dip for crudité or a spread for bread crisps.

When you buy commercial nondairy yogurt, look for the label "Live and Active Cultures (LAC)" from the National Yogurt Association, certifying that it is fermented and contained at least 100 million cultures per gram when it was manufactured. Uncertified yogurts are often heat-treated, which kills beneficial bacteria, or are not fermented at all.

In the Netherlands, soy yogurt has a climate footprint of 0.81 kg CO_2eq per kg.

Dairy Versus Soy Milk for the Climate?

When it comes to the environmental impacts of dairy milk versus plant-based milks, according to Our World in Data, dairy milk emits 3 to 4½ times higher levels of greenhouse gases than plant milks across all metrics. Compared with soy milk, dairy milk uses 14 times as much land, 23 times as much water, and leads to 10 times more eutrophication (fertilizer runoff that causes algae blooms, starving other life-forms of oxygen and creating ocean dead zones). Which plant-based milk is best for the planet? While soy uses a little more land than rice or almond milk, it uses far less water than either and has the lowest level of eutrophication.

Prep time 2 hours to strain the yogurt, plus 15 minutes   Cook time 15 minutes   Makes 1½ cups

2½ cups cultured soy yogurt, strained

1 head garlic, roasted

2 large bunch Swiss chard, leaves only, rinsed and torn crudely

4 to 5 thin young leeks, whites and greens, cut in ⅛-inch slices

Several grinds of black pepper, to taste

1 teaspoon shiro (mild, white) miso paste, or to taste

1. Strain the soy yogurt in a large square of muslin. Use string to tie the yogurt up into a bag and hang it for 2 hours over the sink or a bowl to slowly reduce the amount of watery whey. Strained yogurt's thicker texture provides a richer, creamier mouthfeel.

2. Remove the outer papery leaves on the garlic head. Dry roast the intact head in a 375°F oven for 30 minutes. Cool. Break into cloves, peel them, and slice the cloves thinly.

3. Heat a large skillet over medium-low heat for 3 minutes. Put in the wet, torn, chard leaves, cover, and cook until just wilted and tender, about 5 minutes. Transfer the wilted chard to a strainer, leaving any residual chard juices in the skillet.

4. Place the wilted leaves in a strainer poised over a bowl, drain, and reserve its juices. When the leaves are cool, squeeze out as much liquid as possible. Use a mezzaluna or chef knife to chop the chard into small uniform pieces.

5. Reheat the pan to medium low and stir in the leeks. Cover and sweat the leeks for about 5 minutes, stirring occasionally. If they begin to darken and adhere to the pan, add a tablespoonful or two of the reserved chard juices. The leeks are ready when they are soft, fragrant, and golden here and there.

6. In a bowl combine the chopped wilted chard, sautéed leeks, and sliced roasted garlic. Scrape the strained yogurt from the muslin into the bowl. Stir to combine well. Season to taste with pepper and shiro miso, making sure the miso is distributed evenly throughout the dish. Serve at room temp.

ZAALOUK

Smoky, garlicy, with enticing, complex flavors, Moroccan *Zaalouk* makes a phenomenal salad, spread, or dip. Personally? I love to serve it on bread crisps as a tantalizing appetizer or on a mezze table with other small bites. It is so delicious, I confess, I've had *Zaalouk* for dinner too!

In Morocco, farming eggplant emits 0.12 kg CO_2eq per kg in greenhouse gases, with 21% of emissions from fertilizer production, 38% from in-field bacteria, 12% from off-field bacteria, 4% from soil amendments, 6% from the use of farm machinery, and 17% from irrigation.

The Impacts of Climate Change on Morocco

With climate change, tropical Morocco has become more vulnerable to drought, heat waves, coastal erosion, and desertification. The country also has encountered erratic and violent weather like extreme storms and flooding, which has hurt its agriculture, fisheries, and tourism. Rising sea levels threaten people's lives and livelihoods as well as infrastructure along the coastline. In recent years Morocco has experienced drier winters with declining rainfall, which has exacerbated water scarcity and food shortages. The fourth-largest exporter of tomatoes worldwide, Morocco was forced to impose quotas of tomato exports in 2023; rising agronomic pressures caused by global warming, including repeated droughts, winter cold snaps, and plant pests and pathogens, reduced Morocco's yields of tomatoes, eggplant, peppers, and cucumbers.[50] For how Morocco is fighting climate change, see page 244.

Prep time 20 minutes to 1 hour, depending on roasting technique
Cook time 20 minutes │ Makes about 2 cups

2 to 3 young, firm Italian eggplants

6 large garlic cloves, 2 peeled and sliced, and 4 minced

Up to 2 teaspoons cumin seed, freshly roasted and ground

4 large heirloom tomatoes, gelatinous seed locules removed, roughly chopped, or 1 pound multicolored cherry tomatoes, roughly chopped

Unsalted vegetable broth

3 to 4 teaspoons Harissa (see page 48), or to taste

1 to 2 teaspoons smoked paprika (only for oven-roasted eggplants)

1 organic lemon, zested and juiced

Small bunch cilantro leaves, roughly cut

Small bunch parsley leaves, roughly cut

2 teaspoons shiro (mild, white) miso paste, or to taste

1. Ideally, cook the eggplants whole on a grill or over gas burners to provide smoky flavor notes, characteristic of *Zaalouk*. Cover stovetop burners with foil for an easy cleanup.

2. Cut 1-inch-deep slits in the eggplants here and there. Into each slit insert a slice of garlic.

3. Ignite the burners on medium and lay each eggplant directly on the burners or grill. Rotate the eggplants a quarter-turn every 5 minutes as their skins blacken, to allow them to cook evenly. The total roasting time required is usually 20 minutes but will vary according to the size of each eggplant. When they are done, the eggplants will have softened completely and collapsed.

4. Alternatively, preheat the oven to 400°F to oven roast the eggplants. Lay them whole on cookie sheets lined with parchment paper. Turning them every 15 minutes, roast the eggplants for 50 to 60 minutes, or until they have collapsed, darkened, and become utterly soft.

5. Cool the eggplant slightly, and scrape out their soft flesh. Use a mezzaluna or chef knife to chop their flesh coarsely.

6. Heat a small skillet over medium heat for 2 minutes. Put in the cumin seed, stirring constantly, and toast until fragrant, for 30 to 60 seconds. Do not allow them to smoke or burn or the seeds will be bitter and ruin the dish. Cool and grind into a powder in a coffee grinder.

7. Heat a large skillet for 5 minutes over medium-low heat. Put in the chopped tomatoes and cook for 3 minutes. Deglaze the pan with just a tablespoon or two of broth if the tomatoes begin to adhere to the pan.

8. Stir in Harissa and minced garlic and cook for 3 minutes.

9. Stir in the roasted eggplant pulp and cumin powder. If you roasted the eggplant in the oven, add smoked paprika now.

10. If the mix has dried, add as much broth as needed to create a spreadable consistency.

11. Add lemon juice, to taste, and most of the chopped cilantro and parsley, reserving a few teaspoons for a garnish. Cook for a few more minutes.

12. Turn off the heat and stir in shiro miso paste. Taste and adjust the miso, lemon juice, cumin, and Harissa to your taste.

13. Serve *Zaalouk* warm and garnish with the reserved chopped parsley, cilantro, and lemon zest.

SOUPS, SALADS,
and
SANDWICHES

ASPARAGUS RECOUP SOUP WITH CRISPY CROÛTONS

Here's a delicious way to salvage the tough, woody ends of asparagus spears. They make an exquisitely flavored velvety soup that whips up in minutes. We garnish it with chopped chives, a pinch of chili threads, and some homemade whole-grain croûtons. Asparagus Recoup Soup makes an elegant, delectable first course that smiles on the planet, is nourishing and comforting, and costs very little in time, effort, or ingredients. Using the ends of asparagus stems that normally get tossed in the garbage, Asparagus Recoup Soup is one creative and delicious way to reduce your stream of food waste, a major driver of individual greenhouse gas emissions. While more assertive in flavor, recouping the stems of cauliflower, broccoli, and hardy greens like kale or collards, or the cores of cabbage heads also make very nutritious, tasty, and thrifty blended soups. Cook and season them similarly.

The climate footprint of asparagus grown in U.S. fields is 0.40 kg CO_2eq per kg, 14% of which is linked to fertilizer production, 32% related to N_2O emissions by in-field bacteria, 8% by off-field bacteria, 15% from energy used to drain wetlands for farming, 4% from the application of soil amendments, 3% from pesticide production, 7% from operating farm machinery, and 16% from irrigation's energy requirements.

What a Waste!

The global food system emits about one-third of total annual GHG emissions. According to United Nations Food and Agriculture Organization, one-third of all the food we produce is lost or wasted all across the food supply chain, from the time it is harvested or slaughtered to the landfill. To put this in perspective, in 2017 the amount of GHG emissions produced by food loss and waste amounted to the total combined emissions of the United States and EU that year. A 2023 study in *Nature Food* determined that total food loss and waste amounts to one half of the total GHG emissions from food systems. Meat and animal products account for 73.4% of global food loss and waste emissions, compared with 20.9% from cereal grains and legumes, 3.3% from roots and oil crops, and 2.4% from fruits and vegetables. Because animal products produce significantly higher emissions, the study recommended halving meat consumption and halving the generation of food loss and waste across the supply chain and at waste treatment to reduce total global food waste emissions by 43%.[51]

Prep time 5 minutes to trim, plus 5 minutes to season and blend
Cook time 5 to 20 minutes to cook stems, plus 5 minutes to reheat │ Serves 2

2 (2.25-pound) bags of fresh asparagus spears, lower woody sections only (tops reserved for another dish)

2 teaspoons nutritional yeast, or to taste

⅛ teaspoon fresh grinds of white pepper

2 tablespoons shiro (mild, white) miso, or to taste, diluted in 1 tablespoon warm water to make a thick miso sauce

Garnishes:

A few chives, finely chopped

Several homemade croûtons (recipe on page 113)

A pinch of chili threads or flakes

1. Break off the asparagus stems toward the bottoms to remove the tougher, woodier ends. Simmer in water for 5 to 20 minutes, depending on the stem's thickness and woodiness. Cook until they are entirely tender when pierced with a knife.

2. Drain and reserve the cooking water. Transfer the stems to a high-speed blender. Purée them, adding only as much of the reserved cooking water as needed to create a smooth, velvety textured soup.

3. Season, using a light hand, with nutritional yeast and white pepper.

4. Before serving, reheat on the stovetop or for a minute, covered, in the microwave. Serve in warmed bowls, stirring in a spoonful of diluted miso, or to taste. Garnish with chopped chives, warm croûtons, and if you like, a pinch of chili.

CRISPY CROÛTONS

The fastest way to make croûtons, of course, is to repurpose stale artisanal whole-grain bread or to toast a slice of fresh bread. Then rub it with a clove of garlic and season with fresh grinds of pepper and perhaps a sprinkle of dried thyme leaves.

But, if you are out of bread, here's a tasty surrogate that's simple to make from a quick dough using whole-grain breadcrumbs and potato, seared on a hot, nonstick skillet.

Prep time 5 minutes   Cook time 5 minutes   Makes 15 to 25 croûtons, depending on size

⅔ cup coarse whole wheat bread crumbs

3 teaspoons arrowroot

1 teaspoon nutritional yeast

Several grinds of white or black pepper

¼ teaspoon granulated garlic

¼ teaspoon granulated onion

½ teaspoon dried *herbes de Provence* or dried thyme leaves

1 teaspoon shiro (mild, white) miso paste, or to taste

1 medium yellow potato

1. Mix the bread crumbs, arrowroot, nutritional yeast, pepper, garlic, onion, herbs, and miso paste in a bowl. Taste and adjust the seasonings as you like, then mound the mix on a large cutting board.

2. Cook the potato in a microwave for 3 to 4 minutes until it is tender.

3. While the potato is piping hot, cut it in half, and, using a ricer, squeeze two-thirds of the riced potato pulp onto the bread-crumb mix. Use a fork to distribute the potato throughout the mixture and then use your hands to knead it for a minute into a dough. Add more of the riced potato if the mixture remains too crumbly to gather cohesively.

4. Use a wooden dowel or light rolling pin to flatten the dough to ¼ inch in thickness.

5. Use a straight edge or ruler to square the edges. Cut them into bite-sized 1-inch squares or 1-by-¾-inch rectangles.

6. Heat a nonstick pan for 3 minutes over medium heat. Toast the croûtons for about 2 minutes on each side, lightly browning them.

7. Serve immediately, or if you prepare them in advance, reheat the croûtons before serving in a 300°F oven for 5 minutes.

BLACK-EYED PEAS AND OKRA SOUP

This scrumptious soup is West African in spirit. The culinary traditions of this region make rich use of native peas, beans, and tubers. West African cuisine's history of colonization and the slave trade carried its influence across the Atlantic, inspiring a wealth of Caribbean, Cajun, and *Gulla Geechee* dishes. Tomatoes, onions, and chilies are the foundation here. Two indigenous ingredients *dawadawa* (also known as *iru*, or fermented locust beans) and *melegueta* pepper (grains of paradise) further enrich the soup's flavor. It should be lively and mouth warming, but feel free to tailor the quantity of chili and pepper to suit your taste. For those who *really* like it hot, substitute an even hotter chili like Scotch bonnet or habanero for the cayenne but hold onto your hat if you do!

Dried peas have a low climate footprint on U.S. farms of 0.44 kg CO_2eq per kg, with only 3% related to fertilizer production, 18% to in-field bacteria, 4% to off-field bacteria, 28% due to draining wetlands, 7% from soil amendments, 2% from pesticide production, 31% from operating farm equipment, 3% from energy to pump irrigation water, and 3% from drying the peas. Okra only emits 0.14 kg CO_2eq per kg on U.S. fields, with 13% coming from fertilizer production, 22% due to emissions from in-field bacteria, 6% from off-field bacteria, 22% from draining wetlands, 6% from emissions due to the addition of soil amendments, 2% from pesticide production, 28% from running farm machinery, and 2% from irrigation.

Black-Eyed Peas and Sustainability

Like other legumes, cowpeas attract nitrogen-fixing bacteria and reduce the need for fertilizers. They enjoy a low water footprint and can withstand high heat and drought conditions. New varieties of black-eyed peas are in development to enhance their nitrogen-fixing properties while withstanding drought conditions in the hope that plants like black-eyed peas can enrich and nourish soils, reducing the need for fertilizers for other crops, and improve agricultural sustainability overall.[52]

Prep time 30 minutes | Cook time 30 minutes | Serves 4 to 6

1 pound dried black-eyed peas

2 bay leaves

7 cloves garlic, 3 whole garlic cloves, and 4 garlic cloves ground with ginger into a paste

8 cups unsalted vegetable broth, heated

1 teaspoon dried *dawadawa*, steeped in hot water

1 tablespoon unsalted ground dehydrated soup vegetables

1 tablespoon freshly ground coriander seeds

1 teaspoon freshly ground green cardamom seeds

½ teaspoon freshly ground *melequeta* pepper or black pepper, or to taste

Aka (red) miso, about 1 tablespoon per bowlful, diluted in hot broth, or to taste

1-inch peeled ginger root, ground with the garlic into a paste

1 yellow onion, cut in a medium dice

2 medium carrots, cut in a medium dice

3 stalks celery, cut in ¼-inch slices

1 large green bell pepper, cut in a medium dice

1 (14-ounce) jar or carton whole tomatoes, pulp and purée

1 teaspoon dried thyme or 1 tablespoon fresh thyme leaves

6 allspice berries

1 to 2 fresh cayenne chilies or ⅛ to ¼ teaspoon cayenne powder, or to taste

3 cups unpeeled kabocha squash or peeled African yam, cut in a large dice

1 pound fresh or frozen okra cut in ½-inch slices

5 cups packed spinach leaves

Cilantro leaves and ⅛-inch slices of scallion greens, to garnish

1. Rinse the black-eyed peas and place in a pressure cooker. Add 4 cups water and toss in the bay leaves and whole garlic cloves. Pressure-cook on high for 15 minutes. Then turn off the heat and allow the pressure to release naturally, about 15 minutes. The peas should be tender and intact. Drain.

2. In a separate pot, heat the broth, cover, and maintain on a very low simmer.

3. Place the dried *dawadawa* in a small bowl, add very hot water, and steep.

4. Use a coffee grinder to separately grind the dehydrated vegetables, coriander seeds, green cardamom seeds, and *melequeta* pepper or black peppercorns.

5. For each bowlful you plan to serve, dilute 1 tablespoon of aka miso paste in 2 tablespoons hot broth, stirring to dissolve completely.

6. Heat the oven or a warming drawer to 150°F and put in your serving bowls to preheat.

7. Slice the garlic and ginger. Then use a mortar and pestle or a coffee grinder to grind into a paste.

8. Heat an 8-quart, heavy-bottomed pot for 3 minutes on medium low. Add the onions, carrots, celery, and green pepper and cook for about 5 minutes, stirring occasionally, allowing the vegetables to sweat.

9. Stir in the garlic ginger paste and the tomato pulp and purée, breaking them up with a wooden spoon. Drain the *dawadawa*, and add it with the thyme, allspice, and chilies. Simmer gently for 3 minutes.

10. Now add the squash and the fresh okra, if using. After a minute, add 6 cups of the heated broth and maintain at a gentle simmer.

11. Gently stir in the cooked black-eyed peas. If you are using frozen okra, add it now. Season to taste with freshly ground dehydrated vegetables, coriander, cardamom, and *melequeta* or black pepper. Simmer for a final minute or two to allow all these flavors to meld. The vegetables should all be tender but intact.

12. Stir in the spinach, taste to adjust the seasonings again. If the soup is too dense for your taste, stir in another cup or so of hot broth. Cover the pot and turn off the heat.

13. Serve in your heated bowls. Stir the diluted miso, to taste, into each bowlful of steaming soup, and garnish with cilantro leaves and sliced scallions.

BORSCHT

I've been thinking about my dad today and how much he loved borscht. Earthy and sweet with lightly tangy undernotes, borscht is comforting and an example of homey, nutritious, peasant fare. Borscht is delicious at any time of year but particularly during colder months when beets and other root vegetables and cabbage are at their sweetest. Ukrainian in origin and beloved throughout Eastern and Central Europe, Scandinavia, and even Central Asia, borscht was carried by Ashkenazi Jews throughout the diaspora. Each ethnic group put its own mark on borscht, resulting in infinite variations. Some contain meat, others do not. Some are thick and chunky, others clear and brothy, and some are blended and creamy. Sometimes borscht is served hot, sometimes cold. In its earliest variations, borscht was soured with fermented beets or sour rye berries. Later versions, like this one, add acidity from vinegar and tomatoes instead.

The benchmark climate footprint for beetroot comes from Swedish retail where it generates 0.22 kg CO_2eq per kg in GHG emissions, with 30% from farming, 15% from transport, 1% from processing, 45% from packaging, and 8% from storage. The benchmark for potatoes' climate footprint comes from U.K. retail at 0.28 kg CO_2eq per kg, with 64% related to farming, 10% to transport, 6% to packaging, and 20% to storage.

Climate Change in Eastern Europe

In 2022 the worst drought in 500 years struck much of Europe. In the region's east, lakes and rivers disappeared in Hungary. Poland suffered a devastating blow to its agriculture, suffering 1.35 billion euros in lost revenue. Wildfires overtook Romania with seven times more wildfires than normal. Despite these events, Central and Eastern European countries lag behind the rest of the EU when it comes to decarbonizing their economies and meeting renewable energy targets: GHG emissions in Eastern Europe over the past twenty years have dropped 15% compared to 25% in Western Europe. The key deterrent to transitioning to green economies in Eastern Europe is the region's continued reliance on coal. Progress is also slow because heavy industries comprise a significant part of these national economies. They are major employers and require significant, and expensive, structural overhauls.[53]

Prep time 30 minutes   Cook time 30 minutes   Serves 6 to 8

7 cups unsalted vegetable broth

2 bay leaves

5 whole cloves

2 large potatoes, scrubbed or peeled, cut in a medium dice

½ small green cabbage, cut in a medium dice

3 apple-sized red beets, scrubbed or peeled, cut in a medium dice

1 large onion, cut in a medium dice

1 large carrot, scrubbed or peeled, cut in a medium dice

1 large stalk celery, cut in a medium dice

1 large parsnip or parsley root, cut in a medium dice

1 large leek, well cleaned, cut in ¼-inch slices

3 large cloves garlic, minced

1 teaspoon dried marjoram, or 1 tablespoon fresh, chopped

⅓ cup shiro (mild, white) miso paste, diluted with water, to taste

3 tablespoons tomato paste

3 tablespoons red wine vinegar, or to taste

Several grinds of black pepper

Garnishes: fresh dill sprigs, chopped fresh parsley and/or fresh thyme leaves, or cultured soy yogurt

1. In a soup pot, heat 6 cups of the vegetable broth. When it comes to a simmer, add the bay leaves, cloves, potatoes, cabbage, and beets. Cook at a gentle simmer for 15 minutes.

2. At the same time heat a large skillet on medium low for 3 minutes. Put in the onion, carrot, and celery, stirring occasionally. Cover and gently sweat the vegetables until they release their water in about 5 minutes. Lower the heat if they begin to adhere and deglaze with a spoonful or two of vegetable broth.

3. Add the parsnip, leek, garlic, and marjoram, adding a minimal amount of broth to prevent sticking. Sauté for 5 to 10 minutes longer or until the mix is fragrant and the vegetables are nearly cooked.

4. When the potatoes, beets, and cabbage are nearly soft, add the sautéed vegetables from the skillet.

5. Remove 2 cups of broth from the pot, pouring 1 cup into one bowl and 1 into another. Dilute the miso paste in one bowl, stirring it until it is smooth and pourable. Set the diluted miso aside for now. Dilute the tomato paste into the other, stirring until it dissolves, and then add it back to the pot.

6. Cook the borscht for a few minutes more. All the vegetables should be soft but still intact. Season the pot with wine vinegar and pepper to taste and adjust seasonings as you like.

7. Serve in heated bowls. As you plate the soup, stir in a spoonful or two of the diluted miso paste, to taste. Garnish with the fresh herbs and top with a nice big spoonful of soy yogurt.

CHESAPEAKE CRABLESS SALAD SANDWICH

This tasty, lively salad evokes summer by the sea. It combines hearts of palm in lieu of crabmeat, with fresh grilled corn, red peppers, sweet onion, and celery. Then it is dressed in a luscious egg- and oil-free mayo and Chesapeake Old Bay Spice Blend (see page 38). Stuff it in rolls or pile it high in sandwiches or enjoy it on leafy beds of salad greens. Whatever way you eat it, Chesapeake Crabless Salad makes a delightful lunch or light supper that whips up quickly. It is low in fat, high in fiber, and loaded with lively flavor.

Canned hearts of acai palm sold in U.S. markets have a climate footprint of 0.9 kg CO_2eq per kg. By contrast, crabmeat sold in U.S. shops emits from 10.48 to 15.79 CO_2eq per kg.

Sourcing Hearts of Palm Matters

To protect palm forests, how you source hearts of palm is very important: Choose organic and sustainably grown hearts of palm from multistemmed peach palms or acai palms, which enables the tree to regenerate in two to three years. Avoid hearts of palm from single-stemmed *jucara*, coconut, and sabal palms, which kills the tree upon harvesting and has been responsible for much deforestation in Brazil and elsewhere.[54]

Prep time 20 minutes   Makes 5 to 6 cups

MAYO

½ (14-ounce) package of soft tofu, drained well

1½ teaspoons granulated garlic

1 tablespoon granulated onion

1 tablespoon nutritional yeast

2 teaspoons shiro (mild, white) miso paste, or to taste

A pinch freshly ground white pepper

1½ tablespoons white distilled vinegar

2½ teaspoons Dijon mustard

SALAD

1 (25-ounce) jar organic hearts of palm, rinsed well and drained

2 fresh corncobs, husked, roasted, and sliced off the cob

⅓ cup small diced white or sweet onion

1 to 2 red bell peppers, cut in a small dice

2 stalks celery, or 1 stalk celery plus 1 Persian cucumber, cut in a small dice

1 cup mayo (see above)

Juice of ½ large lemon

1 teaspoon vegan Worcestershire Sauce (see page 62), or to taste

1 to 2 teaspoons Chesapeake Old Bay Spice Blend (see page 38), or to taste

Several grinds of coarse black pepper

½ to 1 teaspoon of your favorite hot sauce, or to taste

1. To make the mayo, combine all the mayo ingredients in a high-speed blender and run on high for 1 minute, scraping down sides if necessary. Taste to adjust its seasonings as you like.

2. Rinse and drain hearts of palm. To simulate shredded crabmeat, use the tines of a fork to shred each heart into irregular pieces.

3. Rest each ear of corn on a gas burner or on a grill, rotating it as it lightly browns on all sides.

4. On a large cutting board, angle the roasted ear and use a sharp knife to slice the kernels off.

5. In a bowl combine the shredded hearts of palm, diced onions, bell peppers, celery, and cucumber, if using.

6. Mix in the cup of mayo and the lemon juice and combine it well.

7. Season to taste with Worcestershire Sauce, Chesapeake Old Bay Spice Blend, and black pepper. Taste as you go. Add a few shakes of hot sauce for additional acid and heat. Taste a final time to adjust seasonings.

8. Refrigerate until use. Chesapeake Crabless Salad will keep about 5 days in the fridge.

9. To build a sandwich, just pile the salad high on slices of a good-quality 100% whole-grain bread or roll, and a tender-leafed butter lettuce.

CREAM OF SHANGHAI BOK CHOY SOUP

I love the simplicity of this delicious, nourishing spring soup. Any bok choy variety will work here but do seek out baby Shanghai choy for its exceptionally sweet and delicate flavor. The seasonings used are minimal to not obscure bok choy's natural sweetness. To finish, we'll brighten and lighten the soup with a splash of soy milk. Cream of Shanghai Bok Choy Soup whips up in a flash and makes a beautiful starter for your next dinner party or a simple supper. Garnish with a little cultured plant-based yogurt and chives and serve warm to better appreciate its superb, nuanced flavors. This soup is a nutritional powerhouse: With negligible fat or calories, it is rich in vitamins C, A, K, and folate, and calcium, phosphorous, and potassium.

Also known as pak choi and Chinese white cabbage, cabbages farmed in China have a low climate footprint at 0.16 kg CO_2eq per kg, making this soup a very climate-friendly choice, with 39% from fertilizer production, 21% from in-field bacteria, 7% from off-field bacteria, 4% from soil amendments, and 26% from the use of farm machinery. For the climate challenges facing China see page 331, and in South China specifically, see page 228. For China's climate policies see page 309.

Prep time 10 minutes   Cook time 10 minutes   Serves 4 for a starter, 2 for a main

1 to 1¼ pounds of Shanghai bok choy, as small as you can find them

½ teaspoon granulated garlic

½ teaspoon granulated onion

2 teaspoons nutritional yeast

⅛ teaspoon white pepper

About ⅓ cup unsweetened soy milk, divided

2 tablespoons shiro (mild, white) miso paste

Low-fat unsweetened cultured plant-based yogurt, chive leaves, and an edible flower (I used chive flower in the photo), to garnish

1. Wash the baby bok choy well to remove any growing media.

2. Blanch for 2 to 4 minutes or until tender. (This is slightly longer than for other bok choy recipes where a crispy-crunchy texture and scarcely cooked leaves are desirable.)

3. Test as you go. Scoop out with a skimmer and plunge the bok choy immediately in an ice bath to halt cooking and brighten its color to a brilliant emerald green. Cool. Reserve ½ cup of the blanching liquid.

4. Transfer the choy to a high-speed blender. Add the granulated garlic and onion, the nutritional yeast, white pepper, ¼ cup of the soy milk, and shiro miso.

5. Blend until entirely smooth and uniform, adding a little of the blanching water, if needed, to facilitate blending. The consistency of the soup should be velvety smooth, and neither dense nor watery.

6. Taste and adjust seasonings as you like. The soup should be flavorful and balanced with a hint of each seasoning perceptible. The soy milk lifts and lightens the color and herbal notes of the boy choy. Feel free to add a little more if you prefer the soup to be lighter and creamier.

7. To serve, warm the soup over low heat, stirring frequently. Turn off the heat when it begins to steam, well before it reaches a simmer. Serve in warmed bowls.

8. Garnish with a spoonful of plant-based yogurt, a few fresh chives with an edible flower or petals strewn on top. Serve immediately.

HERNEKEITTO

Thursday is the day that Finns and Swedes make *Hernekeitto*, a delicious split pea soup. In this version, I celebrate climate-supportive vegetables and sidestep the ham hock. Classically finished with a spoonful of spicy mustard and tender marjoram leaves will take this soup to the next level. Garnish *Hernekeitto* with a dollop of thick cultured soy yogurt for a creamier finish. For a special Nordic meal, serve this soup with Finnish barley *Rieska* flatbread (see page 192), paper-thin chards of Swedish rye sourdough *Knäcke-bröd* (see page 175), or delicious slices of Danish rye sourdough *Rugbrød* (see page 196).

Dried peas farmed in Finland have a climate footprint of 1.56 kg CO_2eq per kg, with only 1% of GHG emissions caused by fertilizer production, 4% from N_2O emissions by in-field bacteria, 1% from off-field bacteria, 2% from emissions from soil amendments, 2% from the production of pesticides, 9% from the use of farm machinery, and 1% from the energy required to dry the peas. Eighty percent of Finland's pea emissions, however, come from the draining of wetlands for farming.

Climate Change in Karelia

The region of lakes, wetlands, and boreal forests that straddles Finland and the Russian Federation has experienced increasing temperatures and sea level rise in recent decades as polar ice caps and glaciers melt. Extreme weather events have become more common, bringing heat waves and drought as well as more extreme storms and flooding. The warming planet has changed the migration routes of wild Barnacle geese, a protected species, putting the birds in direct competition with Eastern Karelian farmers who are trying to protect their crops on their limited tracts of arable land. The Natural Resources Institute of Finland may reserve some fields for the geese but at present the problem persists.[55] For climate change in Sweden, see page 175.

Prep time 30 minutes   Cook time 40 minutes   Serves 4 to 6

1 pound yellow or green split peas, pressure-cooked

1 yellow onion, cut in a medium dice

4 shallots, cut in a medium dice, or 1 entire leek, sliced in half, rinsed thoroughly, then cut in ¼-inch slices

3 bay leaves

6 allspice berries

3 carrots, peeled, cut in ¼-inch slices

2 stalks celery, cut in ¼-inch slices

1 teaspoon dried thyme or 1 tablespoon fresh thyme leaves

2 thin-skinned potatoes, cut in a large dice

For yellow peas only, a pinch of saffron threads

½ teaspoon freshly ground white pepper

Spicy brown or Dijon mustard, to taste

Shiro (mild, white) miso, to taste

Fresh marjoram leaves, dried chili threads, and a dollop of thick cultured soy yogurt, to garnish

1. Rinse the split peas until the water runs clear. Soak them in cool water as you gather your ingredients and prep the vegetables.

2. Drain the split peas and transfer them to a large pressure cooker. Add the onion, shallots, bay leaves, allspice berries, carrots, and celery. Add 6 cups of water. Pressure-cook for 15 minutes, then naturally release the pressure over 15 minutes.

3. Add the thyme and potatoes and simmer gently until the peas are tender and the potatoes are cooked, stirring occasionally to prevent sticking.

4. Remove the allspice berries and bay leaves.

5. If using yellow peas, steep the saffron threads in 1 tablespoon of very hot water for 10 minutes. Stir the vermillion saffron tea into the soup pot.

6. Transfer 4 cups of the peas and soup broth to a stand blender, run until smooth, then add back to the soup pot. Alternatively, transfer 4 cups of the soup to a bowl and use an immersion blender to purée the vegetables and peas, before returning the blend to the soup pot. *Hernekeitto* should be a dense soup but not a mash. If it is too thick, thin it with a little water.

7. Season with white pepper, to taste.

8. Serve in warmed bowls, seasoning each bowl with mustard and miso, to taste.

9. Garnish with fresh marjoram leaves, chili threads, and a spoonful of soy yogurt.

HŌTŌ

One of my favorite Japanese miso soups, *Hōtō* is chock-full of chewy fat whole wheat noodles, chunky Japanese root and green vegetables, and tender tofu—all cooked in a vegan dashi broth. Many Japanese soups and hot pots are served from a shared *nabe* (pot) at the table where each ingredient is grouped in its own section of the soup pot so diners can easily select what they want. For the adventurous, I've included instructions to make homemade noodles, but if you're tight on time, whole-wheat pappardelle works too.

On Japanese farms, taro emits 0.23 kg CO_2eq per kg of GHG, with 24% due to fertilizer production, 12% to in-field bacteria, 8% to off-field bacteria, 11% to the draining of wetlands, 2% to deforestation, 4% to CO_2 released by the addition of soil amendments, 7% from pesticide production, and 32% from the use of farm machinery. Mushrooms farmed in Japan also have a footprint of 0.23 kg CO_2eq per kg, with 37% of emissions from fertilizer production, 22% from in-field bacteria, 15% from off-field bacteria, 4% from draining wetlands, 5% from pesticide production, and 15% from operating farm machinery.

Japan's Climate Challenges

The Climate Action Tracker currently rates Japan's climate policies and targets as "insufficient," and its climate financing as "highly insufficient." The government adopted a Green Transformation Basic Policy in 2023, but rather than prioritizing decarbonization of its economy, it placed greater emphasis on economic growth and energy security. In 2023, Japan failed to endorse the G7's 2030 deadline to phase out coal and is the only G7 country planning to construct new coal-fired power plants.[56] Japan is already experiencing devastating effects from the changing climate, including heat waves, droughts, wildfires, intensified storms, and flooding. Multiple economic sectors, including agriculture, fisheries, infrastructure, and tourism, are threatened. On its present course, economic forecasts predict Japan's economy could shrink 3.72% by 2050 because of its inadequate climate response.[57]

Prep time overnight to soak the dashi broth, plus 1½ hours using fresh noodles or
30 minutes using dry pappardelle | Cook time 30 minutes | Serves 5 to 7

BONITO-FREE DASHI BROTH

1 3-by-3 inch square of kombu seaweed

12 small dried organic or sulfite-free shiitake mushrooms

HOMEMADE NOODLES

1 cup Indian atta flour (whole durum wheat flour)

⅜ cup *besan* (chana dal flour)

⅛ teaspoon ground turmeric

4½ ounces silken tofu, cut in half lengthwise, then cut in ¼-inch slices

1 teaspoon shiro (mild, white) miso paste

Tapioca flour or corn starch, for dusting

Or ⅓ (16-ounce) package dried whole wheat pappardelle

MAKE BONITO-FREE DASHI STOCK

1. In separate glass or ceramic mixing bowls soak the kombu seaweed in 7 cups of water and the dried shiitake mushrooms in 7 cups of water. Refrigerate the bowls overnight.

2. Discard the kombu, and cut the mushrooms in ¼-inch slices, reserving any tough stems, if you like, to make stock at another time. Set the sliced mushrooms aside in a bowl.

3. Strain the kombu and shiitake stocks and combine them into one bowl. This is now our dashi stock.

MAKE HOMEMADE NOODLES

1. In a food processor bowl, combine the atta and besan flours and the turmeric. Add the silken tofu and shiro miso. Run the processor for 2 to 3 minutes or until the dough gathers into a ball.

2. Remove and knead for 10 minutes, adding a bit of atta flour if needed to prevent sticking. Wrap in plastic and rest the dough for 30 minutes.

3. To roll the dough by hand, use a rolling pin to roll the dough into a large uniform rectangle ¹⁄₁₆-inch in thickness, resting the dough for a few minutes. If the dough tightens and resists rolling, rest it for a few minutes. Resume rolling. Then proceed to Step 5.

4. To roll the dough using a pasta maker, cut the dough into quarters, keeping three quarters covered in plastic to prevent drying. Roll each quarter through the widest setting, folding in half and re-rolling about ten times to create a uniform smooth dough. Then use the graduated settings to reduce the dough's thickness to ¹⁄₁₆-inch.

5. Dust each side of the rolled dough with tapioca flour, fold in half widthwise and again in half widthwise.

6. Cut the dough into ½-inch wide strips. Cut noodle length in half. Shake out noodles immediately and set aside in a soft mound on large, clean kitchen towels. Cover loosely with wrap.

SOUP

1 large yellow onion, cut in a very large dice

2 russet potatoes, peeled, cut into 1½-inch pieces

½ large daikon radish, peeled and cut in half lengthwise, then cut in ¼-inch slices

1 large juicing carrot, peeled, cut in half lengthwise, then cut in ¼-inch slices

4 small taros, peeled, cut into 1½-inch pieces

1 (3-foot) burdock root, peeled, cut into 2½-inch matchsticks

8 medium fresh shiitake mushrooms, stems removed, cut in ½-inch slices

1 bunch of fresh *shimeji* or maitake mushrooms, bottoms removed, separated into small clumps

½ medium kabocha squash, seeds removed, cut in 1-inch slices and then in 2-inch pieces

Whole wheat pappardelle (optional), or fresh noodles

1 large bunch of Japanese spinach or other Japanese greens, washed, stems and leaves cut into 2-inch slices

1 (14-ounce) package soft or medium tofu, sliced in half lengthwise and in half widthwise, then cut in ½-inch slices

⅔ cup shiro (mild, white) miso paste, or to taste

MAKE *HŌTŌ*

1. In a large nabe or soup pot, heat the dashi stock.

2. When it comes to a simmer, add the onion, potato, daikon, carrot, taro, and burdock matchsticks. Maintain at a low simmer and cook for 10 minutes.

3. Add the fresh mushrooms, the soaked, sliced, dashi shiitake mushrooms, the kabocha squash, and dry whole wheat pappardelle, if using. Simmer for 5 minutes, pressing the vegetables gently down with a ladle, but do not stir.

4. Shake or lightly brush off any superficial starch and add the fresh noodles, if using. Press the fresh noodles gently into stock. Cook for 5 minutes.

5. Add the Japanese spinach and gently slide in the tender tofu. Cook for 2 minutes longer. Turn off the heat.

6. Place the miso into a large deep ladle. Submerge partially and, using chopsticks, slowly mix the hot liquid with the miso paste in the ladle. As it dissolves, add it to different areas of the pot, gently swirling with chopsticks to disperse. Continue until all the miso is added. Taste and adjust the amount of miso as you like.

7. Serve in the large nabe pot or transfer the soup to pre-warmed bowls, grouping each ingredient by type as best you can.

MINESTRONE *FIORENTINO*

Minestrone means "big soup" and that it is! Most Italian minestrones combine a broad assortment of vegetables, but this Florentine interpretation goes beyond the classic creamy white beans and *cavolo nero* (lacinato kale) to include pumpkin, leeks, and peas too. The squash melts into the broth to create a luscious velvety texture and chestnutty sweetness. This recipe can feed a crowd, but it also freezes beautifully. Cannellini and French *tarbais* beans are delicate white beans that can fall apart when cooked too hot, for too long, or under pressure. Therefore, cook them low and slow as was traditionally done.

Beans farmed in U.S. fields have a climate footprint of 0.46 kg CO_2eq per kg, with 3% from fertilizer production, 16% from in-field bacteria, 4% from off-field bacteria, 25% from draining wetlands, 7% from soil amendment emissions, 4% from pesticide production, 19% from using farm machinery, 10% from the power used to irrigate fields, and 13% from drying the beans.

Why Wetlands Matter

Wetlands are essential to native ecosystems and biodiversity, providing habitats and breeding grounds for innumerable animal and plant species. They connect local waterways to ensure an uninterrupted flow to larger aquatic resources. They help prevent flooding in low-lying areas. Wetlands filter pollutants from surface water and remove carbon from the atmosphere. Over 50% of the world's wetlands have already been sacrificed to agricultural, industrial, and residential uses.[58]

Prep time 1 hour to cook beans and prep ingredients | Cook time 1 hour | Serves 8 to 10

1 pound dried cannellini or *tarbais* beans

1 bouquet garni made of a 4-inch sprig of fresh rosemary, 3 fresh sage leaves, and 2 bay leaves

4 cloves garlic, 2 smashed and 2 minced

2 red onions, 1 small peeled and cut in half and 1 medium cut in a medium dice

2 quarts unsalted vegetable broth, heated

2 medium carrots, cut in a medium dice

2 stalks celery, cut in a medium dice

2 leeks, whites and greens cleaned well, cut in ¼-inch slices

2 russet potatoes, cut in a medium dice, submerged in water to prevent browning

2 medium zucchini, or 1 medium yellow squash plus 1 medium zucchini, cut in a medium dice

1 small kabocha squash, unpeeled, seeded, cut into 1-inch cubes

1 bunch lacinato kale, cut in a ½-inch chiffonade

4 tablespoons tomato paste or 14-ounce jar or carton preservative-free, unsalted whole San Marzano tomatoes, pulp plus purée

1 bunch Swiss chard, cut in a ½-inch chiffonade

¼ savoy cabbage, cut in a ½-inch chiffonade

2 cups frozen green peas

Freshly ground black pepper, to taste

1 tablespoon aka (red) miso paste, diluted in hot broth, or to taste

1. Rinse the dried beans and put them in a pot. Fill the pot with 7 cups of cold water. Bring to a boil, then lower to a simmer. Cook for 2 minutes, turn off the heat, cover, and steep the beans until they swell and sink in the pot, for 20 to 30 minutes.

2. Pour out the water and refill the pot. Add the bouquet garni, smashed garlic cloves, and halved onion. Bring to a boil and lower immediately to a very gentle simmer. Cook until the beans are tender but intact and the broth fragrant, about 30 minutes, or longer for older beans.

3. Pour the vegetable broth into another pot, heat and maintain, covered, at a very low simmer.

4. Heat a 12-quart soup pot for 3 minutes at medium. Put in the diced onions and carrots and sauté them dry, stirring occasionally. As they lightly brown and begin to darken the pot, deglaze it with a minimal amount of broth, scraping up the caramelized sugars with a wooden spoon.

5. Add the celery, leeks, and minced garlic. Sauté for 5 minutes. Drain the diced potatoes and add them, then the zucchini and summer squash, if using, kabocha squash, and lacinato kale. Cook for 5 minutes.

6. Dissolve the tomato paste in ½ cup hot broth. Add two-thirds of the diluted paste to the pot. If using

San Marzano tomatoes instead, add two-thirds of the whole tomato pulp and purée, breaking them up roughly with a spoon or potato masher. In this soup, tomatoes are just another voice in the choir and should not be dominant. We want to add only enough tomatoes to balance the color and flavor of the greens. The final color of Minestrone *Fiorentino* is warm orange, not red.

7. Add the cooked beans and their cooking water, discarding the bouquet garni, smashed garlic cloves, and halved onion. If the soup is overly dense, add as much of the heated broth as required to thin it to a dense but soupy consistency.

8. If using canned beans instead, add the hot broth first before gently stirring in the rinsed and drained canned beans.

9. Preheat the oven to 150°F and insert your serving bowls to warm.

10. Stir in the Swiss chard and cabbage. Cook for another 10 minutes and begin tasting for doneness. All the vegetables should be tender but intact.

11. Stir in the peas. If the soup is too dense, thin it with hot broth. If the color has become green, add some of the reserved tomatoes.

12. Season with black pepper to taste. Cook for a final 2 minutes.

13. Serve piping hot in warmed bowls. Stir in a tablespoon of diluted miso, or to taste. Serve Minestrone *Fiorentino* with a big salad and crusty whole-grain bread.

HINT

To cut greens in a chiffonade, lay a handful of leaves one on top of the other, roll them up tightly like a large cigar, and cut in ½-inch slices, making ribbons of the greens. Herb leaves cut in a chiffonade are rolled and sliced similarly but cut into much finer ¹/₁₆-inch ribbons.

MULLIGATAWNY SOUP

Mulligatawny soup dates to the Raj, the period of British rule in India during the second half of the nineteenth century until independence in 1947. This fragrant peppery soup originated in South India and quickly became a favorite among the British in India and in England alike. While there are many variations, Mulligatawny evolved from a thin, peppery broth into a rich, dense soup filled with puréed lentils, lemon, and spices. It often contains chicken or mutton, but this velvety, climate-happy version is full-flavored with tofu "nuggets" for more nutritional heft and texture. Satisfying and filling, this Mulligatawny makes a great first course or the center of a meal when served with fresh *Rajgira* Roti (see page 186) or Naan (see page 180).

Lentils farmed in the United States have a climate footprint of 0.79, with only 2% from fertilizer production, 15% from in-field bacteria, 3% from off-field bacteria, 26% from draining wetlands, 7% from CO_2 released when soil amendments are used, 2% from pesticide production, 38% from operating farm machinery, 4% from energy used to irrigate fields, and 2% from drying lentils.

Climate Change in India

All of India is at risk to climate change, but the west coast and southern states are especially vulnerable due to local weather conditions, geography, poverty level, population growth, and level of urbanization. According to the 2023 Gross Domestic Climate Risks report by the Cross Dependency Initiative, out of the top fifty global regions with the highest climate exposures, nine are found in India. According to the *Washington Post* and the modeling nonprofit Carbon Plan, India may become the most climate-threatened country by 2030. As the temperature rises, monsoons will become erratic and difficult to forecast. Under World Bank projections, 2°C in warming will make monsoons "highly unpredictable." For India's overall climate performance, see page 42. For how legumes lower GHG emissions and enrich soils, see page 144.

Prep time 30 minutes | Cook time 25 minutes | Serves 6 bowls or 12 cups

1 (14- to 16-ounce) package extra firm tofu, drained

3 tablespoons *Parmigiano Perfetto* (see page 56)

3 teaspoons cumin seed, lightly toasted and ground

3 teaspoons coriander seed, lightly toasted and ground

1 red onion, cut in a medium dice

A splash of unsalted vegetable broth to deglaze pan

1-inch ginger root, peeled and minced

6 cloves garlic, peeled and minced

Leaves from 2 curry sprigs

1 tablespoon whole black peppercorns, or to taste

1¼ cups *masoor* dal (split red lentils), rinsed

4 to 5 whole jarred tomatoes, cut in a medium dice

1½ cups yellow potatoes, peeled, cut in a medium dice

1 teaspoon turmeric powder

¾ teaspoon cayenne chili, freshly ground, or to taste

Juice and zest of 2 organic lemons, or 4 to 5 tablespoons lemon juice, to taste

Shiro (mild, white) miso, to taste

Garnish options: cilantro, lemon zest, a few pink peppercorns, or pinch of chili threads

1. Preheat oven to 350°F.

2. Drain the tofu. Wrap in paper towels to remove some of the surface water but leave damp. Tear the block into irregular, bite-sized pieces.

3. Line a cookie sheet with parchment paper and transfer the tofu pieces to it. Sprinkle on *Parmigiano Perfetto* and toss to coat each piece. Spread the pieces apart and bake for 15 minutes. Stir so they bake evenly. Bake for another 10 to 15 minutes or until they are dried and lightly toasted on their edges. Set them aside.

4. Heat a small skillet for 2 minutes. Separately roast the cumin and coriander seeds very briefly, just until your nose can perceive their aromas. If they smoke or burn, start over. When cool, grind them separately in a coffee grinder and set aside.

5. Heat a large soup pot on medium for 3 minutes. Put in the diced onion and sauté it for a minute or two, until the onion begins to soften and darken the pot.

6. Deglaze the pan with a splash of broth, scraping up the caramelized sugars with a wooden spoon. Add the minced ginger, garlic, and curry leaves, and—for a peppery Mulligatawny Soup—add 1 tablespoon of whole black peppercorns. For a milder soup, add only 2 teaspoons of peppercorns. Sauté for one minute.

7. Stir in the masoor dal, the whole jarred tomatoes, diced potatoes, turmeric powder, 2 teaspoons only of ground cumin, 2 teaspoons only of ground coriander, and cayenne, stirring to combine well. Cook them for 2 minutes to allow the flavors to meld.

8. Add 8 cups of water and bring to a boil. Lower to a simmer and cook until the dal dissolves, about 20 minutes.

9. When the potatoes are soft and the soup is fragrant, use an immersion blender to blend the soup until smooth. Alternatively, you can transfer the soup in batches to a stand blender, leaving plenty of room for the soup to expand as you blend it. Then return the blended soup to the pot.

10. Cook for a final minute. Turn off the heat and stir in lemon juice, to taste.

11. Remove a cup of soup and dissolve ½ cup of shiro miso in it. Stir it back into the pot. Repeat with more soup and miso as needed to suit your taste.

12. Adjust the seasonings by adding more cumin and coriander powder, to your taste.

13. Garnish and serve Mulligatawny Soup in warmed bowls.

NEWFOUNDLAND TRICOLOR SALAD

In this recipe we salute the flag of Newfoundland and Labrador, the ruggedly beautiful easternmost Canadian province with its wild rocky cliffs, puffins, and caribou. We spent a memorable month there and relished its untamed natural beauty and warmhearted people.

Some vegetables are best when they're scarcely cooked at all, making this delightful spring salad with sugar snap peas and Chinese flowering cauliflower a speedy recipe. Thin crisp slices of gorgeous raw watermelon radish add contrast with their striking magenta color and peppery pungency. Serve the salad with Green Goddess Buttermilk Dressing (see page 47), Jade Mayo (see page 50), or a simple oil- and egg-free mayo (see page 123). Garnish with dill or fresh chives.

Green peas and cauliflower generate only 0.27 kg CO_2eq per kg on U.S. farms. Climate data on radishes is currently not available, but daikon sprouts generate a negligible 0–0.1 kg CO_2eq per kg on Swedish farms.

More Peas, Please

Field peas, like all nitrogen-fixing legumes, make excellent cover crops. They sequester carbon, reduce tillage, and improve soil structure and nutrient and water retention. They reduce farmers' need for synthetic fertilizers, whose N_2O emissions spur climate warming. Leguminous cover crops' symbiotic relationship with soil bacteria enables them to convert nitrogen from the air into NH_4 in the soil,[59] thereby lessening the demand for synthetic fertilizers. The nutrient runoff from applied fertilizers in the U.S. Midwest has very negative consequences downstream in the Gulf of Mexico, into which the Mississippi Basin empties. Seventy percent of the nutrient deposits in the Gulf originated from midwestern farms. The algae blooms caused by fertilizer runoff starves the waters of oxygen. Eutrophication has made this the second-largest dead zone in the world, destroying massive amounts of marine life and the livelihoods of fishermen in the Gulf of Mexico.

ABOUT CHINESE FLOWERING CAULIFLOWER

Asian *san hua* is a delightful variant, mild, sweeter, and not crumbly, unlike Western cauliflower varieties, with a loose head and delicious tender stems that are easy to work with. Unlike traditional cauliflower, *san hua*'s pale green stems are as delicious as its flowers, so you can enjoy the entire head without waste. Find *san hua* at your local Asian grocer where it is sold as a whole head. You can also find it (less affordably) at specialty groceries, where the florets are sold separately and called *caulilini*.

Prep time 10 minutes | Cook time 2 minutes | Serves 3 to 4

1 pound fresh sugar snap peas, strings removed

½ small head Chinese flowering cauliflower (*san hua*), cut into bite-sized florets

1 medium watermelon radish, or a small purple daikon radish, cut in $^1/_{16}$-inch slices

Fronds of fresh dill or chopped chives, to garnish

1. Soak the sugar snap peas for 5 minutes in cold water. Fill a pot with water and bring to a rapid boil. Have a large bowl filled with ice water standing by.

2. To strip any fibrous strings off the sugar snap peas, use a paring knife to grab the stem tip and pull it down along the pod. They come off easily.

3. Place all the sugar snap peas at once in the pot. Blanch for about 40 seconds. Test one. It should be just barely cooked. Use a sieve to transfer the peapods immediately from the pot to the ice water. Stir to cool them rapidly. The ice water bath will crisp up the sugar snaps and intensify their green color. When they are quite cool, use the sieve to scoop them out and drain. Place them in a bowl.

4. Repeat with the *san hua* florets, blanching them for 30 seconds. Transfer them immediately to an ice water bath to chill thoroughly. Drain the florets and transfer them to another bowl. Both the sugar snaps and *san hua* florets should be quite crispy but not taste raw.

5. Use a mandolin to slice the watermelon radish, not paper-thin but thin enough to easily chew, about $^1/_{16}$ inch in thickness.

6. Artfully arrange the radish slices, sugar snap peas, and san hua florets on a platter or plate individually. Garnish the plates with fresh dill fronds or chopped chives. Serve chilled or at room temperature and pass around your favorite plant-based dressing.

SALAD WITH BABY ROASTED BEETS AND CITRUS

Juicy, earthy, creamy, peppery, with just the right balance of sweetness and acidity, this salad includes tiny roasted gold and red beets, pink grapefruit, and red mandarin orange. Small colorful radishes, slivers of shallot, and arugula add their peppery sharpness and crunch. Then the whole shebang is dotted with soy *labneh* (yogurt cheese), dill, and scattered pistachio nuts. This salad doesn't require dressing, but if you prefer one, I include one on the next page.

Grapefruit grown in the United States has a climate footprint of 0.11 kg CO_2eq per kg, with 21% of emissions from fertilizer production, 20% from in-field bacteria, 6% from off-field bacteria, 9% from draining wetlands, 2% from soil amendment emissions, 11% from pesticide production, 28% from farm machinery, and 2% from irrigating orchards. GHG produced from orange cultivation in the United States is almost identical to grapefruit grown here. Pistachios grown in the United States have a climate footprint of 2.0 kg CO_2eq per kg, with 13% of emissions coming from fertilizer production, 12% from in-field bacteria, 4% from off-field bacteria, 4% from draining wetlands, 2% from pesticide production, 57% from operating farm equipment, and 7% from powering irrigation pumps. For climate challenges facing the U.S. citrus production, see page 401.

Prep time 3 hours (passive time) to strain the yogurt for *labneh*, 1 hour to roast the beets, plus 20 minutes to prep and compose the other salad elements   Serves 3 to 4

8 baby red beets, peeled, roasted, cut in half or quartered into bite-sized pieces

11 baby golden beets, peeled, roasted, cut in half or quartered into bite-sized pieces

3 cups unsweetened cultured soy yogurt, 2 cups strained for the labneh, plus 1 cup for a dressing

¼ teaspoon granulated garlic

Several grinds or pinch of ground white pepper

1 teaspoon Dijon mustard

2 teaspoons shiro (mild, white) miso paste (optional)

2 cups packed baby arugula

1 red grapefruit, cut in sections

2 red mandarin or blood oranges, cut in sections

1 bunch mixed color or French breakfast radishes, roots trimmed, large or damaged leaves removed, sliced in half

1 shallot, peeled and sliced

Several small sprigs fresh dill

2 tablespoons pistachio nuts

1. Preheat the oven to 400°F. To roast the beets, place the peeled, halved beets in two parchment paper bags, one for the red beets, one for the golden. To make the parchment bag, tear off a large piece of parchment paper, fold it in half, place the beets cut side down and spaced ½ inch apart. Fold up the edges several times and staple them to seal. Place the bags on one or two cooking sheets and roast the beets for one hour.

2. To make the *labneh* cheese, pour 2 cups of the thick soy yogurt onto a 18-inch square of unbleached muslin. Gather up the sides and twist to form a sack, and tie with a piece of string. Suspend the yogurt bag over the sink or in a strainer, placed over a bowl. Strain the yogurt for 3 hours, during which time much of the soy whey will drip away, leaving a dense creamy cheese—and a natural probiotic if you make your own unpasteurized, cultured yogurt.

3. To make a dressing, if using, place 3 small roasted golden beets in a high-speed blender. Add 1 cup of soy yogurt, the granulated garlic, white pepper, Dijon mustard, and shiro miso, if using. Blend until the mix is velvety smooth and uniform. Taste and adjust seasonings as you like.

4. To compose the salad on individual plates, start with a base of arugula and any tiny raw beet leaves if your beets provide them. Place 3 to 4 pieces each of red and golden roasted beets over the greens. Between the beets alternate with sections of grapefruit and orange. Add 3 to 4 radish halves. Sprinkle slices of shallot here and there. Use a small espresso spoon or ½ teaspoon measuring spoon to dot the salad with the strained soy *labneh*. Lastly, add small sprigs of dill and sprinkle a few pistachios.

5. Serve at room temperature with or without the dressing, as you like.

TEMPEH BLT

Let's nix pork bacon's climate impact, not to mention its cholesterol, sodium nitrates, and saturated fat, by making flavorful tempeh bacon. It is full of smoky BBQ flavor and offers hefty climate and nutritional benefits. Tempeh bacon makes a terrific plant-based BLT, but don't stop there. Enjoy it in your tofu scrambles, in chilies, crumbled over salads, and loaded on baked potatoes. Tempeh is a traditional Indonesian food, dating back a thousand years. It is made from soybeans and cultured with Rhizopus oryzae that ferments and binds the soybean substrate into a tidy dense cake. Today there are many tempeh varieties, using other beans and grains; all are excellent low-fat sources of plant protein, fiber, vitamins, and minerals.

Soy tempeh produced in Singapore has a very respectable climate footprint at 0.43 kg CO_2eq per kg—21 times lower than Smithfield pork bacon produced and sold in U.S. shops at 10 kg CO_2eq per kg.

Indonesia's Climate Challenges

Indonesia is the fourth-most-populous country on earth. It ranks among the top 10 highest emitters in GHG, due mostly to deforestation, draining of peatbogs and mangroves, and its reliance on fossil fuels, principally coal.[60] Indonesia is a biodiversity hotspot. Its vast native tropical forests and marine habitats, home to complex ecosystems of flora and fauna, are put at risk by the country's land-use and forestry practices and by the rise in temperature and violent weather. Indonesia's very large communities (180 million people) who live along its extensive coastline are very exposed to sea level rise and flooding. Jakarta is the most vulnerable city to environmental threats in the world.[61] It launched two renewable projects in 2023 but will need to do much more to protect its people and wildlife.[62]

Prep time 1 hour to marinate the tempeh, plus 5 minutes   Cook time 25 minutes
Makes about 35 slices

1 teaspoon cumin
seeds

½ teaspoon freshly
ground asafoetida
(hing) nugget

2½ teaspoons
aged tamari

½ teaspoon
granulated garlic

½ teaspoon
granulated onion

¼ teaspoon freshly
ground black
pepper

2 teaspoons
mesquite liquid
smoke

1 tablespoon
tomato paste

4 tablespoons
Worcestershire
Sauce (see page
62)

1 (8-ounce)
package tempeh,
any variety, cut in
¼-inch slices

1. Heat a small skillet on medium low for 3 minutes. Put in the cumin seed, stirring constantly, and dry roast for about 30 seconds or until it becomes fragrant. Do not over-roast the seeds or they will become bitter.

2. Transfer the cumin seeds and asafoetida nugget to a coffee grinder and process into a powder.

3. To make the tempeh marinade, combine in a blender the cumin-asafoetida powder, tamari, granulated garlic and onion, black pepper, liquid smoke, tomato paste, Worcestershire Sauce, and water. Taste and adjust any of the seasonings as you like.

4. Lay the slices of tempeh flat in a flat-bottomed container and pour the marinade over it. Cover and refrigerate for about an hour.

5. Preheat the broiler on low.

6. Heat a large skillet on medium for 3 minutes.

7. Add the tempeh with the marinade to the skillet. Maintain at a low simmer for 15 to 20 minutes or until the tempeh has softened, adding a little water as needed to prevent it from drying out. After it cooks, the marinade should have thickened to a glaze that coats the tempeh slices.

8. Transfer the tempeh to a baking sheet covered with parchment paper.

9. Using a pastry brush, apply a thick coat of marinade on the tempeh and broil 3 inches from the heat for 5 minutes before flipping. Apply more marinade and broil for an additional 3 minutes on the other side. The tempeh should darken and lightly crisp on its edges but do not allow it to burn.

10. Remove from broiler and brush with marinade again before using it in sandwiches, salads, or other foods.

11. To compose a tempeh BLT, use slices of a good 100% wholegrain bread, spread it generously with Jade Mayo (see page 50) or Green Goddess Buttermilk Dressing (see page 47), Dill Dressing (see page 155), or simple oil- and egg-free mayo (see pages 123). Lay down several slices of tempeh bacon and cover with lettuce and a thick slice of a ripe garden or heirloom tomato.

WINTER PURPLE CABBAGE SALAD

Sweet winter cabbage and Central European flavors inspired this climate-supportive, flavorful salad. I added carrot curls for whimsy, shaved shallot for its sweet heat, capers for their bright briny salinity, dill for warm grassy brightness, and a light sprinkle of caraway for its nutty, mild bitterness. A luscious, creamy dill dressing pulls it all together. This dressing also makes a fabulous alternative to mayo as a spread, dip, or binder for cold vegetable bean, potato, and corn salads. Warm it to serve over baked potatoes or steamed vegetables. Winter Purple Cabbage Salad is loaded with fiber and antioxidants, especially vitamins C and K and sulforaphane, with very little fat. It packs a nutritional punch in every crunchy mouthful.

Every element in this tasty salad supports climate health to the max: Cabbage from U.S. farms emits a low 0.11 kg CO_2eq per kg in greenhouse gases; dried onions and carrots grown in U.S. soils emit a negligible 0–0.1 kg CO_2eq per kg. The benchmark climate footprint for tofu comes from U.K. groceries at 1.4 kg CO_2eq per kg.

Prep time 30 minutes   Serves 3 to 4

SALAD

1 firm head purple cabbage, outer leaves removed, shaved

2 medium shallots, peeled and shaved

2 medium carrots, peeled and shaved

DILL DRESSING

1 (14-ounce) package of soft tofu, drained

2 tablespoons nutritional yeast

2 tablespoons granulated or powdered onion

2 tablespoons lemon juice

1½ tablespoons apple cider vinegar

1½ tablespoons Dijon mustard

1 tablespoon granulated or powdered garlic

2 teaspoons shiro (mild, white) miso paste

⅛ teaspoon freshly ground white pepper

½ cup packed dill fronds, plus more for garnish

¼ cup unsweetened soy milk

½ cup drained nonpareil capers, for garnish

2 teaspoons caraway seeds, for garnish

1. Shave the cabbage and shallots with a mandolin set on ⅛-inch thickness. Use a potato peeler to shave the carrots. Soak the carrot shavings in a bowl filled with very hot water for 5 minutes to soften them to later twist into pleasing curls. Drain the carrot slices when they are quite pliable and pat them dry.

2. In a high-speed blender place the tofu, nutritional yeast, granulated onion, lemon juice, cider vinegar, Dijon mustard, granulated garlic, shiro miso paste, pepper, and dill. Run on high for a minute, scrape down the sides, run for a final minute. The dressing should be thick and rich. Taste and adjust the seasonings as you like. You can use it as is for a spread or dip, or thin it with some soy milk to create a pourable dressing.

3. To arrange the salad on individual plates, first lay down a bed of shaved cabbage, then the shaved shallot. Twist the carrot shavings to make carrot curls and arrange them on each plate. Garnish liberally with capers and dill fronds but with just a light sprinkling of caraway seeds.

4. Spoon or drizzle the dressing attractively on top and serve immediately. Pass around more Dill Dressing at the table.

BREADS, CRACKERS,
and
CRÊPES

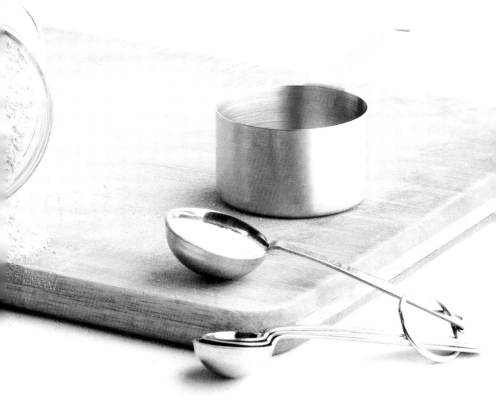

ANISE RAISIN CRISPS

Bread crisps and crackers are fast, delicious alternatives to baking bread. All too often store-bought crackers are ultra-processed, high in fat and sodium, and low in fiber; not so, these crisps. They're climate friendly, nutritious, and fun to make. For crispy crisps, roll the dough thin. For the final pass over the dough, I like to use a *kruskavel* (Swedish rolling pin), whose pointed knobs thin and imprint the dough and prevent bubbles.

Steel-cut oats generate 2 kg CO_2eq per kg at retail in the United States, with 54% from farming, 28% from processing, 12% from transportation, and 6% due to packaging. In the field, oats in the United States have a climate footprint of 0.92 kg CO_2eq per kg, with 30% of emissions related to fertilizer production, 31% from in-field bacteria that digests the fertilizer, 9% from off-field bacteria, 12% from the energy required to drain wetlands for farming, and 10% from farm machinery. Raisins sold in U.S. groceries emit 1.6 kg CO_2eq per kg, with 98% of GHG emissions attributed to agriculture and 2% to processing.

Prep time 30 minutes to make oatmeal, plus 15 minutes Bake time 20 minutes
Makes about 25 to 35, depending on length and width

¾ cup cooked steel-cut oats from ¼ cup dry steel-cut oats and 1 cup water

2 teaspoons aniseed

⅓ cup raisins or currants, chopped

1 cup buckwheat flour, plus more for dusting and rolling

Up to ¼ cup unsweetened almond milk

1. To make the oatmeal, put the steel-cut oats and water in a small heavy-bottomed saucepan. Bring to a boil, then lower to a simmer. Stir periodically to prevent sticking and to encourage the oats to release their starch, about 20 minutes. When the oats are tender but chewy, cover, remove from the heat, and allow the oats to hydrate and release any residue that has adhered to the bottom on the pan, and for the porridge to congeal as it cools.

2. In a medium bowl combine the aniseed, chopped raisins or currants, and buckwheat flour. Rub the flour into the dried fruits, to separate them.

3. Mix in the cooled, cooked oats, using clean hands to incorporate them well.

4. Add only as much almond milk as needed to create a soft, slightly sticky dough. Knead the mix in the bowl for 2 minutes, making sure all the flour is absorbed and the dough is smooth and soft. Flour it on top and cover the bowl tightly with wrap.

5. Preheat the oven to 375°F and place an oven rack on the middle shelf.

6. Cut a piece of parchment paper to fit a large rimless baking sheet.

7. Cut the dough in half, keeping one half in reserve, well covered. Lightly flour the parchment paper. The dough must not be sticky, or it will adhere to the rolling pin. If it sticks, dust with flour and knead it into the dough before rolling.

8. Roll the first piece of dough out directly on the floured parchment until it is between $^1/_{16}$ and ⅛ inch in thickness. As you begin, roll the dough, dust it with flour, flip it over, continue rolling, and repeat. Sprinkle more flour if the dough sticks. Feel it with your hand over the surface to gauge where it might be thicker and require more rolling. When the dough is uniformly flat, for your final pass, roll it once with a *kruskavel* or a docker. If you lack those, prick it all over with the tines of a fork.

9. Use a pizza wheel or blunt butter knife to slice the dough into strips anywhere from 1 to 2 inches in width. Then cut them to the length(s) you like. Using a pastry brush, brush off the surface flour from the raw crisps and parchment.

10. To facilitate crisping, carefully separate each crisp from its neighbor by at least ¼ inch. If your baking tray is sufficiently large, repeat the rolling and cutting with the remaining dough. If not, prepare them on another parchment-lined tray and bake them simultaneously on another oven rack, or bake after the first batch is removed from the oven.

11. Bake for 20 minutes but check it at 15. The crisps are done when they are lightly golden with slightly darker edges.

12. Transfer to a cooling rack. Enjoy Anise Raisin Crisps warm or at room temp. Store any leftover crisps in an airtight container. If over time they lose some crispness from absorbing ambient humidity, simply reheat in a 250°F oven for 5 minutes to crisp them up again.

APPLE RAISIN CRÊPES

Move over Sunday pancakes! Fruit-filled, egg- and dairy-free crêpes are a greener, delicious alternative to pancakes for brunch or dessert. Gluten-free oat and buckwheat make light and tender crêpes. Apple Raisin Crêpes present a terrific opportunity to lighten our individual climate footprint by reducing food waste by using apples that have languished on the counter or in the fridge too long. Even slightly shriveled apples are still nutritious and safe to eat if they show no sign of mold or a broken skin.

U.S. farmed buckwheat emits 1 kg CO_2eq per kg in GHG emissions, with 24% attributable to fertilizer production, 25% to in-field bacteria, 7% for off-field bacteria, 23% to the draining of wetlands, 6% emissions for soil amendments like limestone and urea that release CO_2, 8% to operating farm machinery, and 5% to drying the grain. Oats grown in U.S. fields have a climate footprint of 0.92 kg CO_2eq per kg, with 30% of emissions produced by fertilizer production, 31% from in-field bacteria, 9% from off-field bacteria, 12% from draining wetlands, 3% from soil amendments, 10% from running farm equipment, and 4% from heating the grain to dry it.

Quinoa's Environmental and Ethical Issues

I used to use quinoa flour for these crêpes but stopped when I learned of quinoa's substantial climate footprint—13 kg CO_2eq per kg on South American farms, almost entirely driven (96%) by deforestation. In Peru the footprint is higher at 17 kg CO_2eq per kg. The global demand for this grain over the past decade made quinoa a major income generator for South American farmers. Traditionally, quinoa was cultivated very sustainably, using crop rotation with fallow periods on flat scrub lands that were fertilized by alpacas and llamas. However, as demand exploded, chemical inputs, mechanized equipment, and deforesting mountainsides were employed to ramp up yield. With such strong global demand for quinoa, its price has risen dramatically. While a boon for some farmers, the price put it out of reach of the indigenous populations that depend on quinoa as a staple crop. Moreover, farmers have reduced crop diversity of other native foods in favor of quinoa, negatively impacting the environment, biodiversity, and the health of the local population who have become more reliant on fast and processed foods.[63] If grown sustainably, quinoa is a hardy, drought-resistant, very nutritious food that can be a bulwark against climate change in many regions. As it begins to be grown in Europe and North America, its price may stabilize and hopefully it can become a sustainable option once more.[64]

Prep time 2 hours to strain soy yogurt for a crème fraîche garnish, plus 30 minutes
Cook time 30 minutes | Makes about eight 5½-inch crêpes

FILLING

1 cup mixed raisins, like Thompson, Indian green *Jalpur*, or Indian black raisins (kali kishmish), rehydrated

½ teaspoon freshly ground Ceylon cinnamon

3 apples, cut in a medium dice

⅓ cup lemon juice

¼ teaspoon freshly grated nutmeg

1 tablespoon gluten-free oat flour

BATTER

2 tablespoons apricot paste from ½ cup dried, unsulfured apricots

1 tablespoon flaxseed, freshly ground

½ cup buckwheat flour

½ cup gluten-free oat flour

¼ teaspoon freshly ground Ceylon cinnamon

1 cup unsweetened almond milk

½ cup water

1 teaspoon vanilla extract or ½ teaspoon vanilla seeds

Small spoonful of Soy Crème Fraîche made from 1½ cups soy yogurt, for garnish

Lemon Citrus Powder (see page 41) and freshly grated nutmeg, for garnish

PREPARE THE FILLING

1. Preheat oven to 150°F and insert serving dishes to warm.

2. To rehydrate raisins, place in a small bowl, cover with water, microwave for 1 minute, cool, drain, but reserve the soaking water.

3. Use a coffee grinder to grind Ceylon cinnamon sticks into a fine powder. Measure the amounts needed for both the filling and batter and store any excess in a spice jar placed in a cool, dark cupboard.

4. Combine the drained raisins, Ceylon cinnamon, apples, and lemon juice in a saucepan. Use a nutmeg rasp to grate fresh nutmeg directly into the pan. Taste and adjust seasoning to your taste.

5. Cover and cook over a medium flame, stirring occasionally, for about 10 minutes or until the apples are tender but intact. The apples, depending on the variety, will release some juice. However, if the mixture dries, add some of the reserved raisin water.

6. Stir in the oat flour to thicken the juices and sauce the fruit. Cook for 1 minute. Remove from the heat. Cover to keep the filling warm as you cook the crêpes.

PREPARE THE BATTER

1. Cover the dried apricots with water and microwave for 2 minutes or simmer on a stovetop for 5 minutes. When cool, purée the softened fruit in a high-speed blender, using only as much soaking liquid as required to blend it into a soft, smooth paste.

2. Use a coffee grinder to grind the flaxseed into a powder.

3. In a food processor combine the buckwheat and oat flours, the freshly ground flaxseed, and Ceylon cinnamon. Pulse a few times to mix.

4. Add the apricot paste, almond milk, and vanilla. Run the food processor for a full minute to create a smooth uniform batter. The batter should be thinner than pancake batter to make light crêpes. If it is too thick, thin with a small amount of almond milk.

MAKE SOY CRÈME FRAÎCHE

1. Spoon 1½ cups of soy yogurt onto a square of unbleached muslin. Tie the muslin with a piece of string into a bag and suspend it over the sink for 1½ to 2 hours. Scrape the strained yogurt into a bowl and use a mini whisk to smooth its texture. Refrigerate until it is time to garnish.

COOK AND FILL THE CRÊPES

1. Preheat a large, good-quality nonstick skillet over medium-low heat for 5 minutes. The pan must be fully warmed for the batter not to stick but be careful not to exceed the temperature guidelines for your nonstick pan.

2. With a ¼-cup measuring cup, scoop and pour the batter in the center of the pan. Do not swirl the pan or your crêpes may become too fragile. The crêpe's diameter should measure between 5½ and 6 inches.

3. Cover the skillet and cook for 2 minutes.

4. Uncover the pan and, using a large nylon or silicone spatula, loosen the perimeter of the crêpe to free it entirely; then flip it over. Cook for an additional minute.

5. The first side of your crêpe should be a uniform tan in color. When the second side is cooked, it will be speckled. Adjust the heat if your crêpe is too light or too dark.

6. Transfer the crêpe to a woven place mat or clean kitchen linen and cover lightly with a linen to stay soft and warm.

7. Proceed with the next crêpe. As it cooks, fill the previous crêpe with a few teaspoons of warm filling in a center stripe. Flip over both the left and right sides to cover the filling.

8. Move it to one of the plates in the oven to remain warm.

9. Right before serving, garnish the warm crêpe with a light dusting of Lemon Citrus Powder, freshly grated nutmeg, and a dollop of Soy Crème Fraîche.

CHORNIY KHLIB

Rustic Ukrainian black sourdough rye bread has a crisp crust and a moist crumb. It's robust and earthy with a light sour tang and hint of sweetness. In other words, it is delicious. Enjoy slices of hearty *Chorniy Khlib* with soup, salads, and stews.

The climate footprint for rye on U.S. farms is 0.91 kg CO_2eq per kg, with 25% of emissions driven by fertilizer production, 30% from in-field bacteria, 9% from off-field bacteria, 13% from draining wetlands, 3% from emissions from soil amendments, 13% from the use of farm machinery, and 5% from the energy required to dry the grain. Deforestation is not a factor in the cultivation of rye, and pesticide use is negligible. On Ukrainian farms, by contrast, rye cultivation's climate footprint is lower: 0.45 kg CO_2eq per kg, with 21% attributed to fertilizer production, 28% to in-field bacteria, 8% to off-field bacteria emissions, 5% to draining wetlands, 25% to farm machinery, and 11% to drying.

Ukraine and Climate Change

With a warming planet, Ukraine is increasingly susceptible to heavy rainfall and flooding, mudslides, heat waves, wildfires, and drought. The risks and severity of natural disasters in recent years are rising, causing fatalities, water shortages, and economic losses. The ongoing war with Russia has compounded Ukraine's environmental challenges—the war has caused widespread deforestation across Ukraine, and some of its rich agricultural soils and waterways have been polluted by military sites, materiel, and runoff from coal mines, further compromising some of Ukraine's agricultural output and posing additional health risks for its people.[65]

Prep time 10 to 12 hours to ferment, plus 15 minutes
Bake time 70 minutes | Makes a 500-gram (1-pound) loaf

100 grams (about ⅜ cup) very active rye sourdough starter (see page 199)

130 milliliters (about ½ cup) lukewarm spring water

20 grams (about 2 teaspoons) blackstrap molasses

500 grams (about 3 cups) rye flour, plus more for dusting and to make a slurry

175 milliliters (about ¾ cup) double-strength black decaf coffee, lukewarm

10 grams (about 1 teaspoon) shiro (mild, white) miso paste

50 grams (about ⅓ cup) buckwheat flour

1. A day or two before baking, feed your rye sourdough starter a few times to ensure it is quite active when you use it.

2. In a mixing bowl, mix the water, molasses, and active rye sourdough starter. Add one half of the rye flour, stirring well to combine with a Danish dough whisk or wooden spoon. Cover and allow to rest for 1 hour.

3. Add the coffee and miso paste, dissolving it well, the remaining rye flour, and the buckwheat flour. Wet your hand and knead the sticky dough in the bowl for a few minutes to combine everything well. Smooth it and shape the dough into a ball.

4. Cover the bowl with a lid or wrap and leave it to ferment in a warm corner (ideally around 80°F) for 10 hours in a warmer kitchen, 12 hours in a cooler one.

5. Put a few tablespoons of rye flour in a small bowl and add water to make a slurry. We will use this soon to smooth the surface of the dough before it bakes.

6. Preheat your oven to 500°F. Place a round or oval 3-quart Dutch oven on the middle oven shelf an hour before you bake.

7. Flour a board and transfer the dough to it. The dough will be quite sticky, so shape it with wet hands. Line a bowl, approximately the size and shape of your baking vessel, with parchment paper, leaving tabs that extend beyond the bowl to facilitate moving the dough later.

8. With wet hands, lift the dough and place it in the bowl. Cover lightly with wrap or, better yet, an inverted bowl if you have one that can rest on the bowl rim. While the oven heats up, the dough will puff up considerably.

9. Right before baking, use a bristle pastry brush or your fingers to cover the surface holes with the rye slurry for a smoother, shinier surface. While *Chorniy Khlib* normally is not scored, cutting a few slashes on the top can minimize tearing while baking in its first phase at high heat.

10. Carefully remove the hot baking vessel, remove the lid, and holding the dough by its parchment tabs, transfer both dough and parchment to the hot pot. Cover and return to the oven.

11. Lower the oven temperature to 475°F and bake for 20 minutes.

12. Remove the cover, lower the oven temperature to 420°F, and bake for 50 minutes.

13. Remove the pot from the oven, spill the bread onto a cooling rack, and remove the parchment paper. The bread should have darkened, hardened, and developed a nice, thin crust. It will sound hollow when thumped on its base. If it has not baked adequately, pop the bread back in the oven for an additional 5 minutes and retest it.

14. The bread will continue to develop as it cools. To avoid gumminess, allow the bread to cool fully overnight or for 8 to 10 hours before slicing. Slice *Chorniy Khlib* thinly.

15. Store the black bread on the counter, wrapped in a cotton or linen kitchen towel. It will stay fresh for about 5 days (if it lasts that long).

CORNBREAD

Who doesn't love cornbread? This all-American favorite is comfort food and a staple with deep roots in Native American and southern slave traditions before it spread throughout the country. Cornbread can be sweet or savory, depending on regional preferences, but it is always a welcome addition to any table. This gluten-free cornbread is moist with a light sweetness and crumb. Enjoy it with your chilies, stews, and barbecue or sliced and toasted with a smear of jam for breakfast. Inexpensive, made with but a few humble ingredients, cornbread is easy to make and delightful to eat.

In the United States, sweet corn's climate footprint in the field is 0.45 kg CO_2eq per kg. Fertilizer production accounts for 12% of those emissions, 54% are N_2O emissions from in-field bacteria, 13% from off-field bacteria, 3% from draining wetlands, and 16% from the use of farm machinery. Maize used for corn flour, cornmeal, corn flakes, and animal feed has a similar climate footprint at U.S. farms at 0.43 kg CO_2eq per kg, with 28% related to fertilizer production, 32% from in-field bacteria, 9% from off-field bacteria, 5% from the energy required to drain wetlands for farming, 2% for pesticide production, 11% from running farm machinery, and 10% from the energy used to heat the air to dry corn.

Corn's greenhouse gas emissions is commensurate with its degree of processing before it arrives on grocery shelves. For example, in the United States, packaged yellow corn meal and nixtamalized masa harina share a climate footprint of 1 kg CO_2eq per kg, 66% of which comes from agriculture, 18% from transport, 9% from processing, and 7% from packaging. More processing is involved in making packaged tortillas and corn chips, raising GHG emissions to 4 kg CO_2eq per kg. Corn oil, more processed still, emits 5 kg CO_2eq per kg in GHG.

HINT

For a creamier, sweeter cornbread, use 1⅓ cups of A Better Buttermilk (see page 27), in place of the soy milk and vinegar.

Prep time 15 minutes   Bake time 45 to 55 minutes   Makes 16 to 20 servings

2 ears sweet corn, shucked, roasted, and stripped off the cob

1⅓ cup unsweetened soy milk

4½ teaspoons raw, unfiltered apple cider vinegar

⅓ cup date paste from ¾ cup pitted dates, any variety

1 cup yellow or white cornmeal, medium grind (stone-ground is tastier)

1 cup gluten-free oat flour

2 teaspoons sodium- and-aluminum-free baking powder

½ teaspoon sodium- free baking soda

1. Preheat oven to 400°F/375°F convection.

2. On the burners of a gas range or a grill, lightly roast the shucked corn on the cob, rotating each ear every 10 seconds or so until they are lightly toasted on all sides. Allow the cobs to cool.

3. Position each cob on a large cutting board, and using a sharp chef knife, slice the kernels off the cob. Reverse the knife to scrape off the flavorful corn "milk" liquid too. Transfer the kernels and corny milk to a bowl and set aside.

4. To clabber the soy milk, pour it in a glass and stir in the apple cider vinegar. Set aside for 10 minutes.

5. To make the date paste, cover the dates with water and microwave for 2 minutes. Alternatively, place the dates in a small pot, cover with water and simmer for 5 minutes. Cool. Use a high-speed blender to blend the dates and water into a smooth, uniform paste.

6. In a bowl mix the dry ingredients: cornmeal, oat flour, baking powder, and baking soda.

7. In a separate bowl or measuring cup, combine the clabbered soy milk—or A Better Buttermilk—with the date paste, mixing it very well.

8. Now add the wet ingredients to the dry ones, stirring minimally to combine. Add the grilled corn. Let the batter rest for 10 minutes for the leavening agents to do their magic. The batter should be light and airy.

9. Use a silicon or rubber spatula to transfer the batter to a square 8- or 9-inch glass or ceramic baking dish.

10. Bake the cornbread on the middle rack of the oven for 30 minutes and test with a toothpick. The cornbread is ready when the top is well toasted, golden, and cracked, and when an inserted toothpick comes out clean.

11. Place the baking dish on a cooling rack until it has cooled a little to facilitate slicing.

KNÄCKEBRÖD

A medieval staple from rural Sweden, *Knäckebröd* is a simple sourdough crispbread made from coarse pumpernickel (whole rye) flour, rye sourdough starter, and a sprinkling of seeds. Because it has a very long shelf life, in the past *Knäckebröd* was baked in enormous quantities just twice annually and stored hung on poles under rafters or above the hearth. *Knäckebröd* is rolled very thin and indented with a *kruskavel*, a notched rolling pin that prevents bubbling during baking and gives the crispbread its signature crunchy texture. Homemade *Knäckebröd* is delightfully crispy and light with fabulous nutty rye flavor. Serve plain or top with nondairy *filmjölk*—soy yogurt strained into a spreadable cream cheese—and thinly sliced vegetables or sliced fruit.

In Swedish shops, rye berries have a climate footprint of 0.61 kg CO_2eq per kg, driven entirely by agriculture. In the United States, dark rye flour's climate footprint is 1 CO_2eq per kg, with 66% due to agriculture, 18% from transport, 9% from processing, and 7% from packaging.

Climate Change in Sweden

Climate change is causing air and water temperatures to rise, sea levels to rise, and more extreme weather events like heavy rainfall and flooding. Sweden is among the world's highest consumers of energy per capita, but due to its wide use of renewable energy sources, around 60% of its national energy supply in 2023, its greenhouse gas emissions are relatively low. It ranks in the top 10 countries on Columbia and Yale Universities' Environmental Performance Index. Sweden's goals are to reduce its GHG emissions by 63% by 2030 to reach net zero emissions by 2045, but Sweden is predicted to miss its 2030 target, due both to accelerated warming worldwide and to a relaxing of climate priorities by its current government. In 2021, 76% of Swedes polled were in favor of stricter policies to address the climate crisis.[66, 67]

Prep time 8 hours to ferment the dough, plus 1 hour | Bake time 10 to 12 minutes
Makes eight 8-inch crispbreads

200 grams (about 1½ cups plus 2 tablespoons) whole rye flour

140 milliliters (about ½ cup plus 1 tablespoon) spring water

40 grams (about 2 tablespoons) active rye sourdough starter

7 grams (about 1 teaspoon) shiro (mild, white) miso

10 grams (about 4 teaspoons) seeds, like fennel, anise, caraway

1. Two days before baking, start feeding your rye sourdough starter daily so that it becomes active and bubbly.

2. The night before you bake, mix the rye flour, water, and rye sourdough starter in a mixing bowl.

3. Use a clean hand to knead the mix in a bowl for a few minutes to create a moist and sticky dough. Adjust with flour or water as needed.

4. After 15 minutes, add the miso, mixing it well.

5. Cover with wrap and leave the bowl on the counter to ferment overnight, about 8 hours. The consistency will not have changed greatly.

6. Preheat the oven to 375°F and place a large baking stone on the middle oven rack. If you don't have a stone, insert a large rimless baking sheet, lined with parchment.

7. Transfer the dough to a large cutting board, covered with parchment paper. Roll the dough into a thick snake, then cut it into eight equal pieces.

8. Return the seven dough pieces to the mixing bowl and keep them covered to prevent drying. Use a rolling pin to roll out the first piece on the parchment-lined board, flipping it as you go, sprinkling rye flour if the dough begins to stick. Roll it as thin as you can, to about $^1/_{16}$ inch in thickness.

9. Sprinkle on your seeds of choice and roll them lightly to help them adhere to the dough's surface.

10. For your final pass, use a *kruskavel* to flatten the dough more and create *Knäckebröd*'s signature indentations across the dough's surface. If you don't have one, use a pizza docker or fork to perforate the dough uniformly.

11. Use a cookie cutter or the rim of a sturdy glass to cut out a central hole. Bake it as well to make a tasty cracker.

12. Use a pastry brush to brush off any excess flour from the dough's surface. Then, holding the parchment paper, slide the dough off the parchment and onto a well-floured pizza peel. Use the peel to transfer it immediately to the oven onto the hot baking stone or lined rimless baking sheet.

13. Spritz the dough's surface lightly with water. Bake for 5 minutes. If the *Knäckebröd* is firm enough, flip it over and spritz with water again. The spritzing is optional but does help crisp up the *Knäckebröd* and enrich its color.

14. Begin checking for doneness after 8 minutes. The cut-outs will bake in less time, so begin checking on them after 5 minutes. Remove the *Knäckebröd* when it is firm, golden, and lightly browned on its edges.

15. Transfer the *Knäckebröd* to a cooling rack.

16. Repeat Steps 8 through 15 with the remaining seven pieces of dough.

17. Unless your home is very humid, *Knäckebröd* will stay crispy while unwrapped on the countertop for a few days. They can also be frozen. If they soften, just pop them in a 250°F oven for 10 minutes to crisp up.

NAAN

An Indian yeasted flatbread, naan has its roots in ancient Persia and Central Asia 2,500 years ago. Popular throughout India and indeed, worldwide, naan is ubiquitous in the northern wheat-growing regions of India. Traditionally, naan is made with white flour and cooked on the interior walls of clay tandoori ovens. This nutrient-dense version of naan is made with whole wheat flour and includes no added fats, sugar, or salt. Baked in a regular home oven, they won't have the characteristic tandoori blisters or texture of tandoori-baked naan, but they are still awfully tasty, far more nutritious, and kinder to the planet. Decorate the breads with seeds like sesame, white poppy, and nigella for fun.

Wheat grown in U.S. fields generates 0.67 kg CO_2eq per kg in greenhouse gas emissions with 28% coming from the use of fertilizers, 32% from the N_2O emissions from in-field bacteria, 9% from off-field bacteria, 11% from farming on drained wetlands, 7% from farm machinery, 3% from emissions from soil amendments, 3% from the power required to irrigate fields, and 6% from drying the grain. Wheat farmed in India emits 0.88 kg CO_2eq per kg, with 35% of GHG from fertilizer production, 28% from in-field bacteria, 10% from off-field bacteria, 3% from deforestation, 6% from the CO_2 released by adding soil amendments like limestone and urea, 5% from running farm equipment, 6% from the power required to irrigate fields, and 5% from drying the grain.

Climate Challenges in North India

Warmer, moist air is changing monsoon patterns in the south of India. In India's north, where most of its wheat is cultivated, extreme weather events are becoming more intense and frequent, with heavier rains over shorter time spans, causing flash flooding and landslides. This has caused loss of life and widespread damage to the livelihoods and infrastructure in local communities.[68, 69]

Prep time 60 minutes rise, plus 30 minutes   Bake time 10 minutes   Makes 8 naan

2 teaspoons
date paste
from ⅓ cup
pitted dates

1 flax egg
made from 1
tablespoon
freshly
ground golden
flaxseed

10 grams
(about 1
tablespoon
plus ⅛
teaspoon)
active dry
yeast

½ cup
unsweetened
cultured soy
yogurt

3 to 4 cups
white whole
wheat flour

2 tablespoons
whole seeds,
like sesame,
white poppy, or
nigella

1. To make date paste, cover the dates with water in a small glass container, and microwave for 2 minutes. Alternatively simmer on the stovetop in a small pot for 5 minutes. Cool the dates and use only as much of its soaking water as you need to blend them silky smooth in a high-speed blender.

2. To make the flax egg, grind the flaxseeds in a coffee grinder, then mix them in a small bowl with 2½ tablespoons of water.

3. In a medium-large bowl place 5 tablespoons warm water. Sprinkle on the yeast, and after 5 minutes, stir in the date paste.

4. After another 5 minutes, stir in the soy yogurt and flax egg. Add 5 more tablespoons of warm water and stir well to combine.

5. Mix in 3 cups of white whole wheat flour and either transfer to a board lightly floured with whole wheat flour or to a standing mixer with a dough blade attached. Knead the dough for 20 minutes. The dough will become less sticky with kneading but if it is excessively sticky, dust the board with a little more flour. After kneading, the dough should be soft and supple with little if any stickiness.

6. Place the dough back in the mixing bowl, cover with plastic wrap or a lid, and set the bowl in a warm corner for 1 hour, during which the dough will expand.

7. Preheat the oven to 450°F.

8. Transfer the dough to a lightly floured board. Divide it into eight equal pieces. Return seven pieces to the bowl and cover it well to prevent drying. Knead the dough piece lightly and shape it into a ball. With your fingers flatten it into a 4-by-5-inch disk.

9. Lay the dough disk on a baking sheet lined with parchment paper and cover it with plastic or a slightly damp kitchen linen, as you shape the remaining pieces of dough.

10. Using a 1-inch bristle brush, brush the dough's surface with water and sprinkle the seeds on top of the dough disks.

11. Bake the breads for about 8 minutes or until the naan are golden and toasted in places.

12. Remove the baking sheet and place the naan directly on the oven racks to cook their undersides for an additional 4 minutes.

13. Transfer the baked naan to a large clean kitchen linen and wrap them to stay warm and moist until serving.

POTATO, CORN, AND AMARANTH CRISPS

These crisp breads pay tribute to three of Peru's beloved staples—amaranth, potato, and corn. Gluten-free and high in fiber, protein, healthy omega-3s, and flavor, these chewy crisps are great to serve with both savory and sweet spreads and toppings. Amaranth, an ancient food of Mesoamerica, is a gluten-free pseudo-grain, like buckwheat and quinoa, with a nutty flavor and an impressive nutritional profile: A complete protein, it has the highest level of protein of any grain at 13 to 15%. It is a superb source of soluble and insoluble fiber, calcium, iron, potassium, phosphorus, zinc, and vitamins C and A.

Amaranth flour, produced in U.S. factories, has a climate footprint of 0.69 kg CO_2eq per kg, with 93% of GHG emissions due to agriculture, 3% to transport, and 5% to processing.

Everything Old Is New Again: Amaranth in the Era of Climate Change

Drought-resistant, highly nutritious, and producing low GHG emissions, amaranth is an attractive candidate for a warming planet. Today, rice, wheat, and corn are so dominant that they account for nearly 50% of the world's calories. Over time, over-reliance on these few monoculture crops has made agriculture vulnerable to insect damage and microbial pathogens. Monoculture growing practices have relied on applied synthetic fertilizers, soil amendments, and pesticides, all of which cause soil erosion, nitrogen pollution, eutrophication, pollinator die-off, and biodiversity loss.

As climate conditions worsen throughout the world, farmers are rediscovering their ancient crops, like amaranth. Today, Indigenous farmers in Guatemala, Mexico, and the United States are working together on amaranth projects. Amaranth is also beginning to be cultivated in Europe and Ukraine.[70]

Prep time overnight soak for the amaranth seeds, plus 30 minutes
Bake time 20 to 30 minutes, depending on the crispbreads' thickness
Makes about 70 crisps, roughly 2 by 4 inches

1 cup amaranth, rinsed and soaked

3 tablespoons date paste from ½ cup pitted dates, any variety

2 tablespoons golden flaxseed, freshly ground

Aniseed (a Peruvian preference), or Lime Citrus Powder (see page 41) and ají *panca* powder made from dried red Peruvian *panca* chilies, for garnish

2 teaspoon cumin seed, freshly ground

4½ cups unsalted vegetable broth

1 cup coarse grit instant polenta

1 cup whole potato flour

2 tablespoons granulated onion

2 tablespoons granulated garlic

½ cup nutritional yeast

Several grinds of black pepper

3 tablespoons aka (red) miso paste

1. Amaranth seeds are coated with saponins, a natural, bitter coating, so before cooking, rinse them well in a very fine strainer until the water runs clear. Transfer to a bowl, cover the amaranth with water, and soak overnight. Soaking increases the bioavailability and digestibility of most grains, including amaranth. Drain the amaranth before cooking it in Step 7.

2. Preheat the oven to 450°F and insert a large baking stone on the middle oven shelf about 1 hour in advance of baking.

3. To make the date paste, cover the dates with water and microwave for 2 minutes. Cool. In a high-speed blender blend the softened dates and as much of their cooking water as needed to create a dense paste.

4. Use a coffee grinder to mill the golden flaxseed into a powder.

5. If you want to make chili powder from mild ají *pancas* for a garnish, wipe the coffee grinder out with a paper towel, remove their stems, and grind the dried chilies into flakes or more finely into a powder.

6. Wipe the coffee grinder out again, and put in the cumin seeds, grinding them into a powder.

7. Place the soaked amaranth in a saucepan with 1½ cups of broth. Bring to a boil, cover, lower the heat to cook at a very gentle simmer for about 20 minutes or until the liquid is absorbed. Remove from the heat and allow to sit for another 15 minutes to fully absorb the liquid. Uncover the pot, fluff with a fork, and allow the amaranth to cool.

8. To cook the polenta, heat 3 cups of broth in a saucepan and bring to a boil. Slowly sprinkle in the polenta, stirring constantly to avoid lumps. Cook on low for about 5 minutes or until the polenta is dense. Cover and remove from the heat. Allow the cooked polenta to rest for 10 minutes to fully cook and congeal.

9. When the cooked polenta has cooled sufficiently, pulse it in a food processor to break it up into uniform crumbs.

10. In a large bowl combine the cooked amaranth, polenta crumbs, date paste, ground flaxseed, potato flour, onion and garlic granules, cumin powder, nutritional yeast, and black pepper, mixing it well. Dot the surface with aka miso and, using clean hands, mix in the miso to distribute it evenly throughout the mixture. Taste and adjust seasonings as you like. The dough will be quite sticky.

11. Line a rimless baking sheet with parchment paper. Mound ¼ of the dough toward one end of the lined pan. Cover it with waxed paper to help you see what you're doing and, using a rolling pin, start rolling the dough to spread it uniformly over the parchment. Leave a 1-inch dough-free border on all sides of the baking tray. Feel with your hand as you go to gauge how level the thickness is. Periodically peel off the paper, bending it back low over the dough to cleanly remove the waxed sheet.

12. Observe the dough and add more if needed to fill in any depressions.

13. When you are finished rolling and spreading the dough, you should have a thin, uniform layer. For crispier results, roll the dough closer to $^1/_{16}$ inch thick. For crisps with a chewier bite, roll them between ⅛ and $^3/_{16}$-inch in thickness.

14. Repeat this process using an additional baking sheet, if needed.

15. If your oven is convection and heats very evenly, you can bake multiple trays at once on different oven racks. But keep an eye out to ensure even results. You still may need to swap the trays around. Otherwise, bake the trays on the middle rack, one baking sheet after the other.

16. Regardless of their thickness, remove the baking sheet(s) after 10 minutes.

17. Use a pizza wheel to cut the sheet of dough into crisps. As a guideline use 1½ to 2 inches in width to 3 to 4 inches in length, but feel free to shape them as you wish.

18. Return the sheet(s) to the oven for another 5 minutes. At this point, the dough should be firm on top but still very soft on its underside. Remove the baking sheet(s) from the oven and, using an angled spatula, gently detach each crisp from the parchment paper.

19. Transfer as many crisps as will fit onto the very hot baking stone and bake for another 5 to 10 minutes, depending on their thickness. You will need to bake them in turns to accommodate all the crisps.

20. The crisps are ready when their top edges have browned and the undersides are golden. They may be a little flexible at this stage but will crisp up as they cool.

21. Transfer the crisps to cooling racks and decorate them immediately with a sprinkling of aniseed or a pinch of Lime Citrus Powder and ají *pancas* powder for some zing.

RAJGIRA ROTI

Made from amaranth flour and potato, *Rajgira* Roti are traditional breads eaten on Hindu fasting days when wheat and rice are eschewed, and only certain other foods are permitted. Serve these nutritious roti with a bowl of soy yogurt, instead of the traditional dairy curds, and Green Chutney (see page 44) for a delightful supper or cut into quarters to serve with appetizers.

In U.S. factories, the climate footprint for amaranth flour is 0.69 kg CO_2eq per kg, 93% of which is related to emissions from agriculture, 3% to transportation, and 5% to milling the seeds into flour. Amaranth is resistant to drought. This nutritious crop is being explored in Zimbabwe to improve its climate resistance and food security. To learn more about amaranth's resurgence in the era of climate change, see page 183.

Punjab's Climate Challenges

In recent years, temperatures have risen significantly in Punjab, which straddles both Pakistan and India, and rainfall and groundwater reserves have declined. Floods, droughts, and heat waves are also increasing in intensity, making this region one of the most vulnerable to climate change. In 2022 Punjab suffered severe rains and floods that killed over 1,700 people and injured almost 13,000.[71] The floods that year damaged over 438,000 acres of cropland and orchards, and 50% of its water systems, and destroyed 733,000 livestock.[72] With continued global warming, the yields of all major crops grown in Punjab are expected to decline by 2050: Maize production is expected to drop by 13%, cotton by 11%, and wheat and potato both by 5%, below their 2023 output.[73]

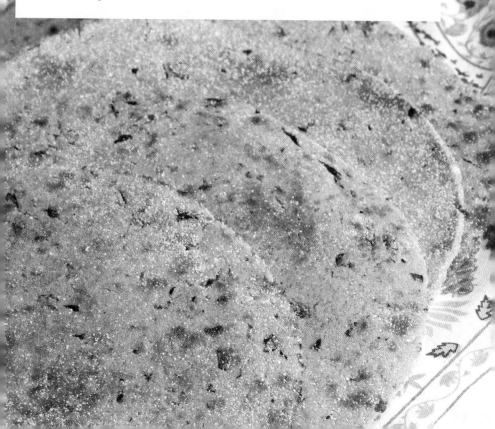

Prep time 20 minutes │ Cook time 20 minutes │ Makes about five 5-inch roti

½ teaspoon cumin seed, lightly roasted and ground

1 cup amaranth flour, plus more for rolling the roti

3 tablespoons cilantro leaves, chopped

1 large green Indian chili, minced

½ inch ginger root, peeled, minced

1 tablespoon soy yogurt

2 teaspoons shiro (mild, white) miso paste

¼ teaspoon freshly ground black pepper, or to taste

⅔ cup russet potato, microwaved and riced from one medium-large potato

1. Heat a small skillet for 2 minutes on medium low. Put in the cumin seed, stirring constantly. As soon as you perceive its aroma, remove the seeds from the skillet to cool. Transfer them to the coffee grinder and grind them into a powder. Place the powder in a small bowl.

2. Place the amaranth flour in a bowl. Stir in the roasted cumin powder, cilantro leaves, minced chili and ginger, soy yogurt, and the miso paste. Add several grinds of black pepper. Mix to combine well, using a spoon to cream the miso paste into the flour by pushing it against the sides of the bowl to break it up and distribute small dots of miso throughout the mix.

3. Microwave the potato until it is very soft, and a fork can penetrate it easily.

4. Peel the potato while it is very hot and, using a potato ricer, squeeze it into your measuring cup and transfer it immediately to the bowl.

5. With a clean hand, knead the mix in the bowl into a soft and smooth dough for about 5 minutes. Add a tablespoon at a time of hot water as needed to make a dough that is dense and smooth, like heavy clay, but not tacky.

6. Heat a good quality nonstick Indian *tava* or nonstick skillet on medium for 4 minutes as you begin to shape the roti.

7. On a cutting board, use your hands to roll the dough into a thick cylinder and divide it into five equal lengths.

8. Keep one piece of dough out and return the rest to the bowl and cover them to prevent drying.

9. The fastest way to make *Rajgira* Roti is to use a small *belan*, or Indian rolling pin, or a length of wooden dowel. Lightly flour the cutting board and roll the piece of dough into a disk about ⅛ to ³/₁₆ inch in thickness. Flip over and dust the roti as you go.

10. *Rajgira* dough is forgiving, but with no gluten, it will crack along its perimeter. That is fine for rustic roti. If you prefer a neater look, cut out the roti using a 5-inch pot cover, and mix the scraps back into the bowl. Cracks and any splits are easily patched with a bit of dough and rolled smoothed.

11. Brush off any surface flour with a small bristle brush and transfer the roti to the hot nonstick skillet. Cook for 1 minute and remove the cover. Use a large nylon or silicone spatula to peek underneath. When the roti is spotted and lightly brown, flip it over to cook the other side. Press down on the roti with the spatula as it cooks to ensure that it cooks evenly. It may puff up in the center with the release of steam. Just keep pressing and rotating the roti as it cooks for 45 seconds to a minute on the second side.

12. When the roti is golden and lightly spotted on both sides, transfer it to a bowl lined with a clean cloth. Cover the roti with the cloth and a pot cover to keep it warm and soft as you cook the others. Then serve immediately.

13. If you have leftovers or if they have cooled completely, reheat them by wrapping them well in cloth and microwaving for 30 seconds before serving immediately.

RIESKA BARLEY BREAD

A flatbread from Finland dating back to the Middle Ages, *Rieska* has as many variations as it does bakers: In olden times, *Rieska* was simply an unleavened hard bread made from barley flour and water, cooked on a hot stone. Nowadays, you are more likely to find it leavened, lightened with buttermilk or milk, and made from rye, wheat, or potatoes, with or in place of barley. These *Rieska* are fiber rich and climate supportive, tender, and very tasty. Serve *Rieska* with steaming bowlfuls of Finnish *Hernekeitto* split pea soup (see page 128) or any soup you like. Or enjoy them sweet, topped with sliced roasted peaches or plums.

On Finnish farms, barley has a climate footprint of 1.2 kg CO_2eq per kg, with 5% of GHG emitted during fertilizer production, 11% from in-field bacteria, 3% from off-field bacteria, 68% from the draining of wetlands for farming, 2% from soil amendments, 6% from operating farm machinery, and 4% from drying the grain. By comparison, on U.S. farms, GHG emissions for barley are 0.84 kg CO_2eq per kg, with 30% from fertilizer production, 33% from in-field bacteria, 10% from off-field bacteria, 7% from draining wetlands, 2% from soil amendments, 9% from running farm equipment, 2% from the power used to irrigate fields, and 6% from drying the crop.

Finland's Ambitious Climate Actions

In 2022 Finland passed the most ambitious self-financing climate target into law, with the goal of reaching net zero emissions by 2035 and becoming net negative by 2040. Worldwide, only South Sudan's target is slightly more impressive but is reliant on international financing for its realization. GHG emissions have been increasing from deforestation from logging over the past decade, which erased Finland's gains from shifting away from fossil fuels. Russia's invasion of Ukraine has accelerated Finland's energy transition, spawning wind power projects, and heating its buildings with renewables to increase their energy efficiency.[74]

Prep time 40 minutes   Bake time 20 minutes   Makes eight 5-inch flatbreads

½ cup cold, congealed oat porridge, made from ¼ cup steel-cut oats

½ cup unsweetened soy milk

1 teaspoon active dry yeast

2 cups thick cultured soy yogurt

1¾ cups barley flour

1¼ cups white whole wheat flour

½ teaspoon sodium-free baking soda

2 teaspoons sodium-and-aluminum-free baking powder

1. An hour before baking, insert a large baking stone or a rimless baking sheet, lined with parchment paper, on the middle oven rack and preheat the oven to 400°F.

2. If you don't have cold porridge on hand, combine ¼ cup steel-cut oats with 1 cup water and simmer on low, stirring occasionally for 30 minutes or until the oats have broken down and thickened. Cool to room temperature.

3. Warm the soy milk to 100°F and pour it into a large mixing bowl. Sprinkle in the yeast, mix, and wait for 10 minutes for the yeast to activate. Stir in the soy yogurt and oat porridge.

4. In a separate bowl, combine the barley flour and white whole wheat flour, baking soda, and baking powder.

5. Using a dough whisk incorporate the flour mix into the yogurt mixture, creating a sticky, very moist dough. Cover, place in a warm, draft-free corner, and allow the dough to rise for an hour.

6. Flour a board very heavily with barley flour. Break off enough dough to lightly shape into a 2½-inch ball, roll it gently into the flour to coat its entire surface. Then gently flatten into a disk ¼ inch thick using your fingers or a wooden dowel.

7. Use a pizza docker or a fork to perforate the *Rieska* well.

8. If you like, emboss a diamond or other simple geometric design on top (a child's grooved rolling pin for clay works well here).

9. Transfer the *Rieska* to a large cutting board and cover with plastic wrap as you prepare the remaining *Rieska*.

10. Use a bristle pastry brush to brush off the surface flour from the breads.

11. Place the unbaked *Rieska*, one by one, on a pizza peel and transfer them to the hot baking stone or lined rimless baking sheet in the oven. Given the size of your baking stone or baking sheet, you may need to bake them in two batches.

12. Use a spray bottle to spritz the *Rieska* in the oven with water.

13. Bake for 15 minutes and check for doneness. When baked, the *Rieska* should be lightly golden all over and sound hollow when knocked. Do not overbake or they may dry out and toughen.

14. As they come out of the oven, wrap the flatbreads in a clean kitchen towel to stay warm and tender until serving.

RUGBRØD

Dark, chewy, deliciously complex Danish *Rugbrød* is the daddy of sour-dough loaves. It is widely adored throughout Scandinavia and in my home too. Once you sample it homemade, you will find commercially made *rug-brød* a poor substitute. This recipe makes a richly flavored loaf chock-full of cracked rye, whole barley, and flaxseeds. Dense *rugbrød* is sliced thin. It is delicious unadorned but really shines when it is smeared with soy skyr, a cultured cream cheese made from strained soy yogurt, and topped with vegetables or fruit.

Rye farmed in Danish fields has a climate footprint of 0.56 kg CO_2eq per kg, with 8% of those emissions emitted during fertilizer production, 25% from N_2O from in-field bacteria, 3% from off-field bacteria, 31% from the energy required to drain wetlands for farming, 2% from soil amendments' CO_2 emissions, 20% from operating farm machinery, and 8% from drying the grain.

Denmark's Climate Risks

Denmark is situated between the North and Baltic Seas. Rising sea temperatures and the melting of sea ice is causing sea levels to rise. Extreme weather, increasing rain-fall, flooding, and storm surge are Denmark's greatest climate risks; its sea levels are projected to rise by 1.2 meters (almost 4 feet) by the end of the century, increasing its coastal flooding risk by 28% by the year 2115. All of the country's flood-prone areas are vulnerable to flooding, primarily from its seas but also from its rivers. Some of Denmark's islands, like Birkholm, are only 2 meters above sea level and are therefore particularly vulnerable.[75]

Prep time 45 minutes | Fermentation time 45 hours | Bake time 80 to 90 minutes
Cool overnight | Makes one 9-by-4-inch loaf | Equipment: A manual or electric grain mill

2 tablespoons ripe rye sourdough starter (see page 199)

1 cup organic rye flour

½ cup spring water

½ cup whole-grain rye berries, cracked

½ cup hulled barley groats, cracked

⅓ cup whole flaxseed or a mix of flaxseed, sunflower, and pumpkin seeds

2 cups spring water

1¼ cups whole rye flour

1 tablespoon unsulfured blackstrap molasses or malt barley syrup

2 teaspoons shiro (mild, white) miso paste

STEP 1: FEED THE SOURDOUGH AND SOAK THE SEEDS

1. Begin feeding your rye mother dough a day or two in advance to ensure it is active and ripe before making *rugbrød*.

2. In a bowl mix the 2 tablespoons of mother dough with 1 cup of rye flour and ½ cup of spring water. Stir well, cover with plastic wrap.

3. Set the bowl in a warm, draft-free spot to develop over 24 hours. Your starter will expand as it ferments, becoming light and bubbly.

4. Use a grain mill on a very coarse setting to crack the rye and barley berries, making as little flour as possible.

5. In a separate bowl mix the cracked grains and seeds with 2 cups of spring water. The seeds and grains should absorb the water and become heavy and saturated.

6. Cover the grains and seeds with plastic wrap and set in a warm, draft-free spot for 24 hours. Observe the bowl after 12 hours. If it has absorbed all its water, add ½ cup more.

7. After 24 hours, drain the seeds and grains.

STEP 2: MIX THE DOUGH

1. In a large bowl, mix the soaked grains and seeds with ½ cup of the fed sourdough starter. Return any excess starter to your container of mother dough and refrigerate.

2. Stir in 1¼ cups rye flour and the molasses or malt barley syrup. Mix until very well combined.

3. Rest the dough for 10 minutes, before mixing in the shiro miso. The dough should be dense and very sticky. If it is dry or crumbly, add a little spring water.

STEP 3: BAKE *RUGBRØD*

1. Preheat the oven to 400°F an hour before baking.

2. Line a bread pan with parchment paper. Use a rubber or silicon spatula to transfer the dough into the pan, spreading it smoothly on the surface and slightly higher at its edges and lower in the center.

3. Cover the baking pan with plastic wrap. Set it in a warm, draft-free spot for 3 hours or until the dough has expanded by one-third and filled your bread pan to capacity.

4. Insert the loaf pan in the oven, and lower the oven temperature to 360°F.

5. Bake for 80 to 90 minutes or until a thermometer measures the bread's internal temp at 210°F. Do not overbake.

6. Remove the loaf from the oven when it is done and place it on a cooling rack. Allow it to cool for 30 minutes in the pan.

7. After 30 minutes, pull up on the parchment paper to gently extract the loaf, leave the parchment attached, and allow the bread to cool for an additional 8 hours or overnight before serving.

8. Store in parchment covering and place in a paper bag to prevent drying. *Rugbrød* also freezes well if it is well wrapped.

9. Slice very thinly and enjoy it plain, served with a hearty soup. As an appetizer or a snack, serve topped with soy skyr and thin slices of cucumber, radish, scallion, and dill, or for a sweet treat, smeared with soy skyr and topped with berries or roasted slices of apricots or plums.

MAKING A RYE SOURDOUGH STARTER

Prep time about 6 days

1. Mix 3½ tablespoons whole rye flour with ¼ cup spring water in a jar that can hold up to 2 cups. Stir well. Cover the container loosely to allow a little airflow. Set it on your counter for 48 hours and stir the mix 3 times a day.

2. Add 2 tablespoons rye flour with 2 tablespoons spring water. Stir well, cover loosely, set aside for 48 hours, stirring 3 times a day.

3. The starter should now begin to show some signs of life with bubbles and froth. If not, repeat Step 2 and give it another 2 days. If it still is unresponsive, it is best to start over.

4. Add 5¼ tablespoons of rye flour and 3 tablespoons spring water. Stir, cover loosely, set aside for 24 hours, stirring 3 times a day.

5. Transfer the starter to a 1-quart container. Stir in ½ cup of rye with only ⅛ cup of water. Cover loosely.

6. After a few hours, your sourdough "mother" should be alive with bubbles and ready for use.

7. To maintain your mother dough, keep it covered and refrigerated, unless you plan to bake daily, in which case you can feed it daily and keep it on the counter.

8. Feed the mother dough with whole rye flour and spring water in a ratio of 2:1 twice per week. The larger your mother grows, the more food/water it will require. Initially, ½ cup flour : ¼ cup water will suffice. Many people retain just a cup of mother dough and discard the rest.

9. Before baking, feed your starter a day in advance and allow it to come to room temp and become active and bubbly.

10. At any point if dark or discolored alcoholic liquid, known as hooch, accumulates on the top of the starter, or if your starter has turned gray on its surface instead of tan, it is a signal that your mother dough needs immediate attention. Pour off the liquid, scrape off the surface, and feed it immediately. If any mold appears on the top, scrape it off together with a measure of healthy sourdough beneath it and feed the remaining mother dough. However, if you have neglected your mother dough to the extent that it does not revive after several feedings, or if it smells unpleasant, it is time to discard it and start anew.

SANGAK PEBBLE BREAD

This fabulous Persian bread dates to the eleventh century when it was the practice of Persian soldiers on their military campaigns to carry a small sack of river stones that they would pile together to make portable ovens upon which to bake *sangak*, their daily bread and staple. Happily, we can make this deliciously chewy sourdough bread today without marching and in the comfort of our kitchens. This version of *sangak* is a sourdough, made with hard spring white whole wheat flour. Nutritious, digestible, light, and chewy, it is absolutely delicious.

You will need about 7 pounds of small (1- to 1½-inch) smooth river stones to line a cookie sheet upon which to bake *sangak*. I suggest you use an old cookie sheet; the super-heated stones may discolor the surface.

Wheat farmed in Iran emits 0.70 kg CO_2eq per kg, with 31% of GHG from fertilizer production, 30% from in-field bacteria, 11% from off-field bacteria, 6% from CO_2 released when soil amendments are applied, 7% from running farm machinery, 10% from the energy used to irrigate fields, and 6% from drying the crop.

Climate Change in Iran

Like other Middle Eastern countries, Iran is hard hit by global warming's rising temperatures, heat waves, reduced precipitation, sand and dust storms, and very serious water shortages. It also has experienced more intense flooding and soil erosion. Rising temperatures together with dam building and irrigation projects have dried up rivers and aquifers, increasing desertification. Over the past twenty years climate-caused internal displacement and migration of Iranians have increased ten-fold.[76, 77] Under these conditions by 2050, parts of Iran may become too extreme to support human life.[78] Iran has not ratified the Paris Climate Agreement of 2015 and does not publish its GHG emissions data. For Iran and its energy policies, see page 29.

Prep time 2 hours to ferment the dough warm, plus 10 hours to ferment the dough cold
Bake time about 10 minutes per flatbread | Makes four 12-inch-long flatbreads

⅔ cup ripe, active whole rye or whole wheat sourdough starter (see page 199)

4 teaspoons date paste from ⅓ cup dates, any variety

1 cup spring water, plus more as needed

2⅔ cups white whole wheat flour

1½ teaspoons shiro (mild, white) miso paste

2 teaspoons each of seeds like nigella, poppy, and sesame to decorate the tops

1. The day before baking, feed your sourdough mother once or twice so that it is quite active and bubbly before you mix the *sangak* dough.

2. Wash and dry the river stones if you are using them for the first time. Toss any broken or cracked stones; they should all be perfectly smooth.

3. To make the date paste, cover the dates with water and microwave for 2 minutes on high to rehydrate and soften the dates. Alternatively, simmer in water on the stovetop for 5 minutes. Cool and purée the dates in a high-speed blender with just enough of the date soaking water required to create a smooth, thick paste.

4. In a mixing bowl use a Danish dough whisk to disperse the date paste in 1 cup of spring water. Use the whisk to mix in the sourdough starter, followed by the white whole wheat flour, combining it well.

5. Cover the bowl with a lid or plastic wrap and rest the dough for 30 minutes. The dough will be too sticky and wet to knead on a board. Instead, we will develop the dough by stretching it and laying it over the other side of the bowl. Rotate the bowl 90 degrees and repeat three times or more until the glutinous strands in the dough tighten and it no longer stretches.

6. Wait 15 minutes for the dough to relax. Mix in the miso paste now by dotting the top of the dough with the miso and stretching and folding the dough over it multiple times until it is integrated and the dough has tightened again. Cover the dough and rest it for 30 minutes.

7. If the dough seems dry as you stretch it, add a little water but just a teaspoon at a time. You will get a feel for this bread as you work with it and make it again in the future. The dough should be soft and sticky but not so wet and sloppy that it lacks cohesion and tears easily.

8. Repeat the stretching and folding with 30-minute rests for another two cycles. In total, the dough will have developed over 2 hours now. Stretch and fold it one more time, cover it, and

refrigerate it to continue fermenting slowly in a cold environment overnight or for about 10 hours.

9. Bring the dough to room temp over 2 to 3 hours, depending on the temperature in your kitchen. You should see that the dough will have risen noticeably since you placed it in the refrigerator.

10. Preheat the oven to 550°F. Cover the bottom of an old cookie sheet with the clean river pebbles and place it on the middle oven shelf.

11. Stretch and fold the dough. Use a plastic dough scraper to remove one-quarter of the dough to shape the first *sangak*. Cover the bowl to prevent the remaining dough from drying.

12. Wet a large dinner plate or oval platter very well and place the piece of dough on it. The platter will need to be very wet to prevent the dough from sticking. Wet your fingers well and begin to stretch and flatten the dough, shaping it into an elongated wedge about 12 inches long and about 5 inches at its wide end. With practice you will be able to work more quickly and can save time by using two wet plates upon which to shape two *sangaks* to bake them together.

13. Very carefully remove the extremely hot cookie sheet and shut the oven door immediately to preserve the high heat. Slide the tip of the dough from one wet plate onto the hot stones on one side of the cookie sheet and slowly retract the plate down the length of the sheet so that, inch by inch, the rest of the dough falls upon the stones. Obviously, if you bake two *sangaks* simultaneously, you will need to leave room on the cookie sheet for a second bread to face in the opposite direction.

14. Sprinkle seeds on top and carefully replace the cookie sheet in the oven.

15. Lower the temperature to 525°F. Bake the breads for 10 minutes. When they are ready, *sangak* flatbreads should be firm, fragrant, golden, and toasted in spots. Use a pair of metal tongs to loosen and lift each baked *sangak* from the cookie sheet to a cooling rack.

16. Allow at least 5 minutes for the stones in the oven to heat up again. Rewet the dinner plates and transfer the next two quarters of dough to each one. Stretch and shape the dough as outlined in Step 12. Transfer them to the hot stones, sprinkle with seeds, and repeat the baking process.

17. As each bread cools enough to handle, about 5 minutes, turn them over, and with a butter knife, dislodge any stones that may have become embedded in the dough during baking.

18. *Sangak* flatbreads are tastiest when they are fresh and warm. If, however, you have any left over, wrap the bread up well in plastic wrap, refrigerate it, and reheat it in a 300°F oven for 10 minutes before serving.

SIDES

A GREENER COLCANNON

Every culture has its comfort food, and colcannon is Ireland's—a marriage of potatoes with kale or cabbage and, traditionally, lots of butter, milk, or cream. Simple, warming, hearty, this climate-happy remake loses the dairy and builds layers of flavor instead, not with fat but with alliums, like onion, leek, garlic, scallions, and chives. The aroma and taste are heavenly, and you have a soothing dish that opens your arteries instead of the other way around. Skip the eggs, boiled ham, and Irish bacon that often share colcannon's table. Serve it instead with a tasty array of seasonal vegetables and doff your cap to Saint Paddy.

This greener colcannon has a very low climate impact: Greenhouse gas emissions from potatoes farmed in Ireland are estimated at 0.17 kg CO_2eq per kg; 0.12 kg CO_2eq per kg for cabbages; leafy vegetables like kale and collards are 0.14 kg CO_2eq per kg. Buying pre-chopped greens at United States grocers, while convenient, increases their climate impact to 0.61–0.92kg CO_2eq per kg, driven primarily by packaging.

Ireland's Climate Challenges

Global warming trends are affecting Ireland with temperatures increasing faster than the global average, bringing warmer weather and more frequent heat waves. Average annual rainfall has risen as well, shifting from spring and summer to substantial precipitation in autumn and winter. According to the U.S. Environmental Protection Agency, sea levels continue to rise, with implications for Ireland's coastal communities as high tides, coastal flooding, and coastal erosion threaten property and infrastructure. More extreme weather, including more intense and frequent storms and greater rainfall, are leading to erosion with "bog bursts" (peat mudslides) becoming more common. Amid its climate and biodiversity crises, Ireland imports more than 80% of its fruits and vegetables. It exports dairy, beef, and live animals. Its dairy output is growing, stressing its ecosystems and water systems. For now at least, Ireland's agricultural priorities and policies are at odds with what is required for ecological resilience and healthy, sustainable diets for its people.[79]

Prep time 30 minutes   Cooking time 30 minutes   Serves 3 to 5

1 head garlic, dry roasted, peeled, and mashed

1½ pounds kale, lacinato kale, cabbage, and/or other hardy greens, cut in ¼-inch ribbons

3 pounds floury potatoes, about 5 medium potatoes, scrubbed and unpeeled

1 large onion, cut in a medium dice

1 medium leek, well cleaned, green and white sections, cut in ¼-inch slices

Dry vermouth or no-sodium vegetable broth to deglaze pot

1 cup unsweetened soy milk

1 bunch scallion and/or Chinese chives, cut in ¼-inch slices

Several big grinds of black pepper

3 tablespoons shiro (mild, white) miso paste, or to taste

1. To dry roast the garlic, remove its outer papery leaves. Bake in 375°F oven for 30 minutes. Cool. Separate its cloves and peel them. Mash the roasted cloves into a pulp with a fork.

2. Bring a large pot of water to a boil, put in the prepped greens separately, cooking each until tender but intact, testing frequently, from 5 to 20 minutes depending on type of green.

3. As each green is ready, use a skimmer to transfer to a colander to drain in the sink.

4. Return the pot to a boil and put in the whole potatoes. When the water returns to a boil, lower to simmer and cook until tender but intact. Do not overcook or their skins will split, and the potatoes can become waterlogged. Begin checking at 15 minutes for doneness. Test periodically by inserting a sharp knife in a potato. When the potato falls off, it is ready. Drain.

5. While they are quite hot, peel the potatoes and immediately rice or mash them in a bowl.

6. Dry the pot and reheat it for 3 minutes over medium-low flame. Put in the onion and leek, stirring frequently. Cover and cook slowly to allow the onion to sweat its liquid and soften.

7. When the onions start to darken the pan and adhere, in 5 to 10 minutes, deglaze the pot with a few tablespoons of deglazing liquid. The onion and leek should be very soft.

8. Lower the heat and add cooked greens, stirring.

9. After a minute add the smashed garlic, mixing it well to distribute it evenly. Stir in the mashed/riced potatoes and mix thoroughly, distributing the garlic and the aromatics throughout the potatoes and greens.

10. Add the soy milk, stirring, and cook for another minute or two to allow all the flavors to blend. The colcannon should be neither dry nor soupy but creamy with the vegetables melting into the potatoes.

11. Mix in the sliced scallion and/or chives and cook for another 2 minutes or until soft. Season with fresh black pepper, to taste.

12. Turn off the heat and season with shiro miso, mixing it well.

13. Serve colcannon hot on warmed plates.

ARTICHOKES EN PAPILLOTE

For the longest time, due to environmental and health concerns, I abandoned big tender artichokes to avoid the butter and oil they are served with. Dipping into a climate-friendly garlicky aioli that is free from egg and oil instead, I now fully savor these gorgeous, nutritious thistles with no regrets. While many might serve these artichokes as a side dish or even a starter, I've (very happily) made a dinner of them too!

I cook the artichokes in a parchment bag, steaming and roasting them in their own flavorful juices that render them soft, moist, and delectable. The chokes also become easy to pluck out. Artichokes pack a nutritional punch: They're loaded with fiber, have negligible calories, and are a great source of vitamin C, magnesium, and calcium. Choose artichokes with their tasty stems attached, the longer the better. Look for globes that are heavy, firm, and "squeak" when pressed for optimal freshness and flavor.

Artichoke hearts from California generate 0.6 kg CO_2eq per kg, 55% of which is due to packaging versus 24% to agriculture, 18% to transportation, and just 3% to processing. Tofu emits 1.3 kg CO_2eq per kg in greenhouse gases: 35% of emissions relate to processing, 29% to agriculture, 24% to packaging, and 11% from transportation.

Perennial Vegetables to the Rescue

Perennial vegetables, like artichokes and asparagus and over 600 other species, are currently underutilized crops: They only use 6% of the world's vegetable cropland at present.[80] Many of these vegetables have higher levels of nutrients. With deeper root systems, they require less water and less tillage. They reduce soil erosion, enrich soils by retaining more nutrients, are better able to withstand pest infestations, and capture much more carbon in the soil. Perennial vegetables and grains also offer an opportunity for plant scientists to widen the limited cultivated gene pool by using perennial vegetables to develop variants that can stand up to the changing climate.[81]

Prep time 30 minutes to roast garlic, plus 20 minutes   Bake time 1 hour   Serves 4

1 small head garlic, roasted intact, then peeled

4 very large, fresh globe artichokes, cut in half lengthwise

8 ounces silken tofu, drained

2 teaspoons lemon juice or more, to taste

2 teaspoons shiro (mild, white) miso paste

A pinch of freshly ground white pepper

5 tablespoons nonpareil capers, drained (optional)

1. Preheat oven to 375°F.

2. To roast the garlic, peel off the loose papery outer skins of the garlic head. Bake whole in the oven for 30 minutes, or until the garlic is soft. Cool. Peel the cloves and set aside.

3. Increase the oven temp to 400°F.

4. Using a serrated knife, or a cleaver and dead blow hammer, cut the artichokes in half lengthwise, leaving the stems attached. To make your parchment bag, tear off a large piece of parchment paper, double the length of your pan and add 2 inches. Fold the parchment in half and reopen. Lay each half artichoke, face down, on the lower half of the parchment. Fold the upper half over them. Fold the cut edge over several times and staple every few inches to seal. Fold over and staple the remaining two open sides to form a sealed bag.

5. Transfer the parchment bag to a cookie sheet and place it on the middle oven rack. Bake for 1 hour.

6. As the artichokes bake, make the aioli. Place the tofu, roasted garlic cloves, lemon juice, shiro miso, and white pepper in a high-speed blender. Run on high for a minute to blend into a dense smooth sauce. Taste to adjust the seasonings as you like. Transfer to a container, stir in the capers, if using, and refrigerate until use.

7. Remove the cookie sheet from the oven. Cut open the parchment bag and move the artichokes to a board, cut side facing up. Use a spoon to remove only the hairy, inedible choke, leaving as much of the delicious heart as possible.

8. Serve the artichokes warm with the aioli at room temp, filling the artichoke cavities with aioli or serving it on the side.

CAULIFLOWER WITH YOGURT SAUCE

This delightful vegetable dish is inspired by vegetarian kitchens in West Bengal and Bangladesh. It is scented with the region's famous simple blend of whole spices, *Panch Phoron* (see page 55). Cauliflower, cabbage, spinach, and sweet peas cook up quickly. Creamy soy yogurt finishes the dish. This is an easy, nutritious side dish and goes beautifully with Naan (see page 180) or *Rajgira* Roti (see page 186).

On Indian farms, cauliflower has a climate footprint of 0.24 kg CO_2eq per kg, with 15% of GHG created by fertilizer production, 34% by N_2O emitted by in-field bacteria, 1% by off-field bacteria, 5% from deforestation, 3% from CO_2 released when soil amendments are applied, 29% from operating farm equipment, and 3% from the energy required to irrigate fields.

Sundarbans Climate Challenges

Sundarbans is a major mangrove forest in the Bay of Bengal, formed by the meeting of the Ganges, Brahmaputra, and Meghna rivers. The Sundarban Reserve Forest is the largest mangrove forest in the world. A complex of ecosystems, including tidal waterways, small islands, and mudflats, it serves as a refuge for over 260 bird species and is critical to supporting endangered species of Bengal tiger, dolphins, Indian python, and estuarine crocodiles. Sundarbans, which straddles Bangladesh and India, is a global climate hotspot: Sea levels are rising at twice the rate of the global average. This area is increasingly prone to high-intensity cyclones, flash floods, and landslides, threatening both human and nonhuman life. More frequent and violent extreme weather events are forcing migrations from the region and increasing the pressures on biodiversity of this uniquely rich and vulnerable country.[82]

Prep time 20 minutes   Cook time 20 minutes   Serves 3 to 5

2 tablespoons *Panch Phoron* spice blend (see page 55)

1 red onion, peeled and thinly sliced

3 tablespoons vegetable broth or water, to deglaze pan

3 cloves garlic, minced

1 medium cauliflower, florets only, cut into bite-sized pieces

1 teaspoon turmeric powder

1 quarter green cabbage, core removed, cut in ¼-inch slices

1½ cups thick, cultured soy yogurt

1 bunch spinach

Several grinds of black pepper

1 cup frozen peas, defrosted

3 tablespoons shiro (mild, white) miso paste, diluted in 3 tablespoons water

1. Heat a large skillet on medium for 3 minutes. Put in *Panch Phoron*, stirring, and cook for a minute until the seeds become fragrant. Stir in the onions, cover, and cook for about 2 minutes, stirring occasionally, until the onions release their water and begin to darken the pan.

2. Deglaze with broth and, using a wooden spoon, scrape up the caramelized sugars from the pan. Add the garlic, cauliflower, turmeric, and cabbage, stirring well. Cover and cook for 5 minutes, adding a minimal amount of broth only if the mix becomes dry. Excess moisture in this dish will dilute its creaminess later.

3. Drain any surface liquid from the soy yogurt and stir it in with the spinach. Grind pepper, to taste. Stir well to combine, cover, lower the heat, and cook for 5 minutes.

4. Finally stir in the peas and cook for 5 minutes.

5. The vegetables should all be tender but intact. Turn off the heat and season with diluted shiro miso, to taste. Serve with warmed whole wheat Naan (see page 180), *Rajgira* Roti (see page 186), or any whole grain you like.

CHOLAR DAL

This beguiling Bengali dal stars chana dal, the skinned and split dal made from brown *desi* chickpeas. This dish combines sweet with a little heat. The sweetness comes from Indian bay leaf, sweet aromatic spices, and delightful Indian raisins. Green and dried chilies lend some gentle heat. Like many Bengali dishes, onion and garlic are supplanted by pungent asafoetida. *Cholar* dal typically fries coconut meat in mustard oil and tempers its spices in ghee. However, this greener and very low-fat version ditches the fats and uses coconut extract instead to perfume the dish.

Nutritionally, all pulses (beans, lentils, and peas) are rich sources of fiber, protein, vitamins, and minerals, making them superb alternatives to meat, fish, and poultry. Legumes are also superb alternatives to animal products for their climate benefits: With low GHG emissions, they sequester carbon in soils, and because they fix nitrogen in the soil, they nourish other crops and reduce the need for synthetic fertilizers.

Chickpeas generate 0.68 kg CO_2eq per kg on Indian farms and chilies emit 0.11 kg CO_2eq per kg in Indian fields. In general, spice mixes sold loose in Indian shops have a climate footprint of 2.0 kg CO_2eq per kg, with 55% attributed to agriculture, 4% to transport, and 42% to processing. Purchasing spices as whole seeds in bulk, versus buying them pre-ground, will lower their climate footprint as well.

Climate Challenges and Responses in West Bengal

West Bengal's long coastline in India is suffering increasing weather variability due to climate change, with temperatures rising and rainfall declining, despite the greater frequency of more severe cyclones and storm surges. The increase in sea levels is causing coastal erosion that threatens communities along the coast and puts their local economies and infrastructure at risk. Water resources are increasingly under pressure during non-monsoon seasons. The government and local communities are working to increase renewable energy in their energy mix, and designing strategies to protect water, agriculture, biodiversity, and health in the region.[83]

Prep time soak for 30 minutes, plus 30 minutes to pressure-cook the chickpeas
and prep the rest | Cook time 20 minutes | Serves 4 to 5

1½ cups chana dal

2 large Indian bay leaves

½ teaspoon Bengal garam masala from a freshly ground 2-inch Ceylon cinnamon stick, 7 green cardamom pods, and 5 cloves

1 teaspoon cumin seeds, ½ teaspoon ground and ½ teaspoon seeds

1 teaspoon coriander seeds, ground

¼ teaspoon asafoetida (hing) nugget, ground

2 tablespoons date paste from ½ cup pitted dates

1½-inch piece of ginger, grated

1 teaspoon ground turmeric powder

2 dried Indian red chilies

1 5-inch Ceylon cinnamon stick

½ teaspoon green cardamom seeds or 1 teaspoon pods

2 whole cloves

2 Indian green chilies, partially slit

½ cup jumbo black *kali kishmis*, green *hunza*, and/or red *monukka* raisins (or other varieties)

2 teaspoons coconut extract

2 tablespoons shiro (mild, white) miso paste, diluted in 2 tablespoons water, or to taste

1. Rinse and soak the chana dal for 30 minutes. Drain and place the dal in a pressure cooker.

2. Add to the pressure cooker 3 cups water and the Indian bay leaves. Heat on high until the cooker comes to full pressure, then lower to medium and pressure-cook for 15 minutes. Turn off the heat and allow the pressure to release naturally, in 10 to 15 minutes. The dal should be soft but intact. Drain, transfer the cooked dal to a bowl, and reserve chana dal's cooking water.

3. Using a coffee grinder, grind the spices for the Bengal garam masala. We will only use ½ teaspoon here. Transfer to a small bowl and use a slightly damp paper towel to clean the coffee grinder. Store the excess in a spice jar and keep in a dark, cool cupboard. It is most potent if used within a month.

4. Use the coffee grinder to grind together the cumin seeds, coriander seeds, and asafoetida nugget. Transfer to a bowl.

5. To make the date paste, add the dates to a small bowl, cover with water, and microwave for 2 minutes. Alternatively, simmer on the stovetop in a small pot for 5 minutes. Cool. Transfer the dates and their soaking liquid to a high-speed blender and blend them into a smooth, soft paste. We will use only 2 tablespoons for this recipe. Store the excess in the fridge in a tightly lidded container and use within a month.

6. In a small bowl combine grated ginger, date paste, turmeric, and freshly ground coriander, cumin, and asafoetida powder. Add about ½ cup of water or more to mix into a slurry.

7. Heat a skillet on medium for 3 minutes. Put in the dried Indian red chili and cook for 1 minute. Add the Ceylon cinnamon stick, cumin seed, green cardamom, and cloves and cook for about a minute, just until they become fragrant. Do not allow the spices to burn or smoke or they will become bitter and ruin the dish.

8. Slit the Indian green chilies about one-third of the way down their length.

9. Stir in the slurry and the slit green chilies. Cook for a minute, adding more water if the mix becomes dry. Mix in the cooked chana dal and enough of its cooking liquid to create a moist but not soupy dal. Stir well to combine. Stir in the raisins, Bengal garam masala, and coconut extract. Cover and cook for 10 minutes to allow all the flavors to meld.

10. Remove the skillet from the heat and stir in the diluted shiro miso, to taste. Taste and adjust seasonings as you like.

11. *Cholar* Dal should be tender, very flavorful, fairly dense, but not dry. It should not be soupy, unlike many other dals. That said, if your dal has become too thick, add a little of the reserved dal cooking water.

12. Serve *Cholar* Dal hot with flatbreads or with cooked whole grains.

FRAGRANT MILLET PILAF

Fluffy grain pilafs have been enjoyed throughout Central Asia, Turkey, the Middle East, and India since the fourth century BCE. Traditionally, pilafs are a rice or wheat dish simmered in stock and fragrant with sweet spices, vegetables, and sometimes meats. Common (proso) millet is simmered in a light vegetable stock scented with *Advieh Berenj* (see page 29), a fragrant Persian spice blend with dried berries and nuts. Saffron, classically used in pilafs, adds its gentle fragrance and gorgeous color. There are many varieties of millet, and they are all richer in vitamins, minerals, fiber, and enzymes than whole rice varieties.

Millets are exceptionally drought tolerant and well adapted to thrive in arid landscapes. U.S. farmed millet has a climate footprint of 0.86 kg CO_2eq per kg, with 25% of emissions from fertilizer production, 28% from in-field bacteria, 8% from off-field bacteria, 17% from draining wetlands to farm, 5% from soil amendments, 2% from farm machinery, 8% from irrigation, and 7% from drying the crop. In contrast, rice farmed on U.S. soil has a climate footprint of 1.7 kg CO_2eq per kg, with 71% of emissions from flooding rice fields, which releases methane produced by soil bacteria. Rice is the only crop that requires routine flooding for its growth. For more on rice, see page 319.

Nut Production and Climate Change

Tree nuts include almonds, chestnuts, walnuts, macadamia nuts, Brazil nuts, cashews, hazelnuts, pecans, and pistachio nuts. Most tree nuts in the United States are grown in Californian groves. Like temperate fruit, nut trees need a sustained winter chill and dormancy to flower and fruit.[84] Warming winter temperatures, earlier springs, more intense heat waves, and reduced precipitation pose risks to nut production. For example, almonds may require as much as 50 to 54 inches of water annually, but existing groves receive only 10 inches, necessitating irrigation from water stores.[85] Past unregulated pumping of groundwater put water availability at risk. The state's Sustainable Groundwater Management Act, passed in 2014, is attempting to redress those abuses and balance water use sustainably.[86]

Prep time 15 minutes   Cook time 20 minutes, plus 10 minutes   Serves 3 to 5

Big pinch saffron pistils

3 cups unsalted vegetable stock, hot

2 carrots, grated

1 cup (2 large) shallots, peeled and sliced

¼ cup dry white wine, to deglaze pan

1 cup common millet, rinsed

2 teaspoons *Advieh Berenj* (see page 29), or to taste

1 cup mixed dried berries like barberries, gooseberries, goldenberries, cranberries, green Indian or golden raisins, and mulberries

⅓ cup whole shelled pistachio nuts and sliced almonds

2 tablespoons shiro (mild, white) miso, diluted in 2 tablespoons hot broth, or to taste (optional)

Parsley and mint leaves, chopped, for garnish

1. To prepare saffron tea, take a big pinch of saffron pistils and crumble them into a small bowl. Pour a tablespoon of boiling water over them and steep as you prep the rest of the ingredients.

2. Pour the vegetable broth into a pot, bring to a boil, cover, and lower the heat to maintain at a very gentle simmer.

3. Use the coarse side of a box grater to grate the carrots.

4. Heat a medium heavy-bottomed stainless steel saucepan for 2 minutes on medium low. Put in the sliced shallots and dry sauté for 3 minutes, stirring occasionally. The shallots will release their water and begin to darken the pan. As they begin to adhere to the pan, deglaze the pan with a few tablespoons of wine, scraping up the caramelized shallot sugars from the pan. Stir in the rinsed millet, *Advieh Berenj*, and saffron tea.

5. Stir in the hot broth and the grated carrots. Bring to a gentle simmer, lower the heat slightly, and cover. Cook the pilaf for 10 minutes. Taste to adjust any seasonings as you like.

6. Now add the mixed dried berries. Cover and cook for another 5 minutes before adding the nuts. Cook for a final 5 minutes. The millet should have absorbed all its liquid and be tender and light.

7. Remove from the heat, season with diluted shiro miso, to taste (optional). Keep covered and allow the pilaf to rest for 10 minutes.

8. Remove the cover. Fluff the pilaf with a fork to gently separate the grains. Cover until use and serve warm. Plate individually or in a warmed serving dish. Garnish with chopped fresh parsley and mint.

GAI LAN WITH LEMON-SCENTED MAYONNAISE

If you are used to the massive flowery heads of Italian broccoli, whose thick stalks play second fiddle, then mild gai lan (Chinese broccoli) may delight you. Its sweet stems play the starring role in this recipe, and you will have to peer closely to spot the demure flowers nestled in the center beneath its dark glossy leaves. Gai Lan makes a delicious and elegant side dish, briefly blanched tender-crisp and dressed in a luscious, environmentally kind mayonnaise, seasoned with Lemon Citrus Powder (see page 41) for enhanced aroma and flavor. Like its fellow brassicas, Chinese broccoli is an excellent source of fiber, protein, calcium, and especially folate. You'll find it in East Asian markets. Choose stalks with very tightly closed florets and dark and glossy leaves.

Broccoli farmed in China has a climate footprint of 0.35 kg CO_2eq per kg, with 34% of emissions related to fertilizer production, 31% to in-field bacteria, 10% to off-field bacteria, 4% from emissions caused by the use of soil amendments, and 20% from farm machinery. The benchmark climate footprint for tofu comes from U.K. groceries at 1.4 kg CO_2eq per kg, 31% of which is driven by agriculture, 34% to processing, 24% to packaging, and 11% to transportation.

South China Climate Risks

Gai lan mainly grows in the south of China, chiefly in Guangdong, Guangxi, and Fujian provinces and Taiwan. Lack of water is a particular risk for China's southern provinces, most of which are reliant on hydropower. Sea level rise is also of concern. More than 650 million Chinese live along its low-lying coastal areas. Sea levels are facing a possible rise of 40 to 60 cm (up to 2 feet) above twentieth century levels by the end of this century.[87] For China's climate policies, see page 309.

Prep time 15 minutes | Cook time 5 minutes | Serves 4 to 6

1 bunch (1½ to 2 pounds) gai lan

1 (14- to 16-ounce) package silken tofu, drained well

2 tablespoons nutritional yeast

1½ tablespoons apple cider vinegar

1½ tablespoons Dijon mustard

1 tablespoon dehydrated or powdered garlic

2 tablespoons shiro (mild, white) miso paste

⅛ teaspoon ground white pepper

1 teaspoon freshly ground Lemon Citrus Powder (see page 41)

1. Soak the gai lan for a few minutes in cold water to remove any grit or soil.

2. Bring a large pot of water to a rapid boil. Transfer all the gai lan at once to the pot, using a large spoon to push its leaves underwater. Blanch for just a few minutes, depending on the thickness of the stems. Test every minute by removing a stalk and tasting a small slice of the stem. As soon as it is tender but still quite crispy, use tongs, a skimmer, or a strainer to quickly transfer all the gai lan to a large bowl of ice water to halt its cooking and brighten its color. Cool completely and drain.

3. To make the lemon mayonnaise, combine the drained silken tofu, nutritional yeast, vinegar, Dijon mustard, granulated garlic, shiro miso, white pepper, and Lemon Citrus Powder in a high-speed blender. Run on high for a minute or until the mayonnaise is well blended and creamy. Taste and adjust any seasonings as you like. Transfer to a container and refrigerate until use. The mayo will thicken slightly as it cools.

4. Gai Lan with Lemon-Scented Mayonnaise is best served warm. Reheat for 30 seconds to a minute in a microwave to warm but not cook it further. Arrange it on a platter and dress with the lemon mayo or serve the mayonnaise separately. Serve immediately.

5. Gai Lan with Lemon-Scented Mayonnaise will keep for about 5 days, refrigerated.

GIGANTES LIMA BEANS

This dish highlights the flavors of Peru with a simple sauté of creamy Peruvian *gigantes* lima beans, roasted cherry tomatoes, and the Peruvian chilies fruity ají *amarillo* and smoky red ají *panca*. Lima beans are an ancient staple in Peru, cultivated even before corn. Nutritional powerhouses, lima beans are very high in fiber, excellent sources of iron, protein, calcium, and other minerals, and are very climate supportive. Serve with a side of roasted ears of corn and a big salad for a scrumptious lunch, light supper, or alongside other Peruvian dishes.

Like all legumes, lima beans fix nitrogen in the soil, helping to nourish the soil and lessening the need for nitrogen fertilizer. Climate footprints for dried beans vary widely by country. In Peru, dried beans like *gigantes* lima beans have a very high (for beans) footprint of 4.4 kg CO_2eq per kg, 93% of which is driven by deforestation that is so damaging to the environment, its ecosystems, and biodiversity. Therefore, source beans from countries like Mexico with 0.31 kg CO_2eq per kg or the United States with 0.46 kg CO_2eq per kg, where no trees are felled to grow beans.

Climate Repercussions in Peru

Peru's glaciers have nearly disappeared at the time of this writing; more than half were lost over the past sixty years. Peru is uniquely susceptible to the devastating effects of a warming planet due to its vast biodiversity and twenty-eight different ecological zones across its very diverse topography. With climate change, heat waves in Peru have become more frequent and fiercer, leading to more extreme wildfires in Peru's bush. Droughts have caused hunger in Peru's more vulnerable areas. Mass internal migrations are occurring with increasing frequency; 700,000 people were displaced in 2023 alone.[88]

Prep time overnight soak of *gigantes* lima beans, plus 1 hour to cook the beans and roast tomatoes and ají *amarillos* | Cook time 15 minutes | Serves 3 to 5

1 pound Peruvian *gigantes* lima beans

2 bay leaves, plus 1 teaspoon freshly ground from 4-5 whole bay leaves

3 large whole cloves garlic, plus 4 cloves of garlic, minced

2 pounds cherry tomatoes, mixed colors, sliced in half lengthwise

1 to 2 frozen ají *amarillo*, defrosted, or to taste

2 teaspoons dried oregano or thyme leaves

Freshly ground black pepper, to taste

½ to 1 teaspoon freshly ground ají *panca* from 1 to 2 whole dried chilies, or to taste

2 teaspoons freshly ground cumin seed

1½ cups unsalted vegetable broth, heated

1 red onion, cut in a medium dice

Juice of 1 lime, or more, to taste

¼ cup unsalted roasted peanuts (optional)

Up to ⅓ cup aka (red) miso paste, dissolved in ½ cup warm water, or to taste

Cilantro leaves cut in a chiffonade (rolled and sliced in thin ribbons), a dusting of Lime Citrus Powder (see page 41) or lime zest, and a sprinkle of aji panca powder, for garnish

1. To prepare the lima beans, rinse, place in a pot, cover with water by a few inches, and soak overnight or for about 8 hours. Drain and rinse.

2. Preheat the oven to 400°F.

3. Return the soaked lima beans to the pot, cover with fresh water, add the bay leaves and whole garlic cloves, and bring to a very low simmer. Like many tender white beans, lima beans are delicate and need to be more steeped than boiled, as anything higher than a gentle simmer can cause the beans to fall apart. The amount of time required to cook them will depend on the age of the beans, but in general, they should simmer very gently for about an hour. They are cooked when their interior is soft, but the beans are still intact.

4. Drain the beans. Remove any broken beans and reserve for another dish like Peruvian Lima Bean Purée (see page 82).

5. While the beans are cooking, oven roast the cherry tomatoes and *amarillo* chilies: Place the whole defrosted ají *amarillo* chilies and sliced cherry tomatoes, cut side up, on a large baking sheet lined with parchment paper. Sprinkle with dried oregano or thyme and grinds of black pepper. Insert the pan on the middle oven shelf and roast them for 25 to 35 minutes, or until the chilies are golden and the tomatoes have softened and begun to caramelize on their cut edges. The chilies may be ready slightly ahead of the tomatoes,

so start checking them at 15 minutes. Remove the tray from the oven and cool. If you are lucky, the roasted *amarillo* chilies and tomatoes will produce some delicious juices; try to recoup them if you can.

6. Lower the oven temperature to 150°F. When it has cooled to this temperature, insert your serving bowls to warm.

7. Cut the roasted *amarillo* chilies in ½-inch slices.

8. Remove the stems from the dried ají *panca* chilies. Use a pair of scissors or a knife to cut them in pieces and grind them in a coffee grinder, pulverizing the chilies, seeds included, into flakes or a finer chili powder. Measure out 1 teaspoon and reserve any surplus in a spice jar. Store it in a cool, dark cupboard, and for greatest potency, use it up in a month.

9. Wipe the bowl of the coffee grinder with a very slightly damp paper towel, then dry it. Add the bay leaves, tearing them as needed to fit in the grinder. Grind to create bay flakes or powder. Measure out 1 teaspoon and store any excess as in Step 8.

10. Clean the grinder again and grind the cumin seeds into a powder.

11. Heat the vegetable broth in a microwave oven or a small pot on the stovetop. Cover it to stay hot.

12. Heat a very large skillet over medium heat for 3 minutes. Put in the onions and dry sauté them for a few minutes until they soften, release their liquid, and begin to darken the pan. Deglaze the pan with a tablespoon or two of the reserved roasted tomato and chili juices if you were able to collect it, or vegetable broth, scraping up the caramelized onion sugars with a wooden spoon. Add the minced garlic, ground cumin seeds, ground ají *panca* chilies, and ground bay leaves.

13. After a minute, stir in the roasted tomatoes and *amarillo* chilies. These chilies are fruity and moderately hot. If you are sensitive to heat, add one chili now and reserve the second until the beans have been added so you can adjust the level of heat to your taste.

14. Add 1 cup of the hot vegetable broth and cook for 5 minutes. Now gently add the cooked *gigantes* lima beans, stirring the sauce over them and taking care not to break them. Season with black pepper, to taste, and cook for 5 minutes to meld all flavors.

15. Turn off the heat. Squeeze on the lime juice, sprinkle in some unsalted peanuts, if using, and season with diluted aka miso to your taste. Taste to adjust all seasonings. Adjust the lime, chilies, cumin, pepper, etc, as you like. Add a little more broth if the mix seems too dry to coat the beans adequately.

16. Serve in warmed bowls. Garnish with slivers of cilantro leaves, Lime Citrus Powder or zest for aroma, and a light dusting of ají *panca* powder for its smokiness and color.

GREEN AND GOLD POTATO SALAD

Baby gold potato wedges meld beautifully with naturally sweet flat Romano and golden wax beans in a creamy tofu mayo. Colorful, crisp radishes add texture, and red onion or shallots and dill round out the flavors in this delightful potato salad. Did you know that eating potatoes cold significantly reduces their glycemic load? Chilling cooked potatoes converts high-glycemic starch into resistant starch that evades our digestion; instead, it is fermented in the gut where it nourishes friendly flora that provide an array of health benefits for gut and metabolic health.

The GHG emissions from leguminous vegetables like Romano and wax beans are 0.14 kg CO_2eq per kg on U.S. farms, with 3% from fertilizer production, 6% from in-field bacteria, 1% from off-field bacteria, 53% from draining wetlands, 14% from amending the soil, 3% from pesticide production, 15% from running farm equipment, and 5% from irrigating the fields. On Italian farms, fresh beans have an even lower climate footprint of 0–0.1 kg CO_2eq per kg, with 3% from fertilizer production, 12% from in-field bacteria, 2% from off-field bacteria, 20% from draining wetlands, 11% from CO_2 released with the addition of soil amendments, 8% from pesticide production, 39% from the operation of farm machinery, and 5% from the power required to pump water to irrigate fields.

How Cover Crops Help

Cover crops, sowed to restore soils when it lies fallow or seeded between rows of crops to discourage weeds, typically include legumes, like beans, peas, clover, and vetch, and grasses, like ryegrass, wheat, rapeseed, oats, and buckwheat. They enrich soils and improve soil structure.[89] They help absorb intense rains, which are becoming more prevalent during climate change, and help reduce nutrient runoff and soil erosion. They increase crop yields, improve crop resilience to disease and pests, attract pollinators, and when turned into the soil at the end of a growing cycle, they become green manure, enriching soil quality.[90]

Prep time 15 minutes | Cook time 30 minutes | Serves 6 to 8

1½ pounds baby Yukon or other gold potato variety

1½ cups colorful baby radishes like purple, French breakfast, and watermelon, cut into small wedges

1 pound young Romano beans

1 pound young yellow wax beans

1 (14- to 16-ounce) package of soft or silken tofu, drained

1½ tablespoons granulated garlic

2 tablespoons granulated onion

1½ tablespoons nutritional yeast

1½ tablespoons apple cider vinegar

1½ tablespoons Dijon mustard

2 teaspoons lemon juice

¼ teaspoon freshly ground white pepper

1 tablespoon shiro (mild, white) miso paste, or to taste

1 medium red onion or 2 shallots, cut into quarters and sliced

¼ cup fresh dill sprigs, chopped, or more, to taste

1. Scrub the whole, unpeeled baby potatoes and radishes. Soak the fresh beans in cool water as you prep the ingredients.

2. Heat a pot of water to a rapid boil. Blanch the Romano beans until just tender. Begin testing after 5 minutes for doneness by tasting a small piece. When they're cooked, use a pair of tongs or a strainer to quickly transfer the beans to a large bowl filled with ice water to halt cooking and brighten their color. When cool, drain the Romano beans, and cut into 2- to 3-inch segments.

3. Add more ice to your ice bath. Bring the pot of water back to a rapid boil. Cook the wax beans until just tender. Begin checking after 3 minutes for doneness. When they're ready, transfer them to ice water to cool rapidly. When cool, drain.

4. Bring the pot back to a rapid boil. Put in the whole potatoes and boil them until they are cooked but still intact. Do not overcook them or their skins will split, and the potatoes can become waterlogged. Begin checking at 15 minutes for doneness. Test periodically by inserting a sharp knife in a potato and holding it up. When the potato can slip off the knife, it is ready. Drain, cut in half, and then cut each half into two wedges.

5. Use a high-speed blender to make mayo. Combine in the blender the drained tofu, granulated garlic and onion, nutritional yeast, cider vinegar, mustard, lemon juice, white pepper, and shiro miso. Purée until very smooth and dense. Taste and adjust any of the seasonings as you like.

6. Gently combine the cooked potatoes, the red onion, and the Romano and wax beans in a very large bowl. Dress them with two-thirds of the mayo, adding more mayonnaise as needed to generously coat the vegetables. Sprinkle the radishes over the surface. Lightly cover with wrap and refrigerate for several hours before serving.

7. Serve this potato salad cold or warm without compromising its resistant starches. Before serving, garnish with lots of freshly chopped dill.

8. This potato salad will keep in the fridge for about 5 days.

MASHUR DAL

Flavorful dals are a mainstay in Bangladeshi home cooking and throughout the Indian subcontinent. Enjoyed both soupy or thick, either way, *Mashur* (red lentil) Dal is delicious, climate supportive, nutritious, economical, and oh so comforting. This dal is fragrant with spices, aromatics, and green chilies. Serve with whole grains, *Rajgira* Roti (see page 186), or Naan (see page 180).

In India, the climate footprint for lentils is 0.86 kg CO_2eq per kg with 5% of emissions attributed to fertilizer production, 14% to in-field bacteria, 4% to off-field bacterial N_2O emissions, 4% from draining wetlands, 24% from deforestation, 35% from operating farm machinery, 12% from the power required to irrigate, and 2% from drying.

Cyclones and Extreme Weather in Bangladesh

According to a World Bank report, the cost to Bangladesh from tropical cyclones in recent years approximates $1 billion annually. Half of Bangladesh's employment is in agriculture. By 2050, it is feared that one-third of agricultural GDP may be lost to extreme weather events like severe flooding, which would pose a grave risk to Bangladeshi livelihoods and provoke food insecurity and water scarcity. By 2050, 13.3 million people may be forced to migrate due to the climate's impacts.

Prep time 30 minutes   Cook time 1 hour   Serves 3 to 4

2 teaspoons unsalted dehydrated soup vegetables, freshly ground

1 teaspoon freshly ground cumin seeds

1 teaspoon freshly ground coriander seeds

1 cup red onions, ½ cup thinly sliced and ½ cup cut in small dice

3 cloves garlic, minced

3 ripe medium tomatoes, cut in a medium dice

2 Indian green chilies, 1 cut into thin strips and 1 chopped

1 cup *mashur* (masoor) dal or whole red lentils

2 whole dried Indian red chilies

1 teaspoon turmeric powder

½ cup cilantro, leaves and stems roughly chopped

1½ teaspoons *Panch Phoron* (see page 55)

several grinds of black pepper

¼ cup shiro (mild, white) miso paste, diluted in ¼ cup water

1. Use a small coffee grinder to grind separately the dehydrated soup vegetables, cumin seeds, and coriander seeds. Place each ground powder in its own small bowl.

2. Divide the sliced onion into two small bowls. We will use one half in Step 9 and the rest to decorate the dal in Step 12.

3. Divide the minced garlic into two small bowls. We will use one half in Step 6 and the other half in Step 10.

4. Reserve half of the diced tomatoes to decorate the dal in Step 12, but we will use the remaining tomatoes earlier in Step 6.

5. Divide the Indian green chili cut into thin strips into halves: the first half to be used in Step 9 and the remaining half to decorate the dal in Step 12.

6. Rinse the dal. Place it with 3 cups of water in a soup pot. Add all the diced onion and chopped green chilies, half of the garlic, half of the diced tomatoes, the whole dried red chilies, ground soup vegetables, cumin, coriander, and turmeric powders. Bring to a simmer, stir occasionally, and cook until the lentils are soft, about 20 minutes for *mashur* dal or 30 minutes for whole red lentils.

7. Stir in the chopped cilantro and cover the pot to keep the cooked lentils warm.

8. Heat a large skillet for 3 minutes over medium heat. Put in *Panch Phoron* and dry roast it for just a minute.

9. Add half of the sliced onion and half the green chili strips to the skillet. As the onions begin to darken the pan, deglaze it with a few tablespoons of water, scraping up its caramelized sugars with a wooden spoon.

10. Stir in the remaining half of the minced garlic. Cook for just 30 seconds before stirring in the cooked lentils. Season with grinds of black pepper.

11. Cover and simmer for the final few minutes to allow the flavors to meld. Remove from the heat and stir in the diluted shiro miso, to taste, and adjust all seasonings to your preferences.

12. Decorate the top of the dal with the remaining sliced onion, green chili strips, and the remaining ½ cup of diced tomatoes. Cover immediately to allow the steam to lightly cook the garnish and to keep the dal warm until serving.

PEAS WITH ARTICHOKE HEARTS

You can never have enough side dishes. This one is Moroccan inspired, perfect for a mezze table or small-plate party. Flavorful and simple to make, it marries tender petite peas with creamy artichoke hearts, and is seasoned with garlic, ginger, green raisins, lemon, and a few brined green olives. We garnish the dish with cilantro, parsley, and mint. Serve alongside other Moroccan greats like *Zaalouk* (see page 104) and on flatbreads, like *Sangak* (see page 201), a Persian bread that is very similar to tafarnout, a pebble bread from the Moroccan town of Skoura.

The Land Institute in Kansas breeds new varieties of perennial crops to better withstand the stresses of climate change. It reports that perennial crops, like artichokes, help increase nutrient retention in soils, reducing the need for synthetic fertilizers and improving the structure of the soil. Artichokes grown on Moroccan farms have a climate footprint of 0.47 kg CO_2eq per kg, with 14% of GHG due to fertilizer production, 54% to in-field bacteria, 15% to off-field bacteria, 3% to soil amendments, 6% to farm machinery, and 7% due to irrigation. In U.S. groceries, artichoke hearts have a climate footprint of 0.6 kg CO_2eq per kg, with 24% from agriculture, 18% from transport, 3% from processing, and 55% from packaging.

Fighting Climate Change in Morocco

Since the 1960s, Morocco's greenhouse gas emissions have significantly risen as its economy has grown. Still dependent on coal and with its natural gas infrastructure still expanding in 2021, Morocco's emissions are expected to flatten by 2030, thanks to its ramping up its decarbonization efforts in key economic sectors, according to the Climate Action Tracker that rated Morocco overall as "Almost Sufficient." Morocco has launched an ambitious solar energy project, one of the world's largest solar projects, and invested in wind farms. Its aim is to produce over half its energy by renewables by 2030, reducing its total GHG by 42%, and to reduce its reliance on fossil fuels significantly, according to a 2023 analysis of Morocco by the Carnegie Endowment for International Peace. To read how global warming is impacting Morocco, see page 105. For how perennial crops help the climate, see page 212.

Prep time 10 minutes | Cook time 15 minutes | Serves 2 to 3

3 cloves garlic, peeled, cut in small pieces

1 inch-long ginger root, peeled, cut in small pieces

⅓ cup green raisins

1 cup white onion, cut into small dice

1 cup unsalted broth, to deglaze pan and moisten the mix

½ teaspoon ground turmeric, mixed with water to make a paste

15 good-quality brined green olives, whole—or for young children, pitted and cut in half

Several grinds white pepper

1 small bunch each of cilantro, parsley, and mint, leaves only

3 cups frozen petite peas, defrosted

2 (10-ounce) jars artichoke hearts (packed in water, not oil), drained and rinsed, larger hearts sliced in half

½ small lemon, sliced thinly, seeds removed

2 teaspoons shiro (mild, white) miso, or to taste

1. Using a coffee grinder, crush and grind the garlic and ginger together to make a smooth paste, adding a few drops of water to facilitate blending, as needed.

2. Soak the raisins in hot water for 5 minutes to soften and rehydrate. Drain.

3. Heat a skillet over a medium flame for a few minutes. Lower the heat and put in the onion. Sweat the onion until it softens and releases its liquid. If the pan has dried and the onions have caramelized, deglaze the pan with a small splash of broth, scraping up the onion sugars from the pan with a wooden spoon.

4. Stir in the garlic-ginger paste, turmeric paste, olives, raisins, and white pepper, mixing well.

5. Use a mezzaluna or chef knife to chop the mint leaves for Step 10. Transfer to a small bowl. Then chop the cilantro and parsley together to garnish the dish in Step 12. Transfer them to a second small bowl.

6. Continue to cook the mixture for 3 minutes. Then stir in the peas and gently add the artichokes.

7. Add broth to create a little sauce in the pan. Cook just a few minutes until hot and fragrant.

8. Scoop out a cup of the mix and transfer it to a high-speed blender. Purée, adding broth if needed, to create a sauce.

9. Stir the sauce back into the pan, coating all the vegetables well.

10. Now add the lemon slice and chopped mint leaves. Cover and cook for the final minute.

11. Remove from the heat. Season with shiro miso. Taste and adjust all seasonings.

12. Serve warm, garnished with chopped parsley and cilantro.

RAPINI E CANNELLINI

If you are a fan of leafy greens with a slightly bitter edge like I am (think arugula and radicchio), you're bound to adore broccoli rabe, aka *rapini.* This comforting beans-greens pairing hails from Puglia, the heel of Italy's southern boot. A little peperoncino for pizzazz, together with onion, garlic, wakame seaweed (in lieu of anchovy), and shiro miso tames *rapini's* bitter notes and balances its flavors. This savory dish makes a splendid lunch or side dish. Choose young broccoli rabe with bright green leaves and tightly closed florets for the most tender, mild flavor. A nutritional power-house, broccoli rabe is loaded with cancer-fighting antioxidants, vitamins K, A, and C, and an array of minerals.

In the vast cruciferous family of vegetables, leafy *rapini* is closer to mustards and turnips than broccoli, despite its deceptive florets. It generates low levels of greenhouse gas emissions and carries a low water footprint: Broccoli rabe's climate footprint is 0.6 kg CO_2eq per kg in U.S. groceries while dried white beans are 1.0 kg CO_2eq per kg.

How the Climate Is Battering Puglia

Climate change is causing increasingly violent coastal storms and shore erosion in Italy's Puglia region.[91] In recent years prolonged heat waves have caused temperatures to rise well over 100°F over sustained periods. Italy's climate is becoming increasing tropical. Warming waters in the Adriatic and Ionian Seas intensify storms, causing storm surge and shore erosion along Puglia's coastline. The hottest temperature recorded in Puglia to date was 116°F in 2007.[92]

Prep time 1 hour to cook beans and prep ingredients
Cook time 25 to 30 minutes | Serves 3 to 5

½ pound white beans, like cannellini, great northern, or heirloom *tarbais*, Marcella, or flageolet, pressure-cooked

2 large sage leaves, a 4-inch sprig of rosemary, and 2 laurel (bay) leaves tied in a cheesecloth bouquet garni

5 large cloves garlic

2 bunches broccoli rabe, soaked, stems trimmed

½ cup Italian parsley, chopped

1 small fresh or dried red peperoncino, or a similar hot red pepper, or to taste

½ teaspoon dried wakame, freshly ground

1 medium onion, any variety, cut in a medium dice

A splash of dry white wine or bean cooking broth, to deglaze pan

Several grinds of black pepper

½ cup shiro (mild, white) miso paste, diluted in water, to taste

1. Rinse the dried beans and put them in a pot. Cover the beans by 3 inches of cold water. Bring to a boil, then lower to a simmer. Cook for 2 minutes, turn off the heat, cover, and steep the beans until they swell and sink in the pot, about 30 minutes.

2. Pour out the water and refill the pot. Add the bouquet garni of fresh herbs and 2 garlic cloves. Bring to a boil and lower immediately to a very gentle simmer. Cook until the beans are tender but intact and the broth fragrant, about 30 minutes, but longer for older beans. The beans are ready when they are plump, tender, fragrant, and intact. We'll use the beans and a few cups of the hot cooking broth below.

3. As the beans are cooking, rinse the *rapini* and soak them in a large bowl of water to revive them for 10 minutes. Discard the bottom few inches of stems that are woody and tough.

4. On a large cutting board, place the parsley, remaining 3 garlic cloves, and the red peperoncino. Use a mezzaluna or chef knife to mince them together into small uniform pieces. The mix should fill ½ to ⅔ cup.

5. Use a small coffee or spice grinder to grind the wakame seaweed leaves into a powder.

6. Heat a large heavy-bottomed stainless steel skillet over medium-low heat for 3 minutes. Put in the diced onion and dry sauté for 2 minutes, stirring. After the onions have released their liquid and

begun to darken the pan, deglaze the pan with a splash of deglazing liquid, scraping up the caramelized onion sugars from the pan.

7. Stir in the ground wakame, the garlic/parsley/peperoncini mix, and a few grinds of black pepper. Cook for a minute and then stir in the broccoli rabe. Add a cup of the herby bean broth, cover, and stew the *rapini* for 20 minutes, turning the *rapini* once or twice. Test for doneness. When the broccoli rabe is almost tender, gently add the cooked beans, taking care not to break them. If the pan is dry, add another cup of bean broth. Cover and very gently simmer until the greens are tender but still intact, for 5 to 10 minutes.

8. Dilute ½ cup shiro miso with water to the consistency of a light batter. When serving the dish, we'll season the plated dish with miso drizzled on top.

9. Taste and adjust seasoning as you like. The dish is ready when the beans and greens are tender, intact, and infused with flavor from the seasonings. Once plated, drizzle diluted shiro miso, to taste, on top. Serve warm with some crusty 100% whole-grain artisanal bread, bread crisps, or crackers.

ROASTED LODI CUPS TWO WAYS

I always get excited when I discover a new offering from Row 7 Seeds, whose plant breeders collaborate with farmers and chefs to come up with new vegetables with exceptional flavor and nutrition. When I happened upon their diminutive Lodi squash, I knew they'd make the perfect addition to the Thanksgiving table. I roasted them simply and stuffed them two ways: One with garlicky, zippy *Spinaci Rifatti* (see page 256), and one with creamy cremini mushrooms and peas.

Winter squashes emit 0.24 kg CO_2eq per kg on U.S. farms, with 7% of emissions coming from fertilizer production, 22% from in-field bacteria, 5% from off-field bacteria, 4% from draining wetlands for farming, 5% from pesticide production, and 54% from running farm equipment. Spinach emits even fewer greenhouse gases at 0.16 kg CO_2eq per kg in U.S. fields, with 30% due to fertilizer production, 30% from in-field bacteria, 9% from off-field bacteria, 10% from draining wetlands, 3% from adding soil amendments like urea and limestone, 4% from producing pesticides, and 14% from operating farm machinery. Mushrooms like cremini are similarly low emitters at 0.15 kg CO_2eq per kg on U.S. farms, with 22% of emissions generated during fertilizer production, 39% from in-field bacteria, 10% from off-field bacterial N_2O emissions, 3% from draining wetlands, 2% from pesticide production, 22% from running farm equipment, and 2% from irrigation.

Winter Squash's Climate Woes

Hotter summers, droughts, and unpredictable rainfall are hurting winter squash yields. After squash ripens in the field, it is left to cure before being harvested. Drought can kill plants in summers, and wet fields will rot the fruit in the fall. In 2020 many British farmers lost half their squash crop due to weather. To hedge, some farmers are diversifying the vegetables they grow and employing regenerative farming techniques to enrich the soil to preserve water and nutrients. However, unless a farmer has indoor facilities to lay out and dry acres of squash, in the face of wetter falls, their challenges will continue.[93]

Prep time 30 minutes | Cook time 30 minutes | Makes 16 filled squash halves

8 Lodi squash

1 teaspoon porcini powder from ¼ cup dried porcini mushroom slices, or to taste

Freshly ground chili de árbol powder, if you like a bit more heat, to garnish

1½ cups unsweetened soy milk

⅓ cup white whole wheat flour

1 teaspoon nutritional yeast

2 teaspoons shiro (mild, white) miso paste, or to taste

Fresh grinds of nutmeg

Several grinds white pepper

¾ pound cremini (baby bella) mushrooms, wiped and cut in ¼-inch slices

½ medium red onion or 1 large shallot, cut in a fine dice

½ teaspoon dried thyme leaves

2 cloves garlic, minced

1 cup petite frozen peas, defrosted

1½ pounds *Spinaci Rifatti* (see page 256)

Lemon Citrus Powder (see page 41), or zest and paprika, to garnish

Fresh chopped chives, to garnish

1. Preheat the oven to 400°F.

2. To prep the Lodi squash, or any winter squash, I like to use a meat cleaver and a dead-blow hammer to neatly split the squash in half lengthwise. Use a melon baller to easily remove the seeds and fibrous strings.

3. On a cookie sheet lined with parchment paper, lay the squash halves face down. Roast them for about 20 minutes but check at 15 for doneness. If a sharp knife easily penetrates the squash, flip them over, change the oven setting to low broil, and broil for about 5 minutes or until the cut edges are golden and caramelized. Remove from the oven and set aside until Step 11.

4. Use a coffee grinder to grind the dried porcini slices into a fine powder. Measure out a teaspoon and transfer any excess to a tightly lidded spice jar. Store in a cool, dark cupboard.

5. Wipe out the coffee grinder with a damp paper towel and dry it. To make chili de árbol powder for a garnish, remove the stems from one or two chilies, and cut them into small pieces with scissors. Use the coffee grinder to reduce them into flakes or a finer powder. Store any excess as described in Step 4.

6. Combine the soy milk, white whole wheat flour, nutritional yeast, and shiro miso paste in a high-speed blender. Use a nutmeg grater to grate about ⅛ teaspoon of nutmeg into the blender container. Do the same with a pepper mill filled with white peppercorns. Run the blender on high to blend the ingredients. Taste to adjust any seasonings.

7. Heat a large skillet on medium for 3 minutes. Put in the cremini mushrooms and onions/shallots, lower the temperature to medium low. Cover and allow the mushrooms and onions/shallots to sweat for 4 to 5 minutes, releasing their liquid.

8. Stir in the thyme leaves, minced garlic, thyme leaves, and porcini powder. Cook for 1 minute.

9. Add the blended white sauce. Raise the heat to medium and stir as the sauce begins to thicken, about 5 minutes.

10. Turn off the heat. Add the peas and season, to taste, adding more shiro miso, if needed, by dissolving it in the hot white sauce and spreading it throughout the pan.

11. Fill half the roasted Lodi cups with *Spinaci Rifatti*, and half with the creamed cremini and peas. Mound each filling slightly in each cup.

12. Heat an oven to 250°F. Fifteen minutes before serving, reheat the filled Lodi squashes to warm thoroughly.

13. Garnish the spinach cups with Lemon Citrus Powder, zest and paprika, or chili de árbol powder. Garnish the cremini cups with chopped fresh chives. Serve hot.

SPINACI RIFATTI

When I lived in Florence, I craved *spinaci rifatti,* garlicky twice-cooked spinach. In Italian groceries everywhere you found sizable balls of spinach, already boiled and squeezed. At home, it was a simple matter then to chop it and sauté it with plenty of oil, garlic, and salt. This remake is craveable but also much more climate friendly and healthier. What's more, it takes no time at all to prepare. Enjoy *Spinaci Rifatti* as a delicious side dish or as a filling for crêpes, plant-based quiches, stuffed pastas, eggless omelets, enchiladas, empanadas, parathas, in appetizers, and stuffed into Roasted Lodi Cups (see page 251).

It's hard to find a dish with a lower climate footprint than *Spinaci Rifatti*. Spinach generates only 0.16 kg CO_2eq per kg on U.S. farms, with 30% of emissions from fertilizer production, 30% from in-field bacteria, 9% from off-field bacteria, 10% from the draining of wetlands, 3% from the application of limestone and/or urea, 4% from the production of pesticides, and 14% from farm machinery.

How to Grow Cold-Loving Spinach when the Mercury Rises

Spinach is a cool-weather crop, preferring temperatures from 55° to 60°F with 12 hours of sunlight. Even young plants can withstand temps as low as 15° to 20°F for brief periods. Warmer temperatures, however, cause spinach to bolt and go to seed, which has precluded spinach as a summer crop and challenges spinach production in many regions, especially as the climate warms. Temperatures in greenhouses during summer can rise as high as 120°F. According to a 2020 study in *Scientia Horticulturae*, scientists are testing micro-mist systems to reduce heat stress on spinach, cool soils, and increase humidity. Yields increased by 30%, and lutein (an antioxidant important to eye health) content increased 140%, compared to conventionally grown spinach. Innovations like micro-misting gives growers new options to grow spinach in hot climates year-round.

Prep time 30 minutes to roast head of garlic, plus 5 minutes
Cook time 10 minutes   Serves 4 to 6

1 large head garlic, dry roasted

1 medium dried Sicilian peperoncino, freshly ground

3 pounds of fresh spinach or Chinese spinach, steamed, or cut-leaf or chopped frozen spinach, defrosted

2½ teaspoons granulated garlic

1 teaspoon granulated onion

2 teaspoons *Parmigiano Perfetto* (see page 56), or to taste

2 tablespoons shiro (mild, white) miso paste, diluted in 2 tablespoons hot water, or to taste

1 teaspoon Lemon Citrus Powder (see page 41) or lemon zest (optional)

1. Preheat the oven to 375°F. To roast the garlic head, remove the head's loose papery skins. Roast it for 30 minutes or until it is quite fragrant and soft. Cool slightly. Peel each clove and place on a cutting board. Use a fork to mash the garlic into a soft, pulpy paste. We will use it in Step 10.

2. Remove the stem from the dried peperoncino. Using a small coffee grinder, grind it into coarse flakes or a finer powder.

3. For fresh spinach, in a large bowl filled with water, wash the spinach multiple times to remove any gritty growing media.

4. If you use bunched spinach, cut off and discard the purple root crowns.

5. Add the wet leaves to a large sauté pan, cover, and over a medium-low heat steam the spinach for just a few minutes until the leaves are wilted and the stems are tender. Cool.

6. Divide the spinach into three portions. With your hands held over a bowl, squeeze each into a ball to remove as much liquid as possible. Repeat for the remaining spinach. Reserve the spinach juice for another dish.

7. Place the three squeezed spinach balls on a large cutting board. Use a mezzaluna or sharp chef knife to chop the leaves and stems into ¼-inch pieces.

8. Reheat the pan over a medium flame for 2 minutes. Put in the chopped spinach and stir to dry it.

9. Season, to taste, with the granulated garlic and onion, the ground peperoncino, and the *Parmigiano Perfetto*.

10. Stir in the roasted garlic paste, incorporating it well into the mix. Cover and cook for 2 minutes to allow all the flavors to meld. Turn off the heat.

11. Season with the diluted shiro miso, to taste, stirring to distribute it evenly.

12. Lastly, sprinkle on a little Lemon Citrus Powder or zest, if using. The lemon aroma and flavor should be light and subtle, not dominate the flavor of this dish. Taste and adjust the seasonings as you like.

TIAN

A splendid dish from Provence, *Tian* is a colorful medley of sliced summer vegetables, cooked to melt-in-your-mouth tenderness in a zesty, chunky tomato-pepper sauce. Its colorful striping is a showstopper. To sop up its delectable juices, I love to eat *Tian* with crusty whole wheat crostini rubbed with garlic and strewn with fresh thyme. *Tian* is a beautiful way to celebrate summer's bounty, served as a festive side dish or playing the starring role, front and center on the plate.

Tian has a low climate footprint: On U.S. farms, onions emit 0–0.10 kg CO_2eq per kg in GHG, eggplants 0–0.1 kg CO_2eq per kg, and zucchini 0.23 kg CO_2eq per kg.

Let's Talk Tomatoes

Although field tomatoes enjoy a low climate footprint in U.S. fields (see page 58), by the time they arrive at market, tomatoes have a higher environmental impact than other vegetables at 1.8 kg CO_2eq per kg. This is due primarily to their handling requirements as a perishable food that requires temperature-controlled transport and special packing and handling to avoid bruising or piercing their tender skins.

Interestingly, minimally processed tomatoes (jars, cans, and cartons) at market generate half the level of emissions as fresh tomatoes: They significantly reduce waste by using tomatoes that may be smaller, misshapen, or blemished. When buying canned or jarred tomatoes, look for the highest-quality San Marzano tomatoes without additives like sodium chloride, calcium chloride, a firming agent, or citric acid. Unpreserved San Marzano tomatoes are picked at their peak, unlike lesser brands, and will be tastier, naturally sweeter, and firmer.

Controlled environment greenhouse and hydroponic tomatoes, at present, have a climate footprint up to 6 times greater than field tomatoes, due to their current over-reliance on fossil fuels for heating, pumping water and nutrients, and light. As our economy transitions fully to renewable energy sources in the coming years, vertical farming's advantages may outweigh its costs: It uses space, nutrients, and water far more efficiently than field-grown tomatoes, producing yields up to 400 times greater per acre than field agriculture. It is protected from microbial contamination like E. coli from animal waste runoff and has far lower exposure to pesticides, treating outbreaks locally with microbes and beneficial insects rather than more toxic conventional means. One day in the not-too-distant future, indoor agriculture may save us from an overheating climate prone to increasingly extreme and erratic weather.[94, 95]

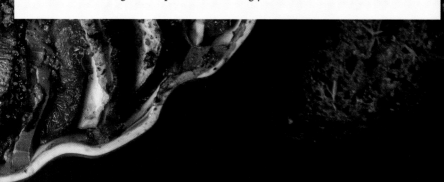

Prep time 40 minutes | Cook time 1 hour 15 minutes
Makes one 10-inch *tian* to serve 8 to 12 as a side dish

TOMATO-PEPPER SAUCE

1 pound mini bell peppers, cored, roasted, cut in a large dice

½–1 teaspoon, freshly ground chili powder from mild dried Espelette, Aleppo, or Kashmiri peppers, or to taste

1 full cup onions, cut in a medium dice

Splash of dry white vermouth or unsalted vegetable broth, to deglaze pan

4 cloves garlic, minced

2 cups jarred or canned sodium- and preservative-free whole tomatoes

1 tablespoon aka (red) miso, or to taste

Fistful of basil leaves, cut in a chiffonade (rolled and sliced in thin ribbons)

TIAN

1½ to 2 cups whole wheat breadcrumbs

2 to 3 small Italian eggplants, stems removed, sliced in ¼-inch rounds

2 medium yellow squash, stems removed, sliced in ¼-inch rounds

2 medium zucchini, stems removed, sliced in ¼-inch rounds

4 to 5 medium ripe fresh tomatoes, stems removed, sliced in ¼-inch rounds

3 to 4 medium onions, peeled, sliced in ¼-inch rounds

2 to 3 cloves garlic, peeled, cut in thin slices

Several fresh grinds of black pepper

2 tablespoons dried *herbes de Provence* or 5 to 6 tablespoons of your own mix of fresh herbs, like rosemary, thyme, summer savory, parsley, tarragon

MAKE THE TOMATO-PEPPER SAUCE

1. Heat oven to 375°F.

2. Place cored mini peppers on a baking sheet lined with parchment and dry roast for 30 minutes or until lightly toasted and collapsing. Cool slightly and cut them in a large dice.

3. While the peppers are roasting, use a coffee grinder to grind mild chili peppers into a powder. Measure out 1 teaspoon and reserve any excess in a spice jar to store in a cool, dark cupboard.

4. Heat a sauté pan for 3 minutes. Dry sauté the diced onion, stirring until it sweats its liquid and begins to caramelize the bottom of the pan. Deglaze with a few tablespoons of deglazing liquid. Stir in the minced garlic, and after a minute add the jarred tomatoes, mashing them crudely with a wooden spoon or potato masher.

5. Stir in the diced roasted peppers, and season with chili powder, to taste. Cook for a few minutes, then turn off the heat and stir in aka miso and basil. Taste to adjust the seasonings as you like.

COMPOSE THE *TIAN*

1. Raise the oven temperature to 450°F.

2. In a stove-to-oven baking pan, spoon in a nice base layer of the tomato-pepper sauce, about ¾ inch thick. Generously sprinkle breadcrumbs over the sauce. If you lack a baking pan that can also cook on a stovetop, place it in a large flat-bottom steamer, filled with ½ inch of water.

3. Alternating vegetables, stack them horizontally on edge along the dish's perimeter. Fit them tightly as the vegetables will shrink as they cook. Depending on the diameter of the vegetables, you should be able to squeeze in two or possibly three concentric rings of stacked vegetables. Stud the vegetables here and there with slivers of the garlic.

4. Cover the pan and bring to a gentle simmer on the stovetop and cook for 30 minutes. Check occasionally to ensure the sauce hasn't dried out. If the pan is dry, add a little water. If your baking pan is sitting in a steamer, steam for half an hour, checking occasionally to ensure the steamer hasn't dried out. Test for doneness by inserting a sharp knife into an eggplant slice; it should penetrate it easily. If it doesn't, cover and cook for an additional 5 minutes, and retest.

5. Remove the cover and transfer the baking pan to a rimmed cookie sheet now to catch any drippings in the oven. Grind pepper on top, and sprinkle the top of the *Tian* generously with more breadcrumbs and your herb blend.

6. Bake, uncovered, for about 30 minutes or until the vegetables become golden and crispy on top.

7. Transfer the pan to a cooling rack and allow the juices to recede and congeal before serving.

8. To serve, spoon and swirl some sauce on the plate. Top with a portion of stacked *Tian*. Serve along with lightly toasted artisanal whole wheat bread. Rub the slices with raw garlic, grinds of pepper, and fresh thyme leaves.

HINT

Choose vegetables that have similar diameters.

MAINS

ASHE JO

Ah, finally the spring equinox arrives with the promise of longer, milder days and rebirth of all life. The season coincides with the Persian New Year celebration of Nowruz, and what better way to honor both than to cook up an iconic Persian stew like *Ashe Jo*. Richly flavored and visually gorgeous, *Ashe Jo* is redolent with herbs, greens, and aromatics. It is made hearty with barley and a medley of legumes. Carrots and a hit of tomato paste add sweetness. Lemon and a cultured, thick, soy *kashk* (yogurt cheese) provides tang. This heady dish wows the senses! Serve with a delightful Persian flatbread like *Sangak* (see page 201) to round out this very satisfying meal.

Ashe Jo is as climate friendly as it is nutritious. At U.S. groceries both chickpeas and kidney beans share a climate footprint of 1 kg CO_2eq per kg, with 23% of GHG emissions coming from agriculture, 11% from transport, 20% from processing, and 46% from packaging. Barley farmed in the United States emits 0.84 kg CO_2eq per kg in GHG, with 30% of emissions from the production of fertilizer, 33% from in-field bacteria, 10% from off-field bacteria, 7% from draining wetlands for farming, 9% from running farm machinery, and 6% from drying the grain. For climate impacts on Iran see page 201. For Iran and its energy policies, see page 29.

Prep time 3 passive hours to strain soy yogurt, plus 30 minutes
Cook time 30 minutes | Serves 5 to 7

3 cups soy yogurt to make *kashk* for the garnish, strained

1 large sweet white onion, like Vidalia or Maui, or 3 to 4 large shallots for the garnish, thinly sliced

10 cups unsalted vegetable broth

1½ cups whole barley (hulled or hull-less, not pearled)

2 bay leaves

2 whole cloves garlic, peeled

1 large red onion, sliced thinly

2 carrots, grated

1 leek, whites and greens, well cleaned, sliced thinly

1 bunch spring onions or scallions, whites and greens, sliced thinly

2 tablespoons dried mint or 1 cup packed fresh mint leaves, cut in a chiffonade (rolled and sliced into thin ribbons)

1½ inch ginger root, grated, or to taste

2 tablespoons tomato paste

1 teaspoon turmeric powder

½ teaspoon freshly ground white or black

pepper, or to taste

1 (15.5-ounce) can unsalted red kidney beans, rinsed

1 (15.5-ounce) can unsalted chickpeas, rinsed

1 pound chopped frozen spinach

1 large bunch dill, roughly chopped

1 cup packed fresh mint leaves, cut in a chiffonade (rolled and sliced in thin ribbons)

1 cup packed parsley, roughly chopped

1 cup packed cilantro, roughly chopped

Juice and zest of 1 medium organic lemon

1 teaspoon Lemon Citrus Powder (see page 41)

1 to 2 teaspoons shiro (mild, white) miso paste per serving, or to taste

Pinch of dry-sauteed sweet onion or shallots, a large spoonful per serving of soy kashk, and a sprinkle of barberries (fresh if available or dried if not) per serving, for garnish

1. To make *kashk*, strain the soy yogurt by pouring it onto a 2 foot square of unbleached muslin. Tie up into a bag with a 2 foot length of string. Suspend the yogurt bag to drain over the sink or in a strainer set atop a bowl for 3 hours. During this time, it will thicken into a creamy cheese with the consistency of sour cream. Scrape it into a lidded container and refrigerate until use.

2. To dirty one fewer pan, let's begin at the end, by dry sautéing the sweet white onion or shallots for the garnish. Heat a large pot over medium heat for 3 minutes. Put the sweet onion in the hot, empty pot and cook for a few minutes, stirring, until the aromatics release their liquid and turn golden. When they dry, darken the pot, and begin to stick, deglaze the pot with a few tablespoons of broth, scraping up the caramelized sugars with a wooden spoon. Continue cooking until the onions dry and crisp up, then remove them from the pot and set aside.

3. To prepare the barley, rinse it, transfer to the pot, cover with water, add the bay leaves and 2 garlic cloves, and simmer for 2 minutes. Cover, remove from the heat, and steep the barley for 30 minutes to parcook it. Alternatively, soak the raw barley in cool water the previous night if you prefer. Drain, discard the garlic and bay leaves, and set aside.

4. Reheat the pot on medium low for 2 minutes. Put in the sliced red onion and sweat it gently for 5 minutes to allow it to soften and release its juices. Add the grated carrot, leek, and spring onions or scallions, and cook for 2 minutes, covered, before adding the dried mint and ginger. Add the parcooked barley, which will absorb the flavors of these aromatics. When the mix dries out, add a few tablespoons of broth. Cook for 5 minutes.

5. Add the rest of the broth now, raise the heat to medium-high to bring to a simmer. Stir in the tomato paste, turmeric, and freshly ground pepper. Then stir in the kidney beans and chickpeas. After another minute add the chopped spinach and chopped dill, fresh mint leaves, parsley, and cilantro. Cover and gently simmer for about 15 minutes.

6. When the barley is tender and the soup has thickened into a stew, *Ashe Jo* is just about ready. Remove from the heat and stir in the lemon juice and Lemon Citrus Powder, if using, to taste. Reserve the lemon zest for the garnish.

7. To plate, ladle the stew into warm bowls, season, to taste, with shiro miso paste. Garnish with the crispy sweet onions or shallots, a big dollop of *kashk*, a sprinkling of barberries, and a pinch of lemon zest. Serve immediately.

BEETY BURGERS

If you find the mushy texture of many plant-based burgers unappealing, then Beety Burgers are for you! These burgers are firm, flavorful, very kind to the climate, and super healthy. Beety burgers live up to their name using a combo of red and golden beets, which create a crispy brown exterior upon cooking yet maintain a pink interior. More important, thanks to the beets, they help us generate nitric oxide, which helps our arteries relax and lowers blood pressure. Top them with Mango Salsa (see page 53) or Salsa Verde (see page 58) and dig in!

Beef and turkey burgers sold in U.S. groceries have climate footprints ranging from 20 to 60 kg CO_2eq per kg. Processed plant-based burgers sold in the United States range in GHG emissions from 3 to 4 kg CO_2eq per kg. Sorghum has a very low carbon footprint at 0.25 kg CO_2eq per kg, and rolled oats are 1.1 kg CO_2eq per kg, making them good, whole-grain choices for our burgers.

Sorghum Takes the Heat

Sorghum is an ancient grain first cultivated in northeastern Africa 8,000 years ago or more. It spread to India, then China, reaching Australia, and eventually the New World in the eighteenth century. Sorghum is a low glycemic grain, packed with flavonoids with antioxidative, anti-inflammatory, and anticarcinogenic health benefits. Long consumed in the Global South, sorghum is finding its way onto plates in the West now for its nutritive and environmental advantages. With deep root systems, sorghum can withstand drought and sequester carbon in the soil. It requires little water for ample yields, making it well adapted to dry, warm conditions. Of all the major cereal grains, sorghum is best able to resist drought. It can even tolerate extreme rain events and flooding, making it a model crop for many regions where traditional staple crops are suffering from weather extremes and dropping yields.[96, 97]

Prep time 35 minutes   Cook time 30 minutes   Makes twelve 3 inch burgers

1 cup raw red sorghum, rinsed

3 cups unsalted vegetable broth

⅓ teaspoon ground cumin seed, freshly ground

1 mounded tablespoon porcini powder, freshly ground

⅛ teaspoon chipotle powder, freshly ground

1 tablespoon flaxseed, freshly ground

⅓ cup oil-free packed sundried tomatoes, rehydrated

1 small golden beet, peeled and grated coarsely, about ¾ cup

1 small red beet, peeled and grated coarsely, about ¾ cup

1 (15.5-ounce) can unsalted red kidney beans, drained and rinsed

½ teaspoon granulated onion

½ teaspoon granulated garlic

Several grinds black pepper

3 tablespoons aka (red) miso paste, or to taste

½ teaspoon apple cider vinegar

1½ teaspoons date paste or blackstrap molasses

½ teaspoon ground sumac

1 teaspoon tamarind concentrate

½ teaspoon liquid smoke or 1 tablespoon smoked paprika

½ teaspoon Dijon mustard

½ cup thick rolled oats

1. To cook the red sorghum, add the grain to a pressure cooker or instant pot. Cover with 3 cups of vegetable broth. Pressure-cook on high for 35 minutes. Turn off the heat and allow the steam to release naturally. Drain. The sorghum should be tender but firm.

2. Preheat oven to 375°F.

3. Use a small coffee grinder to separately mill the cumin seed, dried porcini mushrooms, chipotle chilies, and flaxseeds into powders. Measure each quantity and set aside.

4. Cover the sundried tomatoes with water. Heat for 2 minutes in a microwave or 5 minutes on a stovetop. Cool, drain, chop, and set aside.

5. Depending on the size of your food processor bowl, you may need to process the burger mix in batches and then combine the batches in a large mixing bowl. Pulse the cooked sorghum until most of the grains are chopped roughly. Do not overprocess or you will reduce them to a paste. Transfer the chopped sorghum to a very large bowl.

6. Put in to the food processor the rest of the ingredients, except the oats. Process, scraping down sides, for 15 seconds. Add the oats and process for an additional 15 seconds.

7. Transfer the mix to the bowl with the chopped sorghum. Using very clean hands, mix it well. Taste and adjust the seasonings as desired.

8. Shape patties and place on a parchment-lined cookie sheet. Bake for 35 minutes in a conventional oven or 20 minutes in a convection oven. Flip and bake for an additional 10 minutes or until lightly golden and firm to the touch when pressed.

9. Serve hot. Plate the burgers with your favorite condiments and toppings and dig in.

BLACK AND RED BEAN CHILI AND CHIPS

This bean chili is hearty, satisfying, and alive with flavor, thanks to its Mexican seasonings and mild chilies. A big bowlful makes a satisfying supper scooped up with baked corn tortilla chips. You can also enjoy it in burritos, enchiladas, tostadas, and tacos, topped with Mango Salsa (see page 53) or Salsa Verde (see page 58).

Chilies and peppers farmed in Mexico have a negligible climate footprint of 0–0.1 kg CO_2eq per kg, with 34% of emissions due to fertilizer production, 40% from in-field bacteria, 14% from off-field bacteria, 6% from soil amendments like urea and limestone, and 5% from the energy required to irrigate fields. Mexican-farmed maize emits 0.75 kg CO_2eq per kg in GHG, with 35% of emissions coming from fertilizer production, 32% from in-field bacteria, 12% from off-field bacteria, 7% from soil amendments, 6% from running farm machinery, and 6% from air-drying the corn.

Too Hot for Mexico's Chilies

While chili peppers favor hot, dry climes for optimal growth, even chilies have their limits. Record heat (50°C) and lack of precipitation led to drought in Mexico's dry regions like Sinaloa, Chihuahua, and Michoacán in 2023, depriving chilies of the growing conditions they require. The reduction in the crop's yield reverberated as far as Thailand and Vietnam, creating a shortage in sriracha sauce production. Deforestation and rising greenhouse gas emissions are exacerbating Mexico's drought.[98] In 2020 the Mexican government abolished its Climate Change Fund, pushing the country in the wrong direction in the face of its mounting environmental challenges.[99] For more on Mexico's climate difficulties, see page 313.

Prep time 1 hour | Cook time 30 minutes | Serves 3 to 5

CHILI

1½ teaspoons cumin seeds, freshly roasted and ground

1½ teaspoons coriander seeds, freshly roasted and ground

½ teaspoon allspice berries, freshly roasted and ground

¼ teaspoon ancho chili, wiped clean, freshly ground, or to taste

¼ teaspoon pasilla chili, wiped clean, freshly ground, or to taste

¼ teaspoon guajillo chili, wiped clean, freshly ground, or to taste

¼ teaspoon chipotle chili, wiped clean, freshly ground, or to taste

2 ears corn, lightly roasted and shucked off the cob

1 large onion, cut in a medium dice

Unsalted vegetable broth or dry vermouth, to deglaze skillet

3 cloves garlic, minced

1 teaspoon dried oregano leaves, Mexican if available

1 red and 1 orange bell pepper, deseeded and destemmed, cut in a medium dice

2 to 3 poblano peppers or 1 large green bell pepper, deseeded and destemmed, cut in a medium dice

1 (28-ounce) can whole San Marzano tomatoes

2 teaspoons smoked paprika or ¾ teaspoon liquid smoke

A few good grinds of black pepper

1½ (15.5-ounce) cans unsalted black beans, rinsed

2 (15.5-ounce) cans unsalted red beans, rinsed

⅓ cup aka (red) miso paste, or to taste, diluted in ⅓ cup water

2 tablespoons lime juice

Sliced scallion, roughly cut cilantro leaves, thinly sliced jalapeño pepper, sliced or mashed avocado, and a dollop of soy yogurt, to garnish

CHIPS

1 (7-ounce) package fresh corn tortillas without preservatives, found at local *tortillerias*, and some health food markets and specialty stores

MAKE THE CHILI

1. To coax more flavor and nutritional bang out of the spices and chilies, heat them briefly on a hot skillet before using a coffee grinder to grind them into powder. Cumin and coriander seeds burn and become bitter in a flash, so warm them for 20 to 30 seconds—just until your nose perceives their aromas, then remove them immediately from the pan.

2. Press the chilies on the hot skillet with a spatula for about a minute, flip, toasting them just until they are pliant and fragrant. Do not overcook either spices or chilies or they will become bitter. Cool, grind separately, and measure.

3. To roast the corncobs, rest them on the grates of your stove or grill over a medium heat. Rotate each cob after a minute, roasting them until every side shows very light charring in spots. Allow the cobs to cool. To shuck the kernels off the cob, rest the cob's tip on a cutting board, raise the cob 45 degrees, and using a chef knife, slice the kernels in chunks off the cob. Try to keep the kernels in larger pieces as you gently place the kernels in a bowl.

4. Heat a large skillet or sauté pan over medium heat for 2 minutes. Put in the diced onion. Dry sauté until the onions have softened, lightly caramelized, and their sugars have begun to darken the pan.

5. Deglaze the pan with about 2 tablespoons of deglazing liquid.

6. Lower the heat slightly and stir in the minced garlic and dried oregano. After a minute add the diced fresh peppers and sauté for 1 to 2 minutes.

7. Add the tomatoes with their purée, breaking them up with a potato masher or wooden spoon. Stir in the freshly ground cumin, coriander, allspice, chili powders, smoked paprika, and black pepper.

8. Lower heat to a gentle simmer and cook for 5 minutes. Stir in the beans now and cook for another 10 minutes for all the flavors to meld. If the chili is dense, dilute with a cup or two of hot water.

9. If you plan to serve all the chili at once, stir in some of the diluted miso paste. Taste and adjust the miso, spices, chilies, and lime juice levels to suit your taste. However, if you plan to consume only some of the chili now, plate it in preheated bowls, and stir in a tablespoon or two of diluted miso paste, to taste.

10. Take the skillet off the heat and stir in the lime juice. Gently add the corn kernels.

11. Garnish each bowl with sliced scallion, cilantro leaves, a jalapeño slice or two, a slice or two of avocado, and a dollop of soy yogurt. Surround each bowl with the warm, freshly baked tortilla chips (see below).

MAKE THE CHIPS

1. Preheat oven to 425°F.

2. Use a knife or a pair of scissors to cut each corn tortilla in quarters. Place them on a cookie sheet lined with parchment paper. Toast in the oven until they firm up and turn slightly golden and crisp, about 8 minutes. Keep an eye on them as they can brown and burn in a flash. Remove from oven, and cover with a light cloth to keep warm until serving.

BRAISED SUMMER VEGETABLES
WITH CHICKPEAS

One of my favorite ways to feed a hungry crowd is to braise vegetables with herbs and aromatics and finish them in the oven, where their juices thicken and sweeten. This coaxes forth beautiful flavors that meld in a meltingly delicious ensemble. In this dish we marry tomatoes, peppers, and eggplant with chickpeas to delicious effect. Serve in bowls with whole-grain sourdough bread, or over your favorite whole grains or noodles for a hearty, satisfying meal. Every vegetable in this tasty, eye-catching dish has a low climate footprint.

Like their fellow pulses, beans (0.46 kg CO_2eq per kg) and lentils (0.79 kg CO_2eq per kg), chickpeas are low-carbon-emitting, high-fiber, protein-rich foods, with very little fat. Chickpeas generate 0.55 kg CO_2eq per kg on U.S. farms, with 3% of the generated greenhouse gases due to the manufacture of fertilizers, 17% from the N_2O produced by bacteria in the field, 4% from bacteria off-field, 31% from the draining of wetlands for farming, 8% from the manufacture of soil amendments like urea and limestone to alter soil pH, 5% from the production of pesticides, 28% from the use of farm machinery, and 3% from drying.

Seeking a More Resilient Chickpea

Who doesn't love chickpeas? A rich source of protein and an economically important crop, they are cultivated in more than fifty countries across six continents. Chickpeas, like so many food crops, are susceptible to environmental stressors like excessive cold, heat, drought, and inconsistent rainfall patterns. Both low and high temperatures reduce the viability of pollen and germination. Drought and heat stress can delay or damage their flowers and formation of pods. Under more extreme environmental conditions, crop yields can be reduced by 40 to 45%. Plant geneticists and breeders are working to develop chickpea cultivars with specific traits that perform well under the conditions of drought, heat, and low temperatures to better withstand the environmental pressures brought by climate change.[100]

Prep time 45 minutes | Cook time 45 to 55 minutes | Serves 6 to 8

2 teaspoons unsalted dehydrated soup vegetables, freshly ground

2 pounds cherry tomatoes, cut in half

2 teaspoons dried thyme leaves

2 firm Italian eggplants, cut in ¼-inch discs

⅓ cup aka (red) miso paste, diluted in ⅔ cup water

3 medium sweet onions, peeled and cut in ¼ inch slices

4 cloves garlic, cut in ⅛ inch slices

2 (15.5-ounce) cans unsalted chickpeas, rinsed and drained

Several grinds of black pepper

6 large mixed color bell peppers, cored and cut in ¾ inch slices

Chopped dill, parsley, or chives, to garnish

1. Preheat the oven to 475°F conventional oven/450°F convection oven.

2. Use a coffee grinder to reduce the dehydrated soup vegetables into a powder.

3. In a 12-inch sauté pan lay down a layer of halved cherry tomatoes, cut side up, covering the pan's bottom in a single layer. Sprinkle a teaspoon of the thyme leaves over the tomatoes.

4. Lay down the eggplant discs on top of the tomatoes. Cut a few slices in quarters to fill in the gaps between the eggplant circles. Lightly drizzle some diluted miso across the surface.

5. Lay down a layer of sliced onion as you did with the eggplant.

6. Repeat Step 2 and Step 3 and add the remaining thyme leaves.

7. Press the garlic slices down into the gaps between the eggplant slices.

8. Now sprinkle on a few cups of canned chickpeas. Drizzle more diluted miso over the chickpeas to season. Grind black pepper over the surface.

9. Finally, decoratively arrange the bell pepper slices over the surface. The sauté pan may be filled to capacity now, but cooking will significantly reduce its volume. Mix the dehydrated soup vegetable powder into 1½ cups of water. Pour in just enough of the liquid to cover the bottom of the pan by ½ inch.

10. Cover the pan and simmer on the stovetop for 30 to 35 minutes, or until all the vegetables can easily be pierced with a sharp knife.

11. As the vegetables cook, they will release a fair amount of liquid as well. Use a turkey baster to remove all but ½ inch of liquid at the pan's bottom. Transfer the juices you extract into a small pot.

12. Heat the pot at a gentle simmer to reduce the vegetable juice. This will concentrate its flavor and thicken it. This reduction will be your glazing sauce.

13. While your sauce is reducing, carefully place the sauté pan in the oven, uncovered. Roast the vegetables for 15 to 25 minutes, or until the peppers become slightly wrinkled and lightly toasted on their edges. Remove the pan from the oven.

14. Use a pastry brush to glaze the surface of the vegetables with the reduced vegetable sauce.

15. Serve the braised vegetables hot in warmed bowls. Garnish with some chopped fresh herbs. Pass around the sauce at the table.

BRASSICA BISCUIT BAKE

It is common knowledge that after a first frost is the best time to enjoy brassicas, root vegetables, and hardy winter greens. That's when these plants convert some of their starches into sugars, making them even more delicious. So, on a chilly morning when I happened upon a big, beautiful golden cauliflower and heavy broccoli crowns at my greengrocer's, I couldn't resist buying them. I then built this recipe around them, bathing them in creamy Cheesy White Sauce (see page 36) and baking them atop A Better Buttermilk (see page 27) biscuit.

On U.S. farms, cauliflower and broccoli share a climate footprint of 0.27 kg CO_2eq per kg, with 17% of GHG emitted during fertilizer production, 39% from in-field bacteria, 10% from off-field bacteria, 5% from draining wetlands for farming, and 26% from operating farm machinery.

Can Broccoli Survive?

Broccoli is a temperate plant. It is happiest when its growing temperature averages 62°F, but it begins to deform at 72°F. At 82°F broccoli's tender crown of florets forms a dense head, just like cauliflower. DNA methylation regulates plants' gene expression and is the process at work here. With a warming planet, the cultivation of broccoli is threatened. It is early days yet, but Cornell University and Zhejiang University researchers are exploring a molecular genetics approach to suppress DNA methylation to enable broccoli, and other crops, to thrive at warmer temperatures and be sown in wider regions.[101]

Prep time 30 minutes | Bake time 25 minutes | Serves 8 to 10

3½ cups A Better Buttermilk (see page 27)

1 tablespoon shiro (mild, white) miso paste

2½ cups white whole wheat flour

1 tablespoon sodium-and-aluminum-free baking powder

½ teaspoon sodium-free baking soda

1 large gold, purple, or white cauliflower, cut into florets

4 large heavy broccoli crowns, cut into florets

2½ cups thick Cheesy White Sauce made with 3 tablespoons arrowroot (see page 36)

1 teaspoon *herbes de Provence*

½ cup oil-free whole wheat or gluten-free breadcrumbs (see hint on page 283)

Several grinds of black pepper

1. Preheat the oven to 400°F.

2. Pour 1½ cups of A Better Buttermilk into a mixing bowl. Add 1 teaspoon of the miso paste, stirring well to combine. In a separate bowl, combine the white whole wheat flour, baking powder, and baking soda, mixing them well. Using a wooden spoon or dough whisk, pour the bowl of liquid ingredients into the dry ingredients' bowl and mix to create a loose, sticky biscuit dough.

3. Spread the dough on the base of a 9-by-13-inch glass baking dish. Bake on the middle oven rack for 12 minutes or until the biscuit foundation is firm and golden. Remove from the oven and lower the oven temperature to 375°F.

4. Rinse the cauliflower and cut into uniform-sized florets. Do the same with the broccoli crowns. Reserve the stems for another dish. Steam them separately until just tender, for 5 to 8 minutes, but test frequently to avoid overcooking. When ready, the florets should be easy to pierce with a paring knife but be intact and firm. Allow them to cool.

5. If you are making a fresh batch of Cheesy White Sauce, use 3 tablespoons of arrowroot for a denser sauce. Turn off the heat but cover the sauce to keep it warm.

6. If you are reheating a previous batch of Cheesy White Sauce, warm it slightly in a thick-bottomed saucepan, covered, over very low heat. Stir in the *herbes de Provence*. Whisk occasionally to prevent its burning. Do not exceed 140°F, which is far below a simmer, or the starch thickener in arrowroot will fail and the sauce will become thin. The consistency of the Cheesy White Sauce should be dense, like melted cheese.

7. Transfer the white sauce to a large mixing bowl and stir in the steamed vegetables, making sure to coat them well. Taste and adjust the amount of pepper, *herbes de Provence*, and miso if you need to.

8. Gently spoon the sauced vegetables over the baked biscuit, spreading them evenly across the top. Lightly sprinkle breadcrumbs over the surface and grind black pepper liberally over the surface.

9. Bake for about 20 minutes or until the casserole is bubbly and just beginning to brown here and there.

10. Set the oven broiler to its low setting and broil for 3 minutes or just until the top is golden and lightly crispy.

11. Cool on a rack for about 15 minutes to allow the sauce to congeal to facilitate slicing. Serve on warmed plates.

HINT

If you cannot find oil-free crumbs, it's simple to make your own with any 100% whole-grain bread. Use completely stale slices or tear fresh slices into smaller pieces, place on a cookie sheet, and bake them at 275°F for 30 minutes, stirring occasionally and testing for doneness. When they are ready, the pieces should be completely dry and crisp. Allow them to cool, then toss them in a food processor. Pulse the pieces until you have small, uniform crumbs.

CREAMY TOMATO KORMA

Today, I had a yen for something Indian. With a nod toward both creamy, sweet-spiced Indian kormas and mouth-warming, leafy *saags*, I mixed some culinary metaphors and the outcome sure hit the spot. Unlike many creamy Indian dishes, this one isn't made with butter, ghee, or oils. Instead, its luscious creaminess comes from thick cultured soy yogurt. Seasoned with freshly roasted Garam Masala (see page 42), it is alive with sweet spices and mild Kashmiri peppers. Instead of dairy paneer, I used tender, soft tofu, which I adore. Japanese eggplant and Asian spinach melt into the sauce, round out the flavors, and increase its nutritional density. There is so much to delight the senses. Serve with a whole grain, scented with aniseed or fennel seed, or *Rajgira* Roti (see page 186) or Naan (see page 180).

As a category, spices grown on Indian farms have a climate footprint of 0.52 kg CO_2eq per kg, with 13% of GHG coming from fertilizer production, 14% from in-field bacteria, 5% from off-field bacteria, 14% from deforestation, 40% from running farm machinery, and 9% from irrigation. Processed powdered spice blends and seasonings, as a category, sold in U.S. stores share a very high climate footprint of 30 kg CO_2eq per kg, however. From environmental, health, and culinary perspectives, it is best to buy whole spices directly from reputable, sustainable sources, avoid the risks of adulterated commercial blends, and grind small quantities as you need them.

Climate Threats to Gujarat, India

The warming climate is causing the level of the Arabian Sea to rise annually, threatening the population and infrastructure along the coastline of Gujarat. Inland, Gujarat's varied geography includes arid and semi-arid regions, deserts, hills, and wetlands. With climate change, the region is particularly vulnerable to wide swings in temperatures, drought, extended monsoons, hail, rain, and cyclones. Fifty percent of the population is engaged in agriculture, and farmers have suffered significant losses from extreme rainfall.[102–104]

Prep time 20 minutes | Cook time 30 minutes | Serves 4 to 6

1 teaspoon freshly ground Kashmiri powder from 3 whole chilies, or to taste

3 large cloves garlic, ground into a paste with the ginger

1½-inch ginger root, ground into a paste with the garlic

1 large Indian bay leaf

1 (7-inch) Ceylon cinnamon stick, broken into 3 pieces

4 green cardamom pods, cracked

2 medium yellow onions, cut in a medium dice

2 tablespoons dry vermouth or no-sodium vegetable broth, to deglaze pan

Up to 3 tablespoons fresh Garam Masala (see page 42), or to taste

1 (24-ounce) package or jar strained tomatoes or passata

1 tablespoon tomato paste

2 to 3 teaspoons ground turmeric

2 Asian or 3 young, small Italian eggplants, cut in 1½-inch batons

2 to 3 cups unsweetened cultured soy yogurt

1 pound Asian spinach, stems removed, cut in 1-inch strips, or baby spinach

¼ cup shiro (mild, white) miso paste, thinned with water, or to taste

1 (14-ounce) package of soft tofu, drained and cut into ¾-inch cubes

Cilantro leaves, torn, to garnish

1. To make your own Kashmiri powder, remove the stems and grind 3 medium Kashmiri chilies in a coffee or spice grinder until you have a uniform powder. Measure out a teaspoon and transfer the remainder to a small jar for future use.

2. To make the garlic and ginger paste, peel and mince the garlic and ginger. Transfer both together to a mortar and pestle or a coffee grinder and pound or grind into a soft paste, adding a drop or two of water as needed to facilitate blending.

3. Heat a large skillet or sauté pan over medium heat for 3 minutes. Put in the Indian bay leaf, Ceylon cinnamon, and cardamom pods, stirring, and dry roast for 30 to 60 seconds—just until their aromas waft to your nose. Add the onion, lower the heat, cover the pan, and sweat the onion for about 5 minutes or until it releases its liquid and softens.

4. If the pan dries out or the onions darken, deglaze it with a tablespoon or two of deglazing liquid.

5. Stir in the garlic-ginger paste. Then add 1½ tablespoons only of Garam Masala. Stir in the Kashmiri chili powder, to taste. Continue to cook on low for another minute. Then stir in the strained tomatoes and tomato paste. Cover and readjust the heat to a gentle simmer. Stir in enough turmeric to turn the mixture a deep, rich salmon color.

6. Add the eggplant, cover, and continue to simmer gently until the eggplant is tender but intact, for 10 to 15 minutes.

7. Stir in enough soy yogurt to your desired level of creaminess. The yogurt will lighten the dish's color and flavor.

8. Tasting as you go, stir in as much of the remaining Garam Masala as you like. If the curry has become dry, add enough water for the sauce to become creamy but not watery.

9. Stir in the spinach, cover, and cook for the final 5 minutes.

10. Turn off the heat. Season with the diluted shiro miso, to taste, and adjust any seasonings as you like.

11. Drain any liquid that the soft tofu has released and gently slide the tofu into the pan, spooning the sauce over the tofu rather than stirring the cubes, to avoid breaking them. Cover and steep for a final 5 to 10 minutes so the tofu can absorb all the marvelous flavors.

12. Serve very hot on warmed plates, removing the Indian bay leaf, cinnamon sticks, and cardamon pods as you find them.

13. Garnish with torn cilantro leaves.

FARM MARKET SAUTÉ PROVENÇAL

Inspired by a recent visit to my local farmers market, here is a luscious sauté that nods to the South of France. It includes artichokes, fennel, breakfast radishes, tomatoes, eggplants, green olives, and herbs. Enjoy this simple sauté along with tender white beans like *tarbais*, Marcella, or cannellini, and serve with a crusty whole wheat sourdough bread to sop up its delectable juices. Eating low on the food chain like this is the most effective and kindest way to support the planet. The taste of summer like this never disappoints!

Fennel grown in North America emits 0.60 kg CO_2eq per kg, with 35% of GHG from fertilizer production, 22% from in-field bacteria, 6% from off-field bacteria, 10% from soil amendments' CO_2 release during application, 12% from running farm machinery, and 12% from pumping irrigation water.

Climate Challenges in Provence

Climate change is threatening the South of France in similar ways to the rest of the country. Provence is experiencing warmer temperatures with more frequent heat waves and drought, and lower total precipitation but more intense storms that have caused flooding and landslides. Sea level rise and storms have exacerbated the erosion of beaches along its Mediterranean coastline. Europe is the fastest-warming continent, according to the World Meteorological Organization, and temperatures in France in 2022 were 2.9°C above the 1991–2020 average while rainfall was 25% less compared to the 1991–2020 average. Provence's rich biodiversity is at risk, and invasive species like the tiger mosquito are spreading. With hotter, dryer summers and milder winters, yields from fruit trees, wine grapes, olives, and lavender are under pressure. Vineyards are responding with regenerative agricultural methods: using cover crops to reduce erosion, retain water, sequester carbon, reduce pests, and enrich the soil; expanding the variety of plants in the environs to improve pollination and filter water naturally; and using a few animals only to fertilize the soil.[105]

Prep time 30 minutes to roast tomatoes, plus 20 minutes   Cook time 30 minutes
Serves 4 to 5

½ pound cherry tomatoes, sliced in half, roasted, juices reserved (see Hint on page 291), to deglaze pan

½ teaspoon dried *herbes de Provence*

4 shallots, cut in medium dice

2 slender young leeks, whites and greens, cut in ⅛-inch slices

Up to ⅓ cup juices from the roasted tomatoes (see below) and/or dry vermouth, to deglaze pan

4 cloves garlic, minced

7 small Japanese eggplants, cut in 2-inch sections, each section then quartered

6 baby fennel bulbs, outer leaves, tops, and fronds removed, cut in ¼-inch slices

4 to 5 baby Italian peppers, mildly hot or sweet, cored and cut in ⅛-inch slices

2 bunches French breakfast radishes, cut in ¼-inch slices, greens chopped

½ cup small good-quality brine-cured green olives, unpitted

Small bunch of fresh herb leaves (remove stems if they are not tender), like nepitella, tarragon, parsley, summer savory, chives, chopped, or 1 tablespoon dried *herbes de Provence*

2 bunches Swiss chard or turnip greens, chopped

20 ounces artichoke hearts packed in water, rinsed well, cut in half

⅓ cup aka miso, dissolved in ½ cup water, or to taste

1. Preheat oven to 400°F.

2. Lay the tomatoes, cut side up, on a parchment-lined baking sheet. Sprinkle with dried *herbes de Provence*. Roast for 30 minutes, checking at 20 minutes. The tomatoes are ready when they have softened and become crispy on their cut edges. Do not allow them to burn, however. Cool and store in a covered container if you roast them in advance.

3. Heat a large skillet over a medium flame for 3 minutes. Dry sauté the shallots and leeks for 2 minutes. When they release their water and begin to darken the pan, deglaze it with deglazing liquid, as you scrape up caramelized sugars from the pan.

4. Stir in the garlic and eggplants. After 5 minutes add the fennel and peppers. After another 5 minutes stir in the radishes.

5. Cover and cook on medium low for about 10 minutes or until the vegetables are tender but intact.

6. Stir in the olives and roasted tomatoes and cook for 2 minutes.

7. Now add the herbs and chopped greens. Cover and cook until the sauté is fragrant and the greens are tender. Lastly, gently add the artichoke hearts and cook for a final minute.

8. Remove from the heat. Plate in warmed bowls. Stir a spoonful or two of the diluted miso paste into each bowl, or to taste.

9. Serve immediately and pass around the beans and bread.

HINT

If you roast the tomatoes a day or more in advance and store them covered in the fridge, they will release a delectable, sweet syrup that you can later use to deglaze the pan.

ORZOTTO CON FUNGHI

Hearty, nutty barley (orzo) stars in this luscious, whole-grain cousin to risotto. A comforting, nutritious winter dish, it bursts with wonderful woodsy umami flavors from mixed varieties of mushrooms and herbs. Its creamy texture derives from an oat cream that mimics risotto's velvety mouthfeel while adding nutrition heft. Whole barley is high in dietary fiber beta-glucans and resistant starch, which beautifully supports gut health.

Barley cultivated in the United States carries a climate footprint of 0.84 kg CO_2eq per kg, with 30% of emissions coming from fertilizer production, 33% from in-field bacteria, and 10% from off-field bacteria, 7% from draining wetlands, 9% from operating farm equipment, and 6% from air-drying the crop.

The Beauty of Barley

The cultivation of barley dates back 7,000 years to Egypt, and then spread throughout Mesopotamia, North Africa, Northwest Europe, and ultimately China and Tibet. It was the staple grain among ancient Hebrews, Greeks, and Romans and remained a principal source of nutrition in Northern Europe through the sixteenth century. Barley is the most environmentally adaptable cereal grain, able to thrive in temperate, subarctic, and subtropical climes. It also has the shortest growing period among cereal grains, making it a hardier and more resilient choice, especially for farmers in cooler regions, as the climate warms and weather becomes more erratic and violent.[106]

Prep time overnight soak of dried shiitake mushrooms, plus 1 hour
Cook time 40 minutes   Serves 4 to 6

10 to 12 dried preservative-free shiitake mushrooms, soaked overnight, then cut in ¼-inch slices

2 cups whole barley from hulled or hull-less barley (not pearled)

½ cup salt-free dehydrated soup vegetables

½ cup steel-cut oats

2 teaspoons freshly ground porcini powder from dried sliced porcini mushrooms, or to taste

3 large shallots or 1 large onion, cut in a medium dice

⅓ cup dry vermouth, to deglaze pan

1 tablespoon fresh thyme leaves or 1 teaspoon dried thyme

4 cloves garlic, minced

1½ pounds fresh mixed mushrooms, stem ends trimmed, cut into bite-sized pieces

½ teaspoon freshly ground black pepper, or to taste

Up to ½ cup shiro (mild, white) miso paste, diluted in ⅔ cup tepid water, or to taste

Chopped chives, to garnish

1. In a bowl, cover the dried shiitake mushrooms with water and soak overnight. They will deepen in flavor as they soften slowly. Drain, reserving the soaking water. Remove any stems that have not softened. Cut the shiitake mushrooms in ¼-inch slices.

2. Rinse the barley, transfer it to a medium pot, and fill the pot with water to cover the grains by 2 inches.

3. Bring to a boil, then lower to a simmer and cook for 2 minutes. Turn off the heat, cover the pot, and steep the barley for 30 minutes until the grains swell and sink in the pot. Older barley may take more time.

4. Drain the barley and return it to the pot. Cover again with water and add the dehydrated vegetables. Bring to a boil and lower to a gentle simmer to parcook the barley, about 15 minutes. It should taste undercooked. Do not overcook it.

5. Drain again, reserving the vegetable-flavored broth. Add the shiitake soaking water to the broth, transfer it to a pot, cover, and maintain at a very low simmer.

6. To make oat cream, place the steel-cut oats in a small pot with 2 cups of water. Simmer on low for up to 30 minutes, stirring frequently to avoid sticking and to encourage the oats to release their starches as they thicken. Cool. Process the cooked oats on high in a high-speed blender and or use an immersion blender to create a smooth, thick oat cream.

7. To make porcini powder, use a coffee or spice grinder to reduce the dehydrated porcini slices into a powder. Save any extra porcini powder in a small spice jar and keep in a cupboard away from heat and light. It will remain potent for about 3 months.

8. Heat a very large skillet or sauté pan over medium heat for 3 minutes. Lower heat to medium low and dry sauté the shallots until they release their water and begin to darken the pan. Deglaze the pan with a few tablespoons of vermouth, scraping up the caramelized sugars from the pan.

9. Add the thyme and garlic. Cook for 1 minute, then add the fresh mixed mushrooms and the rehydrated shiitakes. Cover and cook on medium low for about 10 minutes or until all the mushrooms are tender, adding a splash of heated broth to prevent sticking, if need be.

10. Stir in the barley and enough hot broth to make a wet, soupy mix. Cover and allow the barley to absorb the liquid as it reaches a slightly chewy, al dente consistency, in about 15 minutes. Taste the barley every 5 minutes, stirring the mix and adding broth if required to maintain a moist consistency.

11. Season with porcini powder and pepper, to taste. When the barley is nearly ready, stir in as much of the oat cream as you like to make the *Orzotto* rich and creamy.

12. Serve in warm bowls. Stir diluted shiro miso, to taste, to season each bowl.

13. Garnish with chopped chives.

SLOPPY JOES

In this tasty low-carbon makeover, we ditch chopped meat in favor of black soybeans and whole barley. Stewed with onions and peppers in a zesty tomato sauce, spiked with Worcestershire Sauce (see page 62), chili powders, and spices, these Joes are finger-licking good. Instead of serving them on insipid burger buns, how about spooning it over delicious Cornbread (see page 172). Messy and fun to eat, Sloppy Joes bring out the kid in us all. It's sure to become a family favorite.

The different climate impact between using beef versus beans and whole grains is dramatic: Ground beef's climate footprint in the United States is 60 kg CO_2eq per kg compared to soybeans' GHG emissions at 0.44 kg CO_2eq per kg and barley's at 0.84 kg CO_2eq per kg.

The Problem with Livestock

Beef is an extremely resource-intensive food and has a heavy impact on the climate. Estimates of the impact of livestock farming in 2022 range from 11 to 20% of total global GHG emissions, principally methane, CO_2, and N_2O. Global demand for meat rose 25% between 2000 and 2019. If current trends hold, by the end of the century, the consumption of dairy and meat (particularly beef) is projected to exceed over half of future GHG emissions within the food system.[107] In addition to the direct contribution of GHGs by ruminant animals, according to the World Resources Institute, deforestation to create new pastureland and grow feed crops is another key driver of emissions. As carbon stored in trees is released and carbon sinks are eliminated, biodiversity is also put at risk from the elimination of native habitats and the disruption of ecosystems. The negative impacts of climate change on livestock health and on the food supply chain are expected to worsen as climate change advances: Extreme weather events, drought, flooding, and precipitation declines will affect feed and water resources for livestock, increase the risks of disease, and lead to shorter lifespans, according to a 2021 report by Global Food Security.

Prep time overnight soak of black soybeans, plus 1 hour | Cook time 30 minutes
Serves 5 to 7

2 cups cooked black soybeans from 1 scant cup dried black soybeans

2 cups cooked whole (hulled or hull-less) barley from 1 cup whole barley

3 large cloves of garlic, peeled

A handful of Italian parsley leaves and stems

1 medium-large white onion, cut in a medium dice

1 green pepper, deseeded, cut in a medium dice

2 poblano peppers, deseeded, cut in a medium dice

2 jalapeños, deseeded, cut in a small dice

1 teaspoon freshly ground chipotle powder from 1 to 2 dried chilies, or to taste

1 (26-ounce) carton, can, or jar diced tomatoes

¼ cup tomato paste

2 tablespoons homemade Worcestershire Sauce (see page 62)

½ teaspoon yellow mustard powder

½ teaspoon liquid smoke

Several grinds of black pepper

⅓ cup plus 1 tablespoon aka (red) miso paste, or to taste

1. The night before making Sloppy Joes, rinse the black soybeans, transfer them to a medium bowl, and cover with cool water by 3 inches. Soak overnight or for about 8 hours. Drain. Place in a pressure cooker with 6 cups of fresh cool water. Heat on high. When it comes to full pressure and is actively steaming, lower the heat and pressure-cook for 25 minutes. Turn off the heat and allow the pressure to naturally release, about 15 minutes. When the pressure valve drops, open the pot, drain any liquid, and set the beans aside.

2. Rinse the hulled barley. There is no need to soak it in advance. Place in the pressure cooker with 6 cups cool water. Heat on high. When it comes to full pressure and is actively steaming, lower the heat and pressure-cook for 25 minutes. Turn off the heat and allow the pressure to naturally release, about 15 minutes. When the pressure valve drops, open the pot, drain any remaining liquid, and set aside.

3. Place the garlic and parsley on a cutting board. Using a mezzaluna or chef knife, chop finely together.

4. Heat a very large heavy-bottomed stainless steel skillet or sauté pan on medium heat for 3 minutes. Flick a few drops of water on the surface. When the droplets sizzle and

evaporate immediately, put in the diced onions and all the peppers. Lower the heat to medium low and sauté, stirring occasionally, for about 5 minutes. When the onions and peppers soften and release some liquid, stir in the parsley-garlic mix. If the mix becomes dry and begins to darken the pan, deglaze the pan with 2 to 3 tablespoons of water, scraping up any caramelized sugars from the pan, and lower the heat.

5. Remove the stems from the dried chipotle chilies, break them in pieces, and use a coffee or spice grinder to reduce them to a powder. Measure, and store any excess in a glass spice jar in a cool, dry, dark cupboard.

6. Stir in the diced tomatoes and tomato paste, mixing them well. Season with the home-made Worcestershire Sauce, mustard, liquid smoke, grinds of black pepper, and chipotle powder to suit your taste.

7. Now add the cooked black soybeans and cooked barley, combining them well. If the mix is dry, add 2 to 3 tablespoons of water. Cover, maintain at a gentle simmer, and cook for 20 to 30 minutes, allowing the flavors to infuse the beans and grains. Stir occasionally, adding a tiny amount of water if the mixture begins to stick to the pan.

8. If you plan to serve Sloppy Joes on Cornbread (see page 172) or buns, keep the mixture dense to facilitate mounding. However, if you plan to serve in a bowl, add a little water to create a soupier consistency like chili.

9. Taste and adjust any seasonings as you like. If you plan to serve all the Sloppy Joes in a single sitting, turn off the heat and season the entire pan with aka miso, to taste, mixing it well. If you don't plan to use it all, turn off the heat, transfer the amount of the stew that you don't plan on eating to a glass storage container and when cool, refrigerate. Season the rest with a proportionate amount of miso.

10. Spoon immediately on fresh cornbread slices or over toasted whole wheat buns. Or serve in bowls like chili or stew alongside freshly toasted corn tortilla chips.

SPLIT PEA EGGLESS OMELETS

If you have a grain mill, you can create flours out of dried legumes, corn, and whole grains. Split pea flour, for example, makes particularly delicious "omelets" and I love their beautiful, pale green interiors. If you don't have a mill, a high-speed blender may get the job done too, although you won't be able to control the grit of the flour as well as you can with a grain mill. And if you have neither appliance, no worries! You can buy split pea flour online or substitute with another legume or whole-grain flour.

I stuffed these omelets with cauliflower, summer squashes, petite peas, and bell peppers, and seasoned them with a light Cheesy White Sauce (see page 36). They make a delightfully elegant brunch for a lazy Sunday morning or a tasty supper. Feel free to take advantage of other seasonal vegetables to enjoy Split Pea Eggless Omelets year-round.

Chicken eggs carry a climate footprint on U.S. farms of 3.2 kg CO_2eq per kg while dried peas farmed in the United States emit 0.44 kg CO_2eq per kg in GHG.

Climate Change, Poultry Farming, and Bird Flu

Increased extreme weather events, the increase within farm facilities of fires spurred by drought, reduced water availability, and growing thermal pressure on poultry are all examples of the ways that poultry farming is susceptible to the warming climate. The rise in the costs of animal feed and other raw materials and electricity are increasing pressures in the industry.[108] Related to the climate in ways that are not yet well understood, the current, highly pathogenic, and deadly avian flu (H_5N_1), first identified in China in the 1990s, is now a pandemic, threatening wild bird and domestic poultry flocks throughout Europe, Asia, and now North America. Given their crowded, chronic stress conditions, factory-farmed poultry are particularly susceptible. Climate warming is disrupting ecosystems and bird migration patterns and behaviors. As of 2021, H_5N_1 was detected in forty-seven U.S. states, principally circulating among wild birds.[109] At the time of this writing, worldwide, the avian flu has now been detected in farm animals, marine mammals, and some humans.

Prep time 30 minutes │ Cook time 30 minutes │ Makes 4 to 6 omelets, depending on size

FILLING

1 small cauliflower, cut into small florets

4 shallots, sliced thinly

1½ teaspoons dried thyme leaves or 1 tablespoon fresh thyme leaves

Dry vermouth or unsalted vegetable broth, to deglaze pan

1 medium yellow squash, halved lengthwise, then cut in ¼-inch slices

1 medium zucchini, halved lengthwise, then cut in ¼-inch slices

1 red or orange bell pepper or 6 mini bell peppers, cored, cut in a large dice

1 cup baby petite peas, defrosted

Several grinds of white pepper

1½ cups Cheesy White Sauce (see page 36)

Parsley leaves, torn sprigs of dill, or chopped chives and a sprinkle, if you like, of Chesapeake Old Bay Spice Blend (see page 38), to garnish

BATTER

1 cup flour from split peas, roasted

2 teaspoons freshly ground flaxseed

2 teaspoons arrowroot

1 tablespoon nutritional yeast

1 tablespoon sodium-and-aluminum-free baking powder

¼ teaspoon white pepper

½ teaspoon ground turmeric

¼ teaspoon granulated onion

¼ teaspoon granulated garlic

½ teaspoon apple cider vinegar

2 teaspoons shiro (mild, white) miso paste

1¾ cups unsweetened almond milk

1. Preheat the oven to 170°F.

2. Roast the split peas, if using, on a baking tray lined with parchment for 30 minutes. Cool. Grind in a grain mill or high-speed blender into flour. Transfer to a bowl.

3. Blanch the cauliflower florets for 1 minute and taste for doneness. When they are just tender but still crisp, strain from the pot and shock quickly in an ice water bath to halt cooking and crisp up.

4. Preheat a large stainless steel sauté pan over medium heat for 3 minutes.

5. Put in the shallots and thyme, stirring. Lower heat slightly and cook for a few minutes. Once the shallots release their water and begin to lightly brown and darken the pan, deglaze the pan with a small splash of deglazing liquid, scraping up the sugars from the pan.

6. Add the yellow squash and zucchini. Sauté for a few minutes. Now add the red pepper. Cook for 5 minutes.

7. Stir in the blanched cauliflower florets and peas. Cover and cook for a few minutes, just to heat through. Season with pepper. Turn off the heat. Cover to keep warm.

8. Make the Cheesy White Sauce and cover the pot to keep the thickened sauce warm.

9. Lower the oven to 150°F. Insert your serving plates to warm.

10. To make the batter, place the split pea flour, ground flaxseed, arrowroot, nutritional yeast, baking powder, white pepper, ground turmeric, and granulated onion and garlic in a blender. Pulse to combine.

11. Add the vinegar, miso, and almond milk. Run at high speed for 30 to 60 seconds. Set aside for about 10 minutes to allow the baking powder to thicken the batter. The batter should be a little dense but readily pourable, unlike traditional thin crêpe batters.

12. Preheat a large nonstick skillet over a medium-low flame for 3 minutes.

13. Pour about ½ cup of batter into the skillet, swirling the pan to create a 6-inch disk. Cover the pan for a minute and cook until the batter sets and begins to brown along its edges. Cook one side only. Use a very large silicone or nylon spatula to remove the crêpe when the underside is lightly golden, and the surface has lost its sheen. Do not overcook.

14. Transfer the split pea crêpe to a heated plate and pile the sautéed vegetables on one half of the crêpe. Liberally spoon on Cheesy White Sauce, fresh chopped herbs, and for a little kick, a light sprinkle of Chesapeake Old Bay Spice Blend. Fold the crêpe over the filling to make an omelet. Return the plate to the oven or a warming drawer to stay warm as you prepare the other crêpes.

SPROUTED *ORZOTTO* WITH ZUCCHINI AND GOLDEN BEETS

Orzotto is barley's answer to risotto. This one's made with whole (hull-less) barley, giving it a wonderful nutty, toothy texture with a creamy finish from blended whole oats. Barley and oats are both much kinder to the environment than rice (see page 319), higher in fiber, and more nutritionally dense. Spouting the grains before cooking provides added nutritional benefits: As the groats germinate, they release enzymes that increase the bioavailability of vitamin C, folate, minerals, protein, and soluble fiber; drop even lower on the glycemic index; and lower their gluten content nearly by half. And if that weren't enough, germination also speeds cooking time considerably. To save time, cook the oats and grind the dehydrated soup vegetables up to 3 days in advance.

The climate footprint of oats farmed in the United States is 0.92 kg CO_2eq per kg, with 30% of GHG due to fertilizer production, 31% due to the emissions from in-field bacteria, 9% from off-field bacteria, 12% from draining wetlands for farming, 3% from emissions from adding soil amendments, 10% from running farm equipment, and 4% from drying the oats. Barley grown in the United States emits 0.84 kg CO_2eq per kg in GHG, with 30% due to fertilizer production, 33% to in-field bacteria, 10% to off-field bacteria, 7% to wetland drainage, 9% from operating farm machinery, and 6% from the energy used to heat air to dry barley.

Prep time 2 days to sprout the barley, plus 30 minutes
Cook time 30 to 40 minutes │ Serves 4 to 6

1½ cups hull-less or hulled barley

2 cups dense cooked oats from ½ cup steel-cut oats

3 cups flavorful unsalted vegetable broth from ½ cup dehydrated soup vegetables, ground

1 large onion, cut in half and cut in ⅛-inch slices

3 tablespoons dry white vermouth or vegetable broth, to deglaze pan

1 teaspoon dried thyme leaves

4 cloves garlic, minced

2 cups golden beets from bunch with greens, cut in quarters, then cut in ⅛-inch slices

4 medium zucchini, cut in ⅛-inch slices

A few grinds of black pepper

Greens from a bunch of golden beets, leaves and stems cut in 1-inch slices; smallest leaves reserved for garnish

Juice and zest from 1 organic lemon, to taste

½ cup shiro (mild, white) miso paste, or to taste, diluted in ½ cup water

Small beet greens, lemon zest, and sprinkle of *Parmigiano Perfetto* (see page 56), to garnish

1. Rinse the barley groats. Put into a bowl, cover with water, and soak overnight, about 8 hours. Rinse and drain in a strainer placed over a bowl. Continue to rinse and drain the barley in the strainer 4 to 6 times per day over the next 2 days. It's fine to leave the barley on your countertop to monitor its progress. When white tips and some thin white root hairs begin to emerge and the seed coats have softened enough to easily cut through, your sprouted barley is ready to make *orzotto*.

2. To prepare the oats, place ½ cup steel-cut oats in 2 cups water in a small saucepan. Heat to a very gentle simmer, stirring to help coax the starches from the oat groats. Cook until tender, about ½ hour. Cool the pot in cold water to bring to room temp, then use a stand or immersion blender to blend into a smooth creamy dense sauce. Refrigerate.

3. Use a coffee or spice grinder to powder the dehydrated soup vegetables. This makes a great salt-free alternative to bouillon. Mix with 3 cups of hot water in a saucepan. Heat to a very low simmer and cover.

4. Heat a large sauté pan or skillet for 2 minutes over medium heat. Put in the onions and sauté them dry until they turn golden and lightly darken the pan. Deglaze the pan with deglazing liquid. Add the thyme and garlic and cook for a minute before stirring in the sprouted barley. Cook for a minute and add 2 cups of hot vegetable broth.

5. Cover and simmer for about 20 minutes or until the barley is almost tender. Stir in the beets, cover, and cook for 5 minutes. Now stir in the zucchini and cook for another 5 minutes. The barley will absorb liquid as it cooks. If the mix has become dry, add ½ cup broth or more as needed.

6. Check for doneness. When the *orzotto* is close to an al dente toothiness, stir in the blended oats and lower the heat.

7. Season with pepper, to taste. Now add the beet leaves, cover, and cook for the final few minutes.

8. Serve Sprouted *Orzotto* with Zucchini and Golden Beets on warmed plates. Once plated, season each serving with a squeeze of fresh lemon and a few teaspoonfuls of diluted shiro miso (the amount will depend on the serving size). To garnish, scatter a few tiny beet greens on top, a pinch of lemon zest, and a dusting of *Parmigiano Perfetto*.

STIR-FRY WITH CHINESE VEGETABLES

If you are lucky enough to live near an East Asian grocery, you can take advantage of gorgeous Asian vegetables and fruits. This fast stir-fry uses lovely loose-headed flowering cauliflower (*san hua*), with leafy Chinese broccoli (*gai lan*), a medley of mushrooms, slender mauve Chinese eggplant, and crispy snow peas. They are finished in the wok with a traditional Chinese glazing sauce. *Douchi* (fermented black soybeans) add umami yum, Sichuan pepper provides some mouth tingle, and fresh and dried red Chinese chilies lend some pizzazz. Enjoy this colorful, delicious stir-fry with hearty whole grains or whole-grain noodles.

Soy miso pastes prepared in Japan have a climate footprint of 0.57 kg CO_2eq per kg, with 75% of GHG attributable to agriculture, 9% to transport, and 14% to processing. Mushrooms farmed in the United States have a low climate footprint of 0.15 kg CO_2eq per kg, with 22% of emissions produced by fertilizer production, 39% by in-field bacteria, 10% by off-field bacteria, 3% from draining wetlands, and 22% from operating farm equipment.

China's Climate Policies

China's demand for energy and electricity continues to rise. It is not yet known whether its rapid development of renewable energy resources will suffice to enable the country to transition fully away from its reliance on coal and fossil fuels. China has yet to publish meaningful, detailed action plans for its reduction targets. The Climate Action Tracker therefore rates China's climate targets and policies as "highly insufficient" and its target to reach net zero as "poor." Hopefully, more detailed plans and an ambitious road map to decarbonization in China will soon be forthcoming. For China's climate threats see pages 228 and 331. For more on mushrooms and the climate, see page 71.

Prep time 45 minutes | Cook time 20 minutes | Serves 5 to 6

2 tablespoons date paste from ½ cup pitted dates

1 large Chinese eggplant, cut in 4 sections, cut in half lengthwise, then sliced in 4 pieces lengthwise

1 cup unseasoned rice vinegar

1 small or ½ large head flowering cauliflower, cut into florets

½ bunch Chinese broccoli

½ block soft tofu, cut into ¾-inch cubes, simmered in seasoned water

4 tablespoons good-quality fermented tamari, or to taste

1 teaspoon Sichuan peppercorns

4 tablespoons white and/or black sesame seeds

½ teaspoon Chinese dried red chilies (optional)

1 full tablespoon *douchi* (fermented black soybeans)

1 onion, cut in half and then cut in ⅛-inch slices

1 large red bell pepper, seeds removed, cut in bite-sized pieces

3 to 4 tablespoons good-quality unsalted Shaoxing rice wine or sake

4 large cloves garlic, peeled and thinly sliced

1-inch ginger root, peeled and minced

1 fresh red Thai chili, thinly sliced

1 cup *shimeji* mushrooms, tough root ends removed

1 cup oyster or maitake mushrooms, tough root ends removed, caps and stems torn into bite-sized pieces

1 cup shiitake mushrooms, stems removed, caps thinly sliced

1 cup cooking water from blanching the cauliflower and broccoli

¾ teaspoon good-quality fermented black vinegar or unseasoned rice vinegar

⅓ cup aka (red) miso, or to taste

¼ cup cornstarch

1 spring onion or small bunch scallions, whites cut on the bias into ½-inch pieces, greens cut in ¼-inch slivers, for garnish

2 cups snow peas

1. To make date paste, place the pitted dates in a small nonmetallic bowl. Cover with water. Microwave for 2 minutes or cook on a stovetop for 5 minutes. Cool.

2. Transfer the rehydrated dates and their soaking water to a high-speed blender and run for 2 minutes, scraping down the sides of the bowl. The blended paste should be smooth and soft. Set aside 2 tablespoons and reserve the rest for another use in the refrigerator where it will keep for 2 weeks.

3. Prep the eggplant and cover the pieces with rice vinegar to help prevent oxidation.

4. Fill a large bowl with water and two to three trays of ice. Fill a large pot with water and bring to a rapid boil. Blanch the flowering cauliflower florets for 1 minute, scoop them

out with a skimmer and immediately plunge them into the ice bath to halt cooking, crisp the texture, and brighten the color.

5. Repeat with the Chinese broccoli. Reserve the blanching water, cover, and maintain on a very low simmer. When the broccoli is cold, cut it into 2-inch pieces.

6. Soft tofu is very fragile so treat it gingerly. Bring a small pot filled with water to a simmer. Add a teaspoon of aged tamari. Gently transfer the tofu cubes into the pot and simmer for 5 minutes or until the cubes swell slightly. Drain and set aside.

7. On a small, hot skillet, toast the Sichuan peppercorns for a minute, just until they become fragrant. Cool. Grind in a spice or coffee grinder into a powder. Similarly, toast the sesame seeds but for 20 to 30 seconds only. Do not grind them. Finally, toast the dried Chinese chilies, if using. Press them down on the hot skillet to soften and lightly darken. Cool and grind into chili powder.

8. Soak the *douchi* in a small bowl of water as you prep your other vegetables. Drain and chop them.

9. Have all your ingredients prepped and placed in the order in which they'll be added. Heat a wok over medium-high heat for 3 minutes. Put in the onions and toss around for a minute or two until they release their liquid, brown lightly, and darken the pan. Deglaze the pan with unsalted Shaoxing rice wine, and immediately add the garlic, ginger, red Thai chilies, *douchi*, and ground Sichuan pepper.

10. Drain the eggplant, shake off the vinegar, and add to the wok, together with the mushrooms. Toss the wok's contents often to cook evenly for 10 minutes.

11. Use this time to create your finishing glaze by combining 1 cup of the blanching water with the tamari, black vinegar, date paste, aka miso, Chinese chili powder, if using, and cornstarch. Taste and adjust seasoning according to your taste. You should perceive the sauce's heat, acidity, sweetness, and salinity in balance.

12. Add the spring onion or scallion white slices and bell peppers to the wok. After a minute, add the blanched flowering cauliflower and Chinese broccoli, tossing them well.

13. Stir the glazing liquid in the bowl before adding it all to the wok. Toss all the vegetables to coat them well. Cook for about 2 minutes as the glaze thickens and nicely coats the mix. If it dries too much, add a little more blanching water. The stir-fry should not be soupy either. If it is too wet, make a roux with cornstarch and the wok's liquid and stir it into the wok. Taste and make any final adjustments to your seasonings. Add the snow peas, and gently toss.

14. Finally, carefully spoon in the soft tofu. It will fall apart if you toss it around, so instead, spoon the glaze over the tofu to coat it.

15. Serve immediately on warmed plates with whole grains or noodles. Garnish with slivers of spring onion or scallion greens and a good sprinkle of toasted sesame seeds.

¡TOSTADAS *ESTUPENDAS*!

Tostadas make any meal a party. Without animal products or oils, this is a very climate-supportive dish. What makes these tostadas *estupendas* is the array of flavorful toppings you can use atop your oil-free "refried" beans, like mixed roasted onions and peppers, fresh salsa, Cheesy White Sauce (see page 36), guacamole, and soy yogurt. Use some or all, it's up to you. If you have a tortilla press, consider throwing a tortilla party! Friends love to take turns pressing masa harina tortillas. Just pan toast them briefly before loading them up and baking.

In U.S. groceries, instant masa harina, the nixtamalized corn flour used to make tortillas, carries a climate footprint of 1 kg CO_2eq per kg, with 66% of emissions coming from agriculture, 18% from transport, 9% from processing, and 7% from packaging.

Mexico's Climate Challenges

According to USAID and the World Bank, Mexico's geography puts it at risk for extreme weather events like heat waves, flooding, frosts, and cyclones. The warming climate threatens Mexico's aging water, power, and transportation infrastructure, as well as its popular tourist areas on its coastline. Climate change is endangering Mexico's agricultural sector too: Climate Reality Project predicts a 40 to 70% decline in Mexico's cropland by 2030, increasing the country's food and water security risks. Unfortunately, Mexico's climate policies and institutions were weakened under President Andrés Manuel López Obrador and its reliance on fossil fuels increased, according to the Climate Action Tracker. Only 30% of Mexico's electricity relies on renewable sources, in contrast to 60% in the rest of Latin America. Recently, Mexico pledged to reduce its greenhouse gas emissions by 35% by 2030, but it remains the only Group of 20 country that has yet to set a net-zero goal.

For how the climate is affecting Mexico's chili production, see page 273.

Prep time 1 hour | Cook time 15 minutes | Makes 12 tostadas to serve 3 to 4

REFRIED BEANS

1 teaspoon cumin seed, freshly ground

½ teaspoon chipotle chili powder freshly ground from 1 dried chipotle chili, or to taste

3 (15.5-ounce) cans unsalted pinto beans, rinsed

1 teaspoon granulated garlic

1 teaspoon granulated onion

1 tablespoon aka (red) miso paste

½ teaspoon dried Mexican oregano leaves, crushed

FRESH SALSA

1 (16-ounce) package of cherry tomatoes, cut in a medium dice

¼ cup cilantro leaves and stems, chopped

2 scallions, cut in 1-inch slices

ROASTED PEPPER AND ONION TOPPING

2 to 3 poblano peppers, cut in half lengthwise, seeds and pith removed

1 large jalapeño or Fresno pepper, cut in half lengthwise, seeds and pith removed

1 (16-ounce) package of mini bell peppers, cut in half lengthwise, seeds and pith removed

3 medium sweet onions, peeled and cut in ¼-inch slices

SIMPLE GUACAMOLE

1 ripe avocado, peeled and mashed

2 tablespoons lime juice

OTHER INGREDIENTS

1½ cups Cheesy White Sauce (see page 36)

1 cup unsweetened cultured soy yogurt

12 fresh corn tortillas, made from corn, water, and lime with no preservatives

Chopped cilantro leaves and sliced scallion, for garnish

MAKE REFRIED BEANS

1. Use a coffee or spice grinder to grind a teaspoon of cumin seeds into a powder. Wipe out the bowl with a paper towel and grind a dried chipotle chili into a powder. Measure ½ teaspoon of chipotle powder and reserve any extra in a tight jar for another use.

2. Combine the pinto beans, 1 teaspoon each of granulated garlic and onion, ground cumin and chipotle powders, aka miso, and Mexican oregano in the bowl of a food processor. Run for 1 minute. Scrape down the sides of the bowl. The purée's texture should be thick but creamy. If the mix is dry, add a tablespoon or two of water and reprocess. Taste and adjust the seasonings as you like. The bean purée should be flavorful and lightly spicy.

MAKE THE SALSA

1. Mix the diced tomatoes, chopped cilantro, and sliced scallion in a medium bowl.

ROAST THE PEPPERS AND ONIONS

1. Preheat the oven at 425°F/400°F convection.

2. Lay the peppers, cut side up, on a large cookie sheet lined with parchment paper. On a second sheet lined with parchment, lay the onion slices. Roast the peppers for 10 to 15 minutes or until they are lightly toasted and softened. The onions may take a few minutes longer.

3. Remove the peppers and onions when they have softened and lighted browned on their cut edges. Cool. Peel off the poblanos' skins, which should be easily removable.

4. Lay the roasted peppers and onions on a large cutting board, and crudely chop with a mezzaluna or chef knife.

5. Keep the oven at 425°F to toast the tortillas (see below).

MAKE A SIMPLE GUACAMOLE

1. Add the peeled and pitted avocado to a bowl, mash with a potato masher or fork until smooth or chunky, as you prefer.

2. Season with lime juice to flavor and to retard browning.

WARM THE CHEESY WHITE SAUCE

1. If you make a fresh batch of Cheesy White Sauce, use 2 tablespoons of arrowroot. After it thickens, remove it from the heat and cover the pot to stay warm. For Cheesy White Sauce made in advance, reheat it now over low heat, whisking occasionally until it is just warm. Turn off the heat well before it comes to a simmer.

2. For tostadas, the sauce should be neither too thick nor runny. We want to be able to sauce the tostadas without dripping. If the warm sauce is too dense, dilute it with a tablespoon of almond or soy milk. If too thin, make a slurry with 1 to 2 teaspoons of arrowroot in water before heating it in the sauce to thicken.

MAKE AND PLATE THE TOSTADAS

1. Line two to three cookie sheets with parchment paper. Place the tortillas without overlapping and bake in the oven for 6 to 8 minutes—just until they have dried, stiffened, and begun to very lightly toast.

2. Remove the tortillas from the oven.

3. Set the oven to low broil.

4. Spread a very thick layer of the refried pinto beans over the toasted tortillas.

5. Then spoon on a thick coating of Cheesy White Sauce.

6. Broil the tostadas on low for a few minutes, just until the sauce turns golden. Keep a close watch. Do not over-broil or the beans and sauce will dry out and the tostadas will burn.

7. Remove from the broiler and load each tostada up with the pepper mix, fresh salsa, a dollop of guacamole, and soy yogurt.

8. Plate ¡Tostadas *Estupendas*! and serve immediately, garnishing the tostadas with chopped cilantro and slices of scallion.

CELEBRATIONS

ARTICHOKE *KHORESH* WITH SAFFRON RICE

This lovely Persian stew is scented with dried Persian limes, saffron, and lots of herbs. Serve it alongside a mound of fragrant saffron rice (see page 321) and a side of thick Yogurt with Chard, Leeks, and Garlic (see page 102) for a Persian-themed supper.

Lemons and limes grown in Iran produce 0.24 kg CO_2eq per kg in greenhouse gas emissions, with 33% caused by fertilizer production, 27% from in-field bacteria, 10% from off-field bacteria, 6% from the manufacture of soil amendments, 13% from the energy used to run farm machinery, and 10% from irrigating orchards. Rice grown on Iranian farms has a climate footprint of 1.3 kg CO_2eq per kg, 14% of which is related to fertilizer manufacture, 6% from in-field bacteria, 5% from off-field bacteria, 8% from the use of farm machinery, 8% from the energy used to irrigate, 4% to dry the grain, and 52% from the methane released from flooding rice paddies.

Rice's Methane Problem

According to the World Population Review, over half of the world's people consume rice as a daily staple. It provides 20% of total calories globally. So great attention is paid to the greenhouse gas emissions of this widely consumed crop. While far lower than animal products (4.0 kg CO_2eq per kg at U.S. retail versus 30 kg CO_2eq per kg for chopped beef sold in the United States), the emissions generated by all varieties of rice are problematic because of rice farming's growing practices: Fields are flooded to kill weeds and spur growth. When water blocks the oxygen supply from the air to the soil, anaerobic fermentation by microbes in the paddies produces high levels of methane (CH_4), which is released into the atmosphere.

The development of greener rice varieties and more climate-friendly cultivation techniques are underway to make rice lower emitting and higher yielding. Look for these choices to purchase when they become available. Moreover, because rice absorbs so much groundwater in its cultivation, it is more likely than other crops to absorb high concentrations of heavy metals like arsenic from contaminated soils. Rices from California, Pakistan, and India are safest at present.

To learn about how the climate affects saffron production, see page 355. For how the climate is affecting Iran, see page 201, and for Iran's use of energy, see page 29.

Prep time 30 minutes | Cook time 1 hour | Serves 4 to 5

Pinch of good-quality saffron threads and 2 tablespoons hot water, for steeping

2 Persian dried limes

2 cups unsalted vegetable broth

12 fresh baby artichokes, as small as possible, stems included, or 10-ounce jar of artichoke hearts packed in water, or 12 ounces frozen artichoke hearts, defrosted

2 onions, cut in a medium dice

3 cloves garlic, minced

3½ cups celery, about 5 stalks, cut in ¼-inch slices

1½ cups cooked chickpeas from 1 (15.5-ounce) can, no sodium

1 cup mixed fresh herbs, like mint, parsley, dill, cilantro, and basil, chopped

Several grinds of black pepper

2 tablespoons shiro (mild, white) miso paste diluted in 4 tablespoons hot water, or to taste

Additional fresh chopped herbs and either lemon wedges, lemon zest, or Lemon Citrus Powder (see page 41), to garnish

1. To make a saffron "tea," use a mortar and pestle to finely crush the saffron in a small bowl. Add 2 tablespoons hot water and allow to steep until use.

2. In a small bowl cover the dried limes with boiling water and steep for about 20 minutes or until softened. Discard the soaking water and puncture the limes in a few places with a skewer or chopstick. Set them aside.

3. Put the broth in a small pot, cover, bring to a boil, and lower the heat to maintain at a very gentle simmer.

4. Tiny fresh artichokes have no chokes to remove. To prep, slice off the bottom of their stems, and remove the outer leaves until you reach the pale interior layers. We will cook them whole. If using jarred, canned, or frozen artichoke hearts, rinse gently and leave whole if they are less than ¾ inch wide. Slice larger hearts in half lengthwise.

5. Heat a large skillet over low heat for 3 minutes. Put in the onions, cover, and allow to sweat and soften for 5 minutes, stirring occasionally. Stir in the garlic, celery, chickpeas, raw artichokes, if using, and one tablespoon of saffron tea. If the mix is dry, add a few tablespoons of the heated broth. Cook on low for 10 minutes, during which time the vegetables will soften, and their flavors will blend.

6. Add the heated broth now and the punctured, soaked dried limes, and cover. Bring to a simmer. Now add the chopped mixed herbs and cook for 45 minutes.

7. Add the frozen, jarred, or canned artichokes, if using. Cover the pan and cook for a final 10 minutes.

8. Season, to taste, with black pepper and the diluted shiro miso. Stir in the remaining saffron tea.

9. Garnish with chopped fresh herbs and either a squeeze of fresh lemon or sprinkling of lemon zest or Lemon Citrus Powder.

SAFFRON RICE

Most Persian rice recipes include plenty of oil and butter. This greener version uses whole basmati rice and excludes added fats.

Prep time 15 minutes   Cook time about 70 minutes   Serves 4 to 5

½ teaspoon saffron threads steeped in ⅓ cup hot water

2 cups brown basmati rice

Several grinds white pepper, or to taste

2 tablespoons shiro (mild, white) miso paste, diluted in 4 tablespoons hot water (optional)

1. "Bloom" the saffron in a tea, as described in the Artichoke *Khoresh* recipe on page 320.

2. Wash and rinse the rice in cool water several times until the water is clear. Persian saffron rice is made in two stages: First it is partially cooked in boiling water; then it is steamed. Fill a pot with water and bring to a boil. Add the rice and cook at a slow boil for 10 minutes. Drain and submerge in cold water to halt its cooking. Drain again. Add the pepper and miso, if using, and toss the rice well with clean hands to gently spread the seasonings evenly throughout.

3. Pour ⅓ cup of water in a medium-sized heavy-bottomed (multi-ply) stainless steel pot with a tight-fitting lid. Add half the saffron tea and stir in 1 cup of the boiled rice well. Now start adding the remaining boiled rice, spooning it in gently with a large mixing spoon. Be careful not to compact the rice. Mound it lightly, higher in the pot's center, lower at its perimeter, until all the rice is added. Pour the remaining saffron tea over the rice mound. Use a chopstick to poke 10 to 12 holes in the mound to facilitate its steaming evenly.

4. Cover and cook on low for about 30 minutes. The trick is to know your stove. Since we are not using oils or butter, we need to steam the rice very gently to avoid burning the bottom. If your nose senses any hint of burning, lower the heat immediately, and add ¼ cup water to the rice.

5. After 30 minutes the rice will be steamed but damp. In its final cooking phase, the rice absorbs its excess liquid, leaving the grains plump, light, and fluffy. Place a clean absorbent dishcloth under the lid and close tightly. Cook for a final 25 to 30 minutes over very low heat. The cooked rice will be speckled white and gold and smell fragrant.

6. Plate and serve the saffron rice with Artichoke *Khoresh* and serve hot.

BEET BUCKWHEAT CRÊPES

Midsummer, when you find both spring and early summer vegetables in the market, is a good time to enjoy these elegant, delicious crêpes. The rose-colored batter combines beets with buckwheat. The crêpes are filled with asparagus, French radishes, and petite peas, bathed in luscious Cheesy White Sauce (see page 36). For plating, the crêpes rest in a puddle of puréed sweet peas and parsley. The dish's pinks and greens evoke summer blossoms, making this a splendid entrée or first course for a June luncheon with friends or an elegant dinner.

The benchmark climate footprint for root, bulb, and tuberous vegetables like beet-root farmed in the United States is 0.11 kg CO_2eq per kg, with 27% of emissions coming from the production of fertilizer, 25% from in-field bacteria, 7% from off-field bacteria, 4% from draining wetlands for farming, 4% from the production of pesticides, 28% from operating farm machinery, and 4% from pumping water for irrigation.

The Beauty of Buckwheat

Buckwheat, a pseudocereal, is a seed like amaranth and quinoa. Gluten-free and high in fiber and antioxidants, buckwheat is integral to Asian and European cuisines and enjoyed as groats, flour, and noodles. Buckwheat is very hardy and can handle floods, heat, and drought. It is far more drought resistant than wheat, grows even in nutrient-poor soils and uses water more efficiently, making it a viable wheat alternative as the climate warms.[110] Researchers at the University of New Hampshire are testing a new variety of buckwheat, Tartary, which holds even more promise. With a similar profile to common buckwheat, it self-pollinates and is easier to breed, an advantage where pollinator populations are under threat.[111]

Prep time 80 minutes | Cook time 20 minutes | Makes six 7-inch crêpes

VEGETABLES

1 bunch asparagus, woody ends removed

1 cup petit peas, blanched if fresh, defrosted if frozen

1 bunch radishes, cut in wedges

1 cup Cheesy White Sauce (see page 36)

Microgreens, to garnish

PARSLEY-PEA PUDDLE

Cloves from 1 head garlic, dry roasted

1 cup tightly packed parsley leaves, stems removed

¼ cup petit peas, blanched if fresh, defrosted if frozen

⅛ cup shelled walnuts

⅛ cup nutritional yeast

A pinch of ground white pepper

CRÊPE BATTER

2 cups beet purée from 3 to 4 medium red and gold beets

1 tablespoon golden flaxseed, freshly ground

1½ cups buckwheat flour

1 tablespoon nutritional yeast

½ teaspoon granulated onion

½ teaspoon granulated garlic

⅛ teaspoon freshly grated nutmeg

A pinch of ground white pepper

½ cup unsweetened almond milk

½ teaspoon shiro (mild, white) miso pate

BLANCH THE VEGETABLES AND PREPARE THE CHEESY WHITE SAUCE

1. Submerge the asparagus, fresh peas, and radishes separately in boiling water, each for 1 minute or less. Test at 30 seconds for doneness.

2. Remove and plunge the blanched vegetables immediately in an ice bath to halt cooking. Drain when cool. Blanching intensifies vegetables' colors and gives them a tender-crisp texture.

3. Warm the Cheesy White Sauce but do not overheat or it will thin.

PREPARE THE PARSLEY-PEA PUDDLE

1. Preheat the oven to 375°F.

2. To roast the garlic head, peel off loose outer skins. Place in the oven and roast for 30 minutes. Cool and peel cloves.

3. Combine roasted garlic cloves, parsley, peas, walnuts, nutritional yeast, water, and white pepper in a high-speed blender. Run at high speed to purée. The consistency should be dense but spreadable. Taste and adjust seasonings as you like.

4. Lower the oven to 150°F. When it reaches this temperature or 30 minutes before serving, insert your serving dishes to warm.

MAKE THE CRÊPE BATTER

1. Peel, slice, steam the beets until tender, about 8 minutes but begin checking at 5 minutes. When done, the beets should easily be pierced with a knife and offer no resistance.

2. Use a coffee grinder to reduce the golden flaxseed to a powder.

3. Combine buckwheat flour, ground flaxseed, nutritional yeast, granulated onion and garlic, grated nutmeg, and white pepper in a high-speed blender. Pulse to combine.

4. Add the steamed beets, almond milk, and shiro miso. Blend for a minute, scraping down the sides of the container. The batter should be thinner than pancake batter but not as thin as a typical crêpe batter, so that it easily spreads in the pan when swirled. To thin it out, if needed, slowly add up to ¼ cup of water. Taste and adjust the seasonings.

CREATE THE CRÊPES

1. Heat a good-quality large nonstick skillet over medium heat for 4 minutes.

2. Pour ½ cup of crêpe batter in the center of the pan, tipping and swirling the pan to spread the batter in as wide a circle as possible. Cover for 1 minute. Remove the cover and cook for 1 more minute. If the batter is still too thick to spread on the hot pan, add a bit more water and mix well.

3. Ease a nonmetallic flat spatula under the edges around the crêpe to loosen it. Flip and cook for another minute.

4. Transfer the crêpe to a woven straw mat and cover with a clean kitchen towel. Repeat until all crêpes are cooked.

PLATE THE CRÊPES

1. As each crêpe cooks, you can begin to fill and plate those that are ready. Take one of the plates warming in the oven.

2. Add a ladleful of parsley–sweet pea sauce to the center of the plate and with the back of the ladle spread it on the plate.

3. Place a cooked crêpe on a cutting board, spread some Cheesy White Sauce on top, arrange several blanched asparagus spears, radish wedges, and peas in the center, and roll it up.

4. Carefully transfer the filled crêpe onto the center of the sauced plate. Return it to the low temperature oven until serving.

5. Garnish with a few sprigs of microgreens and serve.

CASSOULET, REIMAGINED

This rustic casserole hails from Languedoc-Roussillon in southeast France. Traditionally, cassoulet is made with duck, pork skin, goose, and sausage in a base of creamy white French *tarbais* beans, leeks, and fresh herbs. All that cholesterol and saturated fat makes my arteries ache, so I devised a far greener and healthier alternative: Incorporating an aromatic mix of French vegetables, fresh herbs, spices, greens, and the beans, this cassoulet is slowly baked until it creamily melts in your mouth. Its heavenly herbal and garlicky aromas permeate the house. I like to top it with slabs of 100% whole wheat sourdough bread, toasted and rubbed with garlic and thyme. Cassoulet, Reimagined is a welcome dish when the weather turns cold and rainy, and you are stuck indoors. It is the perfect occasion to putter around the kitchen, making a splendid, comforting rustic French dish, and filling your home with intoxicating aromas.

Whole wheat bread sold in U.S. groceries has a climate footprint of 1 kg CO_2eq per kg, with 39% of greenhouse gas emissions generated during agriculture, 12% from transport, 22% from processing, and 24% from packaging. Dried white beans sold in U.S. shops also have a footprint of 1 kg CO_2eq per kg, with 23% of emissions produced during agriculture, 11% in transport, 20% during processing, and 46% from packaging.

The Vineyards of Southeast France

Languedoc-Roussillon sits between mountains to its north and south and the Mediterranean Sea to its east. It is home to the highest percentage of organic vineyards in France, thanks to its drying winds, sunny clime, and rich volcanic soil. For over a decade, rising temperatures, hailstorms, heat waves, and drought have caused grapes to ripen too early and burn, altering their flavors, raising the grapes' pH, and increasing their alcohol content, according to a France24 report in 2022. The grape harvest is occurring weeks earlier than thirty years ago. To help counter these damaging climate effects and safeguard vineyards, wine producers are exploring heritage varieties, designing hybrids with more resilient traits, and testing the viability of relocating vineyards to other regions.

Prep time 2 hours │ Cook time 1¼ hours │ Serves 4 to 6

1 pound dried *tarbais* white beans (order online)

2 to 3 quarts unsalted vegetable broth

Handful of fresh sage leaves or sprigs

9 large cloves garlic, peeled, 4 left whole, 4 smashed , and 1 to rub on toast

2 beefsteak or large heirloom tomatoes, thickly sliced

Several sprigs of fresh thyme

1 cup shallots from 2 large shallots, cut in ¼-inch slices

1⅓ cups carrots, cut in a large dice

1⅓ cups celery, cut in a large dice

Sprigs of rosemary, sage, thyme, bay, and parsley, tied in a bouquet garni

Dry vermouth, dry white wine, or unsalted vegetable broth, to deglaze pot

4 cups leeks from 1½ leeks, well cleaned and cut in a large dice

4 whole cloves

Whole nutmeg

8 whole black peppercorns

4 juniper berries

1 large russet potato, peeled, cut in a large dice

8 ounces of cremini mushrooms, cut into quarters

4 cups lacinato kale, rolled and cut in ¼-inch ribbons

1½ (14-ounce) cans of small artichoke hearts packed in water, drained and rinsed

1 to 2 teaspoons porcini powder from sliced dried porcini mushrooms

3 tablespoons aka (red) miso, or to taste, dissolved in ⅓ cup hot broth or water, or to taste

Several grinds black pepper, or to taste

3 to 4 slices of stale or toasted artisanal 100% whole wheat bread (sourdough is my favorite)

Fresh thyme sprigs

1. Preheat the oven to 375°F.

2. Rinse the beans, place in a 4-quart Dutch oven or ovenproof pot, and cover with 3 inches of water and bring to a boil. Lower the heat and simmer for 3 minutes. Cover, turn off the heat, and steep the beans for about an hour or until all the beans have swelled and sunk to the bottom. Drain. Refill the pot with broth, covering the beans with 2 inches of broth. Add the handful of sage and 4 whole garlic cloves. Bring the pot to a boil, then lower the heat to a gentle simmer. Cook the beans until they are tender but intact. This may take 30 minutes to an hour, depending on the freshness of your beans.

3. Line a large cookie sheet with parchment. Place the slabs of tomatoes on the parchment. Strew some of the fresh thyme sprigs over the tomatoes, reserving some for Step 11. Bake for 30 minutes or until the tomatoes have begun to dry, and their edges have begun to crisp and brown. They should be tender and fragrant. Cut each slice into quarters and set aside.

4. Lower the oven temperature to 325°F.

5. Heat a large sauté pan, chicken fryer, or Dutch oven that can hold up to 4 quarts on medium heat for 3 minutes. Put in the sliced shallots, lower the heat to medium low, and
dry sauté for a few minutes, stirring. Add the diced carrot, celery, and bouquet garni.

6. After the aromatics have released their liquid and begun to darken and adhere to the
pan, deglaze with a minimal amount of deglazing liquid. Then add the 4 smashed garlic
cloves, diced leeks, cloves, whole peppercorns, and juniper berries. Grate nutmeg generously on top. Stir gently. Add a little broth if the mix is dry.

7. In a few minutes stir in the diced potatoes, cremini mushrooms, and sliced lacinato
kale.

8. After a few minutes incorporate the whole artichoke hearts and roasted tomatoes, and
gently stir in the beans with enough of their cooking water to cover all the vegetables.
Simmer for 5 minutes to allow the flavors to meld.

9. Remove the bouquet garni. Stir in porcini powder and dissolved aka miso. Add 2 to 3
grinds of black pepper on top. Taste and adjust seasonings as you like.

10. Cover the pan and transfer to the oven. Bake for an hour.

11. Remove from the oven and uncover the pan. Rub the toast with the remaining clove of
garlic. Place the toasted garlic bread slices on top, basting the bread with some of the
cassoulet's pan juices. Sprinkle the remaining sprigs of thyme on top and continue to
bake for a final 15 minutes, uncovered, until the cassoulet's juices are bubbling, and the
casserole is very fragrant.

12. Serve in warmed Italian soup bowls. To plate, place a slab of cassoulet's garlicked bread
slab in each bowl, cover with the cassoulet's beans, greens, vegetables, and broth. Pass
around the pepper mill at the table.

DI SAN XIAN, THREE EARTHLY TREASURES

A homey dish from China's northeast Dongbei Province (Manchuria), *Di San Xian*'s three earthly treasures refer to its classic ingredients: peppers, potatoes, and eggplant. Typically prepared with a lot of processed cooking oil, each "treasure" is typically deep-fried before being stir-fried with more oil in a mild sauce of garlic, ginger, and spring onion. In this cleaner and greener makeover, I ditch the oil entirely, toasting each chunky vegetable instead in nonstick skillets before combining and glazing them in an aromatic finishing sauce and garnishing helpings with freshly toasted sesame seeds. Serve *Di San Xian* with your favorite whole grain or whole-grain noodles.

Potatoes at U.S. distribution centers have a climate footprint of 0.28 kg CO_2eq per kg. Eggplants on U.S. farms have a footprint of 0–0.1 kg CO_2eq per kg. Peppers cultivated on U.S. farms also generate a negligible 0–0.1 kg CO_2eq per kg.

China's Climate Threats

In February 2023, Al Jazeera reported that sixteen of the world's twenty most vulnerable climate regions sit in China, with extreme heat and drought most pronounced in the southern and eastern provinces. These regions are increasingly susceptible to wildfires, water shortages, and sea level rise along the coast. Northern China, on the other hand, has been battered by heavy rainfalls and floods, which have caused significant damage and loss of life, according to the World Meteorological Organization. In June 2022, the government released a new policy document to respond to its climate risks with the goal of modernizing the monitoring and adaptation at every level of government to improve the country's climate resilience and protection of its people, infrastructure, agriculture, the economy, and society. The report emphasized the need for agriculture to adapt by introducing crops that are more stress resilient and higher yielding.[112]

Prep time 30 minutes Cook time 40 minutes Serves 3 to 4

1 pound russet or yellow potatoes, roll cut in 2½-inch pieces

2 young, firm Chinese eggplants or small, young Italian eggplants, roll cut in 2½ inch pieces

1 cup white vinegar or more to cover the cut eggplant pieces

1½ teaspoons dense date paste from ½ cup pitted dates

¼ cup freshly toasted sesame seeds, for a garnish

2 teaspoons unsalted dehydrated soup vegetables, freshly ground

2 green bell peppers (classic) or 1 green and 1 red, deseeded and cut in large triangles

1 cup scallions from 2 white bulbs of spring onion or white sections from a bunch of scallions, sliced thinly

Up to ⅓ cup unsalted Shaoxing Chinese rice wine, sake, or unsalted vegetable broth, to deglaze pan and use in the glazing sauce

4 large cloves garlic, very thinly sliced

1-inch fresh ginger root, peeled and cut in very thin matchsticks

4 teaspoons good-quality fermented aged tamari

¾ cup water

¾ teaspoon Chinese black vinegar or unseasoned rice vinegar

1 tablespoon cornstarch dissolved in 1 tablespoon water, to make a slurry

2 teaspoons aka (red) miso paste, diluted in water, or to taste

1. Roll cut is a dicing method for many Chinese stir-fries. It creates vegetable pieces of equivalent sizes with angled sides. Roll cuts increase each piece's surface area for more even, faster cooking. To roll cut, make a diagonal cut, roll the vegetable a quarter turn (90°), make the next angled cut, and continue rolling and cutting until all pieces are cut.

2. Rinse the potatoes after they are roll cut. To prevent oxidation and remove their surface starch, soak the cut potatoes in water as you prep the other ingredients.

3. After roll cutting the eggplants, toss them in a bowl and add white vinegar, covering each piece well to prevent oxidation. The eggplants will tend to float. Keep them submerged by placing a smaller plate or bowl on top to weigh them down.

4. To make the date paste, cover the pitted dates with water and microwave for 2 minutes or simmer on a stovetop for 5 minutes. When cool, blend in a high-speed blender with as little of the soaking water as required to create a smooth, dense paste. Measure 1½ teaspoons and reserve the rest for another use. Date paste, well covered, will keep in the fridge for about 2 weeks.

5. To toast the sesame seeds, heat a small skillet over low heat, put in the

seeds, stirring frequently as they lightly toast and become fragrant, in about a minute. Do not overcook or allow the seeds to smoke or they will become bitter. Transfer to a small bowl and reserve for the garnish.

6. To make the soup vegetable powder, grind a tablespoon of dehydrated soup vegetables in a coffee or spice grinder. Store any extra powder in a tight-lidded jar in a dark, cool cupboard to use in other dishes in place of bouillon.

7. Heat a good-quality large nonstick skillet over medium-low heat for 3 minutes. If you have two skillets, you can save time by heating them both. Dry the potatoes very well and lay each piece flat on the skillet, spaced from one another. Cover and cook for 4 to 5 minutes on each side. Each surface will become golden, and the interior will parcook. When all sides are golden and a knife penetrates them easily, transfer the potatoes to a plate and set aside.

8. Repeat this cooking method with the peppers. We only want to partially cook the peppers, leaving them still crunchy while toasting their edges, so these will take less time. Flip after a minute or two and cook for another 2 minutes. When they are lightly browned but still firm, transfer them to another plate and set aside.

9. Dry the eggplant pieces and cook them as you did the potatoes, covering the skillet(s) and turning the pieces this time after 3 minutes until the eggplant pieces are tender and lightly toasted on all sides. Remove these too from the pan.

10. Place the sliced whites of the spring onion or scallion in the pan, stir for a minute or two until they have released their liquid and begun to caramelize and darken the pan.

11. Deglaze with a tablespoon or two of deglazing liquid, scraping up the onion sugars from the pan. Mix in three-quarters of the sliced garlic and all the matchsticks of ginger. Cook for a minute. Add the tamari, the rest of the Shaoxing rice wine, and after a minute, add ¾ cup of water.

12. When the mix returns to a simmer, add the date paste, ground soup vegetables, and black vinegar, mixing them in well.

13. Stir in the browned potatoes, then the eggplant and peppers, coating them well with the sauce. Add the remaining sliced garlic.

14. Stir the cornstarch slurry, then stir it into the pan, coating all the vegetables well as the glaze thickens, in about a minute.

15. Finally, turn off the heat and season with the aka miso, to taste.

16. To serve, mound the *Di San Xian*, family style, on a warm platter or on individual plates. Garnish with a good sprinkle of freshly toasted sesame seeds or pass them around at the table.

EGGPLANT-ZUCCHINI TORTE

This melt-in-your-mouth torte makes an elegant gluten-free entree or appetizer to satisfy a holiday crowd. It contains alternating layers of creamy eggplant and summer squash with a tender buckwheat-potato dough. Doused with red, white, and basil sauces, it is bursting with flavor. Any excess dough makes fabulous crackers too. All the torte's ingredients are low carbon-emitting, rest assured, and despite its creamy, rich flavors, this low-fat dish is kind to our bodies too. To help you manage your time, the sauces and vegetable fillings can all be made in advance.

At U.S. distribution centers, potatoes' climate footprint is 0.28 kg CO_2eq per kg, with 73% of emissions coming from agriculture, 7% from processing (washing), and 20% from storage. Buckwheat flour sold at U.S. retail has a climate footprint of 1 kg CO_2eq per kg, with 66% coming from agriculture, 18% from transportation, 9% from processing, and 7% from packaging.

Prep time 2 hours   Bake time 45 to 55 minutes
Serves 8 to 12 from a 9-by-13-inch baking dish

3 cups Cheesy White Sauce (see page 36)

3 cups *Sugo Senza Carne* (see page 60)

1½ cups Arugula Pesto (see page 31)

VEGETABLES

2 young Italian or Graffiti eggplants, sliced ³/₁₆ inch thick

4 zucchini, sliced ³/₁₆ inch thick

4 yellow squash, sliced ³/₁₆ inch thick

DOUGH

2 large russet potatoes, boiled or microwaved whole

4 cups buckwheat flour, plus more for dusting

⅓ full cup golden flaxseed, freshly ground

4 tablespoons nutritional yeast

2 teaspoons granulated onion

2 teaspoons granulated garlic

2 teaspoons dried oregano

A big pinch white pepper, freshly ground

1 teaspoon shiro (mild, white) miso paste

PREPARE THE CHEESY WHITE SAUCE

1. Just warm the white sauce in a saucepan. Do not overheat or the arrowroot's starches will break down and the sauce will become watery. The sauce should be dense but pourable, neither overly thick nor runny.

PREPARE THE RED SAUCE

1. Warm the *Sugo Senza Carne* over low heat.

PREPARE THE ARUGULA PESTO

1. When making Arugula Pesto, its density should be spreadable with a knife and not at all watery.

PREP THE VEGETABLES

1. Use a mandolin or stand mixer vegetable sheet cutter to cut uniform slices or sheets of eggplant, squash, and zucchini ³⁄₁₆ inch thick.

2. Steam the eggplant, zucchini, and squash separately until just fork tender, about 3 to 4 minutes. Do not overcook.

MAKE THE DOUGH

1. Preheat oven to 350°F.

2. We want to use the potatoes while they are very hot to soften and hydrate the dough, so cook them right before mixing the dough and keep them well covered until use.

3. Combine the buckwheat flour, ground flaxseed, nutritional yeast, granulated onion and garlic, dried oregano, and white pepper in the bowl of a food processor. Pulse several times to combine well. Add shiro miso. Peel the hot potatoes. Use a ricer to squeeze the pulp immediately into the processor bowl. Run the processor for 1 to 2 minutes or until dough forms and gathers into a ball. The dough's texture should be very soft. Remove the dough and wrap in plastic to prevent drying.

COMPOSE THE TORTE

1. Use a 9-by-13-inch glass or ceramic lasagna pan.

2. Sprinkle a little buckwheat flour on a large board and roll out one-third of the dough to a thickness of ³⁄₁₆ inch. As the dough begins to adhere to the board with pressure, lift it and dust it with flour. Repeat the dusting as needed while you roll out the dough.

3. Cut a rectangle of dough to fit the pan. Spread a thin layer of *Sugo Senza Carne* on the

bottom before placing the first layer of dough to prevent sticking. Trim the dough to fit the pan, if required, returning excess dough to the wrapped dough.

4. Add another thin layer of *Sugo Senza Carne,* then sliced eggplant, then a layer of Cheesy White Sauce. Drop a few spoonfuls of Arugula Pesto on top, spreading it thinly (an offset spatula works well here).

5. Roll out half of the dough that remains to ³⁄₁₆ inch in thickness. Transfer it to the pan and trim to size.

6. Repeat Step 4, but this time, top the *Sugo Senza Carne* with zucchini slices instead of eggplant, followed by the Cheesy White Sauce and a few spoonfuls of the Arugula Pesto.

7. Roll out the remaining dough. Add it to the pan and trim. Wrap any dough trimmings in plastic to make crackers later, if you like (see below).

8. This time, top the *Sugo Senza Carne* with slices of yellow squash, more Cheesy White Sauce, and spoonfuls of Arugula Pesto.

9. If you have enough unused dough and room in your pan, you can add more layers but stop at three-quarters of an inch below the rim: The torte needs room to expand as it cooks although it will contract again as it cools.

10. Finish constructing the torte with a final layer of *Sugo Senza Carne*, dotted with some Cheesy White Sauce and more Arugula Pesto.

11. Cover with parchment paper, then cover covered with foil. Bake for 45 minutes or until the torte's juices are bubbling. Remove the parchment and foil and cook for a final 10 minutes to lightly toast the top.

12. Transfer to a cooling rack and allow the tort to rest for 20 to 30 minutes before plating. This allows the sauces to set and will facilitate slicing.

MAKE THE CRACKERS

1. Raise the oven temperature to 375°F.

2. Roll out any remaining dough to ¼-inch thickness.

3. Cut out shapes with your favorite cookie cutters or a pastry wheel. Spritz with water or brush with almond milk and sprinkle with *Parmigiano Perfetto* (see page 56), pepper, onion flakes, or whatever suits your fancy.

4. Line a cookie sheet with parchment paper and bake the crackers for 8 to 10 minutes. Check them after 5 minutes to ensure that they don't overbake. The crackers are ready when they are golden and puffy. Cool briefly on a rack.

IMAM *BAYILDI*

In Turkish, Imam *Bayildi* means "the imam was overcome," and once you have tasted these braised, stuffed eggplants, it's easy to see why. Normally, the dish's eggplants are saturated with olive oil, making it less than ideal for the planet or our arteries and waistlines, but don't worry—these Imam *Bayildi* intensify their flavor instead with roasted tomatoes and peppers, herbs, and spices. Topped with rich and creamy cultured soy yogurt, the dish is then garnished with fresh mint. Mop up the sauce with whole-grain flatbreads like *Sangak* Pebble Bread (see page 201), *Rajgira* Roti (see page 186), Naan (see page 180), or *Rieska* Barley Bread (see page 192).

Imam *Bayildi* is a very climate-friendly dish. Eggplants grown on U.S. farms have a climate footprint of 0–0.1 kg CO_2eq per kg, and peppers cultivated on U.S. farms also generate a negligible 0–0.1 kg CO_2eq per kg.

Turkey's Climate Threats and Policy Responses

Turkey is highly exposed to climate change with the frequency and intensity of wildfires, landslides, windstorms, heat waves, and droughts, which have all increased over recent decades. In 2021, the worst rainstorms and fires in centuries forced evacuations and destroyed lives and infrastructure. Its fishing industry, tourism, and shipping access to the Black Sea were impeded by the largest outbreak in sea mucilage, exacerbated by warmer, slower-moving ocean currents. The World Bank reports that Turkey's availability of fresh water is inadequate and by 2030 it may become scarce if current policies continue, threatening agricultural yields, jobs, and food security. The Climate Action Tracker rated the comprehensiveness of Turkey's National Determined Contribution (NDC) target, updated in 2023, as "poor." Its current climate policies will lead to increased GHG emissions and fall short of its stated objectives. Turkey remains heavily reliant on fossil fuel imports. It has the world's third-largest coal pipeline and plans to become a fossil gas hub. As a result of Turkey's climate policies and actions, its targets, and climate financing, the Climate Action Tracker has given Turkey an overall rating of "critically insufficient."

Prep time 1 hour | Cook time 30 minutes | Serves 4

1 teaspoon cumin seed, freshly roasted and ground

1 ½ pounds cherry or small ripe tomatoes, cut in half

1 ½ pounds mini multicolored bell peppers, cored

¼ cup packed Italian parsley

6 cloves garlic, peeled

Full ½ cup tomato paste

2 tablespoons aka (red) miso, or to taste

1 large or 2 medium onions, peeled, cut in half, and thinly sliced

Dry white wine, dry vermouth, or unsalted vegetable broth, to deglaze pan

½ teaspoon freshly ground black pepper, or to taste

4 young Italian eggplants

2 cups unsalted vegetable broth

About ½ cup cultured soy yogurt

¼ cup mint leaves, cut in a chiffonade (rolled and sliced in thin ribbons)

1. Preheat oven to 375°F.

2. Heat a small pan on low for a few minutes. Put in the cumin seeds, tossing or stirring them for 30 seconds or just until they become fragrant. Do not allow them to smoke or burn or they will become bitter. Transfer immediately to a small bowl to cool. Use a coffee grinder to reduce the seeds to powder.

3. Place the tomatoes, cut side up, and the cored mini peppers on separate cookie sheets, each lined with parchment paper. Roast the peppers for about 30 minutes or until they are lightly toasted and begin to collapse. The tomatoes may take an additional 5 to 10 minutes to dry and brown on their cut edges.

4. Set aside 1 full cup of the roasted peppers to make a pepper-tomato paste (see Step 8). Cut the remaining peppers in thin slices, capturing their juices if you can. We will use these for the filling (Step 10).

5. Lower the oven temperature to 350°F.

6. Strip the parsley leaves from their stems, reserving the stems for another dish.

7. On a cutting board, finely mince the garlic and parsley leaves together using a mezzaluna or chef knife.

8. Place the reserved roasted full cup of peppers in a high-speed blender. Add the tomato paste and 1 teaspoon of aka miso and blend. Add water as needed to create a smooth, dense sauce. This is our pepper-tomato paste.

9. Heat a large skillet for 3 minutes over a medium flame. Dry sauté the onions over low heat until they sweat and soften. When they begin to adhere to your pan, deglaze with a few tablespoons of deglazing liquid, scraping up the dissolved caramelized sugars with a wooden spoon.

10. Add the minced garlic and parsley, the remaining sliced peppers, plus 2 tablespoons of pepper-tomato paste. Cook for a minute.

11. Add the cumin and black pepper, stirring well. After a minute, add the roasted sliced tomatoes and their juices.

12. Cook for 10 minutes, just until all flavors have melded and the sauté is fragrant, but before the tomatoes disintegrate and become saucy. Season with aka miso, to taste, and adjust seasonings as you like. This will be our filling.

13. To prepare the eggplants for braising, cut off the stems but leave the caps intact. Remove the tough sepals. Using a chef knife make a deep slit—but not all the way through— extending from the base of the eggplants to ¾ inch before reaching the caps.

14. Place the eggplants in a large sauté pan. Add broth to cover ½ inch up the sides of the pan. Cover and gently simmer on the stovetop for about 40 minutes. Larger eggplants may require 5 to 10 minutes more. Rotate them every 10 minutes in quarter turns so that all sides are exposed to the liquid to cook them evenly. The eggplants are ready when they are soft and just beginning to collapse. Their interiors should be soft and fully cooked.

15. Add a little water to the remaining pepper-tomato paste, if needed, to dilute it from a paste into a sauce. Use this to coat the bottom of your baking dish. Carefully transfer each eggplant from the sauté pan onto this saucy bed with their slit sides facing up.

16. Gently pry open their cavities, taking care not to tear the eggplants, and stuff them with enough sautéed filling to form a mound on top. Generously spoon the pepper-tomato sauce on top of each stuffed eggplant.

17. Bake the Imam *Bayildi* until they are hot and bubbly, about 20 to 25 minutes.

18. Serve them hot on warmed plates. Garnish with a dollop of soy yogurt, topped with ribbons of mint.

JAPCHAE

If you're looking for a tasty, vegetable-packed, gluten-free dish, *Japchae*'s got you covered. This Korean standard is a fun party dish. It features delightfully slippery *dangmyeon* noodles made from sweet potato starch, and is brightly colored with carrots, sweet peppers, and spinach. Feel free to add seasonal vegetables as I did with summer zucchini. Each vegetable is briefly steam-fried to crispy perfection, the noodles are boiled, and the mix is dressed with an aromatic sauce. Then the whole shebang is tossed like a salad. Typically, *Japchae* is garnished with strips of omelet, but we'll spare the chickens, the planet, and our arteries here with a chickpea omelet. Serve with a side of steamed edamame and broccolini to further elevate this delicious, very satisfying meal with added fiber, protein, and antioxidants.

Dangmyeon or sweet potato noodles sold in U.S. shops have a climate footprint of 0.6 kg CO_2eq per kg, with 24% of those emissions related to agriculture, 18% to transportation, 3% to processing, and 55% to packaging.

South Korea's Climate Performance

According to the International Energy Agency, South Korea, like other countries in its region, has experienced an acceleration in surface temperature over the past fifty years. Sea temperatures have also risen, fueling the intensity, frequency, and destructiveness of typhoons and tropical cyclones. Our World in Data reported that in 2022, South Korea's GHG emissions per capita ranked among the top twenty countries worldwide. South Korea's President Yoon Suk Yeol, in office since May 2022, has moved the country away from its 100% renewable energy target, which it deemed too expensive, and revitalized its nuclear energy program instead. Its current mitigation planning does not have the speed or "stringency" to prevent its emissions from exceeding 1.5°C of temperature rise, according to the Climate Action Tracker, which rated South Korea's overall climate performance and targets as "highly insufficient."

Prep time 40 minutes │ Cook time 20 to 30 minutes │ Serves 4 to 6

⅓ cup white sesame seeds, lightly toasted

1 tablespoon soft date paste from ¼ cup pitted dates, any variety

½ cup besan (Indian gram chickpea flour) or chickpea flour, dissolved in ½ cup water

¼ teaspoon turmeric

½ teaspoon shiro (mild, white) miso paste

3 cups fresh shiitake or mixed mushrooms, tough stems removed, cut in ¼ inch slices

2 large carrots, cut in 3/16 inch matchsticks

2 small young zucchini, cut in 3/16 inch matchsticks

2 medium, red, yellow, or orange bell peppers, cored and cut in 3/16 inch matchsticks

1½ cups spring onion, whites only, or white onion, cut in 3/16 inch slices

4 large cloves garlic, minced

1½-inch ginger root, peeled and minced

2 tablespoons good-quality fermented tamari

⅓ teaspoon black pepper, freshly ground, or to taste

3 tablespoons aka (red) miso, diluted in 3 tablespoons water, or to taste

1 pound Asian or European spinach or 2 bunches Swiss chard leaves only, well washed, cut in 3-inch slices if necessary

1 (12-ounce) package of *dangmyeon* noodles, available in Korean groceries and online

Toasted sesame seeds and sliced chickpea omelet, to garnish

1. To toast the sesame seeds, heat a large nonstick skillet over medium heat for 3 minutes. Put in the seeds, stirring constantly for 2 minutes until they become fragrant and golden. Do not overcook or they may become bitter.

2. To make the date paste, cover the dates with water in a small bowl and microwave for 2 minutes or cook on the stovetop for 5 minutes. Cool and blend the dates and soaking water in a high-speed blender until very smooth.

3. To make the chickpea omelet, combine the flour, ½ cup water, turmeric, and shiro miso in the blender and run until very smooth. Reheat the nonstick skillet, covered, for 3 minutes over a medium low heat. When a drop of water flicked over the surface skips across the surface, the pan is ready. Pour in the batter and twirl the skillet to spread the batter into a thin, large round disk. Cover and cook until the batter loses its sheen, after 1 to 2 minutes. Use a wide silicon or nylon spatula to loosen the omelet and transfer it to a clean kitchen towel to cool. Square off its edges and cut in ½-inch strips. This will be our "omelet" garnish.

4. We cook each vegetable type individually and *only* as long as each variety requires. Because we are not using oil, we will use the nonstick skillet

and a water spritzer simultaneously to lightly fry and steam the vegetables so they are each cooked crispy-tender, pliant but not limp. We will cook the mushrooms, however, until they are soft, plump, and juicy.

5. Reheat the skillet on medium for 2 minutes. Put in the sliced shiitake caps, spritz some water over them, cover and steam-fry for a minute, stir, and repeat until the mushrooms are juicy and soft, in 4 to 5 minutes. Transfer to a small bowl or plate. Reheat the skillet. Cook each vegetable type consecutively, watching, spritzing, stirring, and testing. The carrots will take about 4 minutes, the zucchini from 2 to 3 minutes, the peppers about 2 minutes, and the onion about 3 minutes. Do not undercook the mushrooms or overcook the vegetables.

6. Fill a 6-quart pot with water and bring to a boil. Put in the spinach leaves and blanch them for 1 minute only. Scoop them out with a strainer and submerge in ice water to halt their cooking and brighten their color. Swish around to cool, then drain them and squeeze out their water well, then form a ball. Cut the ball in ¾-inch slices. Reheat the skillet. Put in the blanched spinach with 1 teaspoon of the minced garlic, spritz, cover, and steam-fry as before. Remove the spinach when it is tender, about 1 minute; if using chard, cook it for 3 minutes. Transfer the cooked greens to a bowl.

7. Now for the dressing: Reheat the skillet. Spritz the skillet before putting in the ginger and remaining minced garlic. Cook for a minute, then stir in the tamari, date paste, black pepper, and ¾ cup water. Turn off the heat and stir in the aka miso, dissolving it completely. Taste to adjust the seasonings as you like.

8. Reheat the 6-quart pot to a boil. Cook the noodles for 7 minutes. The noodles are done when they taste cooked but are still chewy. Drain in a colander, shaking them out well, before transferring to a very large bowl. Use scissors to cut the very long cooked noodles in half or thirds.

9. As soon as they are cool enough to handle, dress the noodles with all the dressing. Toss it like a salad with very clean bare hands or food prep gloves.

10. Mix in each of the cooked vegetables, distributing them well and coating them with the sauce. Lastly, complete *Japchae* by adding toasted sesame seeds, reserving some for the garnish.

11. Transfer *Japchae* to a serving platter or plate individually, garnishing with slices of the chickpea omelet and sprinkling more sesame seeds on top.

M'NAZALEH

M'nazaleh is a flavorful vegetarian stew from Palestine. Although it sometimes includes lamb or chicken, *M'nazaleh* often is enjoyed meat-free. Our version stars eggplant and chickpeas cooked in a very fragrant tomato sauce, redolent with spices. To make *M'nazaleh* even greener and healthier, instead of frying eggplant in oil, which it soaks up like a sponge, we roast it in a parchment bag, rendering it soft and tender with a crispy exterior. Seasoning the stew with freshly roasted *Baharat* spice blend (see page 34) knocks it right out of the ballpark. *M'nazaleh* makes a delicious addition to your meze table or as supper, served with a whole-grain flatbread like *Sangak* Pebble Bread (see page 201) or a fluffy whole-grain pilaf.

On Palestinian farms, chickpeas generate 0.52 kg CO_2eq per kg in GHG emissions, with 5% coming from the production of fertilizer, 17% from in-field bacteria, 5% from off-field bacteria, 15% from the production of pesticides, 29% from farm equipment operations, 25% from the energy used to irrigate fields, and 3% from air-drying the crop.

Palestine's Climate Crisis

According to the World Bank's ReliefWeb report of December 2023, the warming climate is reducing water, food, and energy resources in Palestine and stymying economic development. Restrictions on the movement of its people and goods, its recurrent, violent conflicts with Israel, and the lack of sovereign control over its resources, together with its unplanned urban development, population growth, and weak public services, have increased the exposure of its people to climate shocks, especially among the poor and in overcrowded, underserved urban centers. Climate models predict that water will become increasingly scarce, especially in Gaza, as sea levels rise, risking the contamination of aquifers and groundwater with salt water. The ongoing Israeli-Hamas conflict has created new and infinitely greater challenges for the Gazans. The West Bank faces climate risks too as its population growth increases its demand for energy and water, putting ever more pressure on its public services.

Prep time 1¾ hours | Cook time 30 minutes | Serves 4 to 5

3½ cups cooked chickpeas from ½ pound dried or 2 (15-ounce) unsalted cans, rinsed

8 cloves garlic, 2 whole and 6 minced

Several sprigs fresh herbs like sage or rosemary, tied in a bouquet garni

2 pounds young eggplants, cut in ¾-by- ¾-inch batons, then cut in 2-inch lengths

2 yellow onions, cut in a medium dice

Up to ¼ cup dry vermouth or white wine, to deglaze pan

1 (28-ounce) can organic whole tomatoes, pulp and juice

2 tablespoons *Baharat* (see page 34), or to taste

A large fistful of parsley leaves, chopped for the stew and the garnish

⅓ cup red aka (red) miso paste, diluted in ½ cup water, or to taste

1. If using dried chickpeas, cover with water in a medium pot, boil for 2 minutes, then steep for an hour.

2. Drain and refill the pot with the chickpeas and water to cover them by 3 inches. Toss in the whole garlic cloves and bouquet garni. Bring to a boil, then lower to a simmer, cooking the chickpeas until tender but intact, in about 30 minutes, although older chickpeas may require more time. Drain and set aside. If using canned chickpeas, rinse and drain.

3. Preheat your oven to 400°F.

4. To roast the eggplants, tear off parchment paper double the length of a cookie sheet and fold in half. Arrange the eggplants in one layer (you may need to use multiple pans).

5. Fold over the open edges twice. To seal the parchment bag, staple the folded edges every 6 inches.

6. Roast the eggplants for an hour or until the batons are soft when pierced with a knife and have a lightly toasted exterior. Use scissors to cut the bag open to release steam.

7. Heat a large skillet over medium-low heat for 3 minutes. Dry sauté the onions for a few minutes until they release their liquid and begin to darken the pan.

8. Deglaze the pan with a few tablespoons of deglazing liquid, scraping up the caramelized onion sugars with a wooden spoon. Stir in the minced garlic, and after a minute, add the tomatoes, pulp and juice, breaking them up into smaller pieces with the back of a spoon.

9. Simmer the sauce for 10 minutes, then season, to taste, with *Baharat*.

10. Stir in the cooked chickpeas and roasted eggplant. Cook for a final 10 minutes to allow the flavors to meld.

11. Remove the pan from the heat and stir in a generous amount of chopped parsley.

12. Serve *M'nazaleh* in warmed bowls, seasoning each with teaspoons of diluted miso, to taste. Garnish with additional chopped parsley.

OKONOMIYAKI

Okonomiyaki are Japanese savory griddle cakes. They are a meal in themselves. These delectable, thick, plate-sized patties have a crispy exterior and are tender and moist inside, like crabcake. *Okonomiyaki* means "as you like it" and, indeed, variations abound. This one is much kinder to the planet than traditional *Okonomiyaki*: We ditch bonito flakes, eggs, and pork belly in favor of flavorful mushrooms, aromatics, and vegetables from land and sea. We will garnish ours with a zesty barbecue sauce and an oil- and egg-free Japanese-style mayo to be greener and cleaner. *Okonomiyaki* also makes smashing canapés when miniaturized and served on whole wheat slider buns.

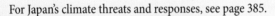

Naigamo (Japanese yam) has a climate footprint of 0.21 kg CO_2eq per kg on Japanese farms, with 26% of GHG emissions the result of fertilizer production, 13% from in-field bacteria, 9% from off-field bacteria, 6% from draining wetlands, 8% from pesticide production, and 35% from operating farm machinery.

For Japan's climate threats and responses, see page 385.

Prep time overnight for dashi broth, plus 1 hour
Cook time 50 minutes   Makes 4 full-sized *Okonomiyaki* or about 16 minis

BONITO-FREE DASHI BROTH

1 3-by-3 inch square of dried kombu

4 dried preservative-free shiitake mushrooms

JAPANESE BARBECUE SAUCE

1 teaspoon Chinese 5-spice powder

4 tablespoons vegan ketchup

4 tablespoons homemade Worcestershire Sauce (see page 62)

4 tablespoons vegan oyster sauce

JAPANESE-STYLE MAYO

1 teaspoon date paste from ½ cup pitted dates

1 cup silken tofu

2 teaspoons garlic granules

⅛ teaspoon wasabi powder or wasabi paste

2 teaspoons unseasoned rice vinegar

¼ teaspoon aka (red) miso paste

2 teaspoons shiro (mild, white) miso paste

2 teaspoons shiitake powder

½ teaspoon smoked paprika

⅛ teaspoon ground turmeric

OKONOMIYAKI

5-inch piece of *nagaimo* (Japanese yam), peeled and grated

1 teaspoon date paste from ½ cup unpitted dates used to make Japanese-style mayo

1 cup oat flour

¼ teaspoon sodium-and-aluminum-free baking powder

1 teaspoon shiro (mild, white) miso paste

¼ cup red pickled ginger, chopped, plus more for garnish

½ green cabbage, cut in a large dice

1 bunch Japanese spring onion or 1 large bunch scallions, greens and whites, cut in ⅛-inch slices

1 large bunch Asian chives or 1 bunch scallions, cut in ⅛-inch slices, reserving ½ cup for garnish

1 bunch Japanese spinach, or regular spinach, stems removed, chopped into medium pieces

Dashi broth's rehydrated shiitake mushrooms, tough stems removed, cut in half and thinly sliced

3 fresh shiitake mushroom caps, cut in half and thinly sliced

½ cup puffed Khorasan wheat cold cereal, sold under the brand name Kamut

Japanese barbecue sauce, Japanese mayo, sliced scallions, pickled ginger, and *aonori* seaweed flakes, for garnish

MAKE BONITO-FREE DASHI BROTH

1. To make the dashi broth, place the kombu seaweed and dried shiitake mushrooms in a bowl. Fill with 1 cup water, cover the bowl with wrap, and soak in the fridge overnight. Squeeze out the mushrooms, remove the stems, cut in half, and slice the caps thinly. We will use them in Step 5 of Make *Okonomiyaki* (below). Discard the kombu. This slightly viscous liquid is our dashi broth.

MAKE JAPANESE BARBECUE SAUCE

1. In a bowl, combine the 5-spice powder, vegan ketchup, homemade Worcestershire Sauce, and vegan oyster sauce, mixing them well.

2. Taste and adjust the sauce ingredients as you like.

MAKE JAPANESE-STYLE MAYO

1. To make date paste, cover the pitted dates with water and microwave for 2 minutes or cook on the stovetop for 5 minutes. Cover the bowl and steep the dates for 10 minutes to soften. Purée the dates with some of the soaking water in a high-speed blender until smooth. Use 1 teaspoon in the following step and 1 teaspoon in Step 3 of Making *Okonomiyaki* (below). Any remaining date paste will keep in the fridge for 2 weeks or can be frozen for up to 3 months.

2. Combine 1 teaspoon date paste with the other mayo ingredients in a high-speed blender. Run on high speed to make a smooth, creamy spread.

3. Taste and adjust any seasonings as you like.

4. Spoon the mayo into a squeeze bottle or pastry bag to decorate when plating.

MAKE *OKONOMIYAKI*

1. Use a vegetable peeler to peel the skin off the *nagaimo*. If it irritates your skin, wet your hands with vinegar or wear gloves. Then use a box grater's largest holes to grate the *nagaimo*. Place it over a bowl as you grate it; the yam will dissolve into a thick, viscous liquid.

2. In a large bowl, mix the oat flour and baking powder.

3. In a separate bowl, combine grated *nagaimo*, dashi broth, and 1 teaspoon date paste, mixing them well. Then whisk the liquids into the dry mix, whipping a little air into it.

4. Cover the bowl with wrap and refrigerate it for at least an hour.

5. Remove the bowl from the fridge and gently fold in the chopped pickled ginger, cabbage,

spring onion, chives, spinach, and both the rehydrated shiitakes used to make the dashi broth and the fresh shiitakes.

6.   Preheat a large nonstick skillet over medium heat for 5 minutes.

7.   Heat the oven to 150°F. Insert your platter or individual serving plates, to warm.

8.   Fold the puffed Khorasan wheat cereal (Kamut) into the bowl. Pour as much of the batter into the hot skillet as you need for the size you desire.

9.   Using two large nylon or silicone spatulas, quickly shape the batter into a 1½-inch-high disk.

10. Cover the skillet. Cook for about 6 minutes or until you see that the bottom of the cake is golden brown and has developed a nice crust. Adjust your heat if it browns too quickly or slowly.

11. Use the large spatula to flip the *okonomiyaki* over, reshaping it if required. Cover the pan and continue to cook it for another 5 to 6 minutes or until the bottom is golden and crisp.

12. Transfer the cake to the oven serving dish or dishes to stay warm as you cook the remaining *okonomiyaki*.

13. To garnish, use a pastry brush to apply a coating of the Japanese barbecue sauce over the surface. With the squeeze bottle, squirt the Japanese-style mayo in zigzags on top. Garnish with sliced scallions, pickled ginger, and *aonori* seaweed flake.

TAHCHIN

Persian *Tahchin* is a gorgeous, crispy, saffron-infused baked rice cake, typically filled with chicken and made with dairy yogurt, butter, oil, and eggs. But not this one! This fragrant, delicious *Tahchin* is climate friendly and low in fat. It is fragrant with warm spices and orange and layered with dried fruits and a sprinkling of almonds and pistachios.

Tahchin, like any great holiday dish, has many steps and takes time to make, but it sure is worth it: It will fill your home with intoxicatingly wonderful aromas of orange, rose, and saffron. A showstopper, it makes a beautiful centerpiece for any table, and particularly for a Persian-inspired meal. However, because currently available varieties of rice generate more greenhouse gas emissions than other whole grains, I reserve *Tahchin*, and other rice dishes, for special occasions.

At U.S. retail, most dried fruits, like apricot, cranberry, plums, goldenberries, and mango, all share a climate footprint of 4 kg CO_2eq per kg. with 62% of emissions related to agriculture, 5% to transport, 25% to processing, and 8% to packaging.

Saffron's Climate Risks

Iran is the world's leading source for saffron, with the harvest centered in the region of Khorasan. In 2023, yields were down 40%, rocking domestic and global saffron markets. Extreme weather, starting with a freezing winter, lack of rain in spring, and followed by scorching summer heat reaching 122°F (50°C), is blamed for the crop's failure, which threatens the livelihood of 100,000 local families who reside in this arid desert area.[113] For more on the environmental impacts of rice, see page 319. For how the climate is impacting Iran, see page 201. For Iran's use of energy, see page 29.

Prep time 1 hour to soak the rice, make the orange purée, steep the saffron tea, and strain the soy yogurt, plus 1 hour to prepare the filling, parcook the rice, and compose the cake
Bake time 1 hour 10 minutes   Makes an 8-inch cake, 8 servings

2 cups brown basmati rice

1 teaspoon good quality saffron threads

3 tablespoons date paste from ½ cup pitted dates, any variety

1 organic orange, tips trimmed, cut first in quarters, then each piece in half

½ organic lemon, tips trimmed, cut in quarters

1 tablespoon Persian *Advieh Berenj* spice blend (see page 29)

2 cups unsweetened soy or almond yogurt, strained for 1 hour

1 flax egg from 1 tablespoon freshly ground golden flaxseed mixed with 3 tablespoons water

¼ cup fresh barberries, preferably, or ¼ cup dried barberries, soaked and drained

⅓ cup almond flakes

⅓ cup unsalted shelled pistachio nuts

1 cup dried unsulfured apricots, cut in ¼-inch strips

½ cup dried Bing cherries

½ cup oil- and sugar-free, unsulfured dried cranberries

2 cups orange juice

¼ cup fresh pomegranate arils

1 tablespoon arrowroot

2 teaspoons shiro (mild, white) miso paste

1. To make the brown basmati rice, wash it in a large bowlful of water and rinse several times until the water is clear. Refill with cool water and soak for 1 hour, then drain. To cook, bring a pot of water to a boil. Put in the soaked rice. Cook over a low boil for 10 minutes and test. The rice cooks quickly and we only want to parcook it here. Drain and cool completely in a bowl of cold water. Drain again and set aside.

2. To prepare the saffron, pulverize the threads into a powder using a spice grinder or small mortar and pestle. To make saffron tea, steep the ground saffron in ½ cup very hot water to release its color and flavor.

3. To make the date paste, put the pitted dates in a small pot, cover barely with water, and simmer for 5 minutes. Alternatively, add them to a small bowl, just cover with water, and microwave for 2 minutes. Cool. Use a high-speed blender to purée the dates with only as much of their soaking water as necessary to make a dense, uniform paste.

4. To make the orange purée, cut off the white pithy top and bottom of the orange and ½ lemon. Cut each fruit in quarters, and then each orange quarter in half.

5. Transfer the fruit to a pot and add 1¼ cups water, the date paste, and, for now, just 1 teaspoon of both the saffron tea and *Advieh Berenj*. Cover and simmer on low for about 45 minutes, stirring occasionally, or until the fruit is extremely soft. Cool slightly. Transfer to a high-speed blender and run on high to make a velvety smooth, fragrant purée.

6. To strain the soy or almond yogurt, spoon it onto a 2-foot square of unbleached muslin. Gather up the corners to form a sack and tie it tightly with string. Suspend the bag filled with yogurt over the sink or place it in a strainer over a bowl, allowing its liquid to drain through the cloth. Allow it to strain and thicken for 1 hour.

7. To make the flax egg, grind the flaxseed in a spice or coffee grinder into a powder. Transfer to a small bowl. Stir or whisk in 3 tablespoons of water. The "egg" will soon congeal into a soft paste.

8. If using dried barberries, soak them in lukewarm water for about 15 minutes, then drain.

9. Now, let's cook the fruit and nuts. Heat a large skillet over medium-low heat for 3 minutes. Put in the almonds and pistachios, stirring constantly, just until they become fragrant and lightly toasted, in 4 to 5 minutes. Add the apricots, cherries, and cranberries, stirring. Warm them in the pan for 2 minutes to soften. Stir in the orange juice, 2 teaspoons of saffron tea, and 1 teaspoon of *Advieh Berenj*. Cover. Lower the heat to gently simmer for an hour, during which time the fruit and nuts will absorb the spices and juice and become fragrant, soft, and plump. Uncover, stir in the barberries and the orange-lemon purée. Remove the pan from the heat. When cool, stir in the pomegranate arils.

10. Preheat the oven to 400°F and place a rack in the middle of the oven.

11. To compose the *Tahchin*, cut out 2 parchment disks to line the bottom and top of an 8-inch springform pan. Cut a 2½-inch-wide strip of parchment to line the sides of the pan, overlapping the parchment to help it stay in place as you fill the pan.

12. In a bowl, mix 3 heaping tablespoons of the thickened yogurt with 1 tablespoon of saffron tea and 1 cup of the parcooked rice. Spoon this mix onto the bottom and line the sides of the pan, as best you can.

13. Now, in a larger bowl mix the rest of the soy yogurt with the rest of the saffron tea, 2 teaspoons of *Advieh Berenj*, the flax egg, arrowroot, and shiro miso. Stir in the remaining parcooked rice and using clean hands, mix it until well combined. The rice mix should be moist and a little sticky, which will enable it to bind together into a cake.

14. Layer an inch of this rice mix on the pan bottom, smoothing it flat and gently pressing it to eliminate any voids. Follow with a ½-inch layer of the mixed cooked fruits and nuts, leaving a ¾-inch rice border along the perimeter of the pan, which should be lined with the rice mixture applied in Step 12.

15. Repeat with another layer of rice and fruit. Finish with a layer of the remaining rice. We will use the remaining fruit to decorate the *Tahchin* right before slicing and serving.

16. Cover the pan with the second parchment disk and press down lightly over the rice mix to firm it up and eliminate voids. Cover the pan tightly with aluminum foil or an ovenproof lid. The *Tahchin* is baked upside-down. After it is cooked, we will flip it and remove the pan and parchment sheets.

17. Bake the *Tahchin* for 1 hour.

18. Raise the temperature to 500°F and move the *Tahchin* to the lowest possible oven rack for the final 10 minutes of baking to crisp its bottom.

19. Remove the cake from the oven and place the pan on a cooling rack. Remove the foil and parchment disk liner.

20. When it is sufficiently cool to handle, place a serving plate over the pan and hold it firmly on top and bottom. Flip the pan over. Center the *Tahchin* on the plate, open the springform and remove the pan entirely. Peel off the second parchment disk.

21. Allow the *Tahchin* to cool almost completely, for about 20 minutes. If you blow a small fan on it, you can reduce the cooling time considerably.

22. Before serving, decorate the top with the remaining cooked fruits and nuts. The *Tahchin* will slice beautifully.

SWEETS

BERRY BITES

Purple sweet potatoes, blackberries, rolled oats, vanilla, and dates fashioned into chewy, little squares. These climate-friendly treats are tasty, healthy, and simple to make. Enjoy them in lunch boxes, as an afterschool snack, or a post-workout pick-me-up.

Sweet potatoes grown in U.S. soils have a climate footprint of 0.19 kg CO_2eq per kg. Fourteen percent of the emissions are driven by fertilizer production, 29% from in-field bacteria that consume the fertilizer, 6% from draining wetlands to farm, and 38% from the energy required to power farm machinery.

Sweet Potatoes' Sweet Climate Story

Sweet potatoes are tropical vegetables. They are able to tolerate heat better than many other crops. Plant breeders are testing new varieties of sweet potato to be high yielding and even more resilient.[114] For example, the orange-freshed sweet potato developed at the International Potato Center, a project funded by the Gates Foundation, is packed with micronutrients, matures quickly, doesn't require a lot of water, and is tolerant to drought and disease. It is biofortified to provide fiber, carbohydrates, and enough vitamin A to protect against blindness, diarrhea, and immune disorders—valuable attributes particularly for smallholder farms in the Global South. This is one good-news climate story to celebrate.[115]

CHOOSING VANILLA?

Whole and ground vanilla seeds have twice the potency of vanilla extract. I love using it instead of extract whenever I do not want any extra moisture added to a dish or I am cooking for anyone who needs to avoid alcohol. Look for whole or ground vanilla seeds, sometimes labeled as vanilla powder, but make sure it contains only ground vanilla seeds without added sugar, fillers, or preservatives.

Prep time 20 minutes │ Bake time 45 minutes │ Makes about fifty 1½-inch squares

1 cup date paste from 1½ cups pitted dates, any variety

1 cup packed Stokes or Okinawan purple sweet potatoes

1 teaspoon vanilla seeds or ground vanilla seeds

½ cup sodium-and-aluminum-free baking powder

½ cup unsweetened soy milk

1 teaspoon shiro (mild, white) miso paste

1½ cups rolled oats

1 (12-ounce) package of fresh blackberries, rinsed and air-dried

Fresh or dried blueberries, for garnish

1. Preheat the oven to 375°F.

2. To make date paste, add the pitted dates to a glass container, cover with water, and microwave for 2 minutes. Alternatively, simmer on a stovetop for 5 minutes. Steep until the dates have softened. Cool. Then transfer the dates and as much of the soaking water as you need to blend into a dense purée in a high-speed blender. Run on high for a minute or two until the paste is smooth and uniform, scraping down the sides of the bowl if you need to.

3. Microwave the whole purple sweet potatoes for 5 to 10 minutes, depending on their size. Alternatively, bake in a 425°F oven for 40 to 60 minutes, depending on their size. When cooked, you should easily be able to pierce them with a fork. Do not overcook, however, or the flesh will become dry and tough. Peel, mash, and press the mashed pulp firmly to measure 1 cup.

4. In the bowl of a food processor, combine the sweet potato mash, date paste, vanilla seeds, baking powder, soy milk, and shiro miso. Run for a minute. The mix should be smooth and uniform. Taste to adjust any seasonings as you like.

5. Transfer the mixture to a bowl. Stir in the rolled oats.

6. Tear off a piece of parchment paper to line the bottom and sides of an 8-by-8-inch glass baking dish. Wet and crumple the parchment first before distending it; it will then conform more easily to the sides of the dish.

7. Scrape the mixture into the lined baking dish. Level and smooth the surface with an offset icing spatula. Press each blackberry a little into the batter, spacing them about 1 to 1¼ inch apart.

8. Bake for 45 minutes and check for doneness. The berry bites are ready when they are lightly toasted on the edges of the dish and a toothpick comes out clean.

9. Remove from the oven, and remove the loaf out of the baking dish by lifting up the parchment liner.

10. We are looking for a texture that is moist and a little chewy, but not gummy, so allow the loaf to cool completely before gently tugging the parchment paper down from the sides of the loaf and slicing.

11. Use a wet, clean, sharp knife to cut into small, bite-sized squares, each with a blackberry, cleaning and rewetting the knife as you proceed.

12. Troubleshooting: If upon cutting the bites you find them to be too moist and gummy, simply pop them back into the oven and bake for an additional 10 to 15 minutes.

13. To serve, arrange the berry bites on individual plates or a larger serving tray. Strew some blueberries around them for fun.

CHERRY NESTS

I adore cherries and came up with this dainty pastry made of nothing but a bit of date-sweetened, vanilla-scented dough, a smear of jam, and whole cherries: light as a feather and bursting with cherry goodness. Fruit filled, whole grain, and without added fats, cherry nests are healthy enough for a child's lunch box and elegant enough for company. Cherry trees, like all trees, are the best carbon-capture technology we have right now. Enjoy these climate-supportive, healthy delights for breakfast, snacks, and dessert.

U.S. cherries have a climate footprint of 0.61 kg CO_2eq per kg at farms. Only 4% of those emissions are linked to fertilizer production, 8% to in-field bacteria, 2% from off-field bacteria, 5% from draining wetlands for farming, and 6% to pesticide production. A high 72% of emissions is due to the use of farm machinery, however.

Climate Threats to Cherry Production

Washington, Oregon, and California grow about 90% of the U.S. cherries. The vagaries of climate-induced extreme weather from climate change have caused smaller yields in recent years. In 2021, heat waves struck early in spring, causing sun and heat damage that stunted fruit growth in Washington. In 2023, Oregon's crop suffered heavy losses of fruit due to ice storms, excessive heat, and smoke from wildfires while in neighboring California record cold and rain delayed the cherry harvest for weeks, creating a glut when its fruit arrived at market concurrently with Oregon's crop.[116] The predicted future trend for the Northwest is hotter temperatures during the day and night, which will threaten the growth and health of fruiting trees. To protect them, farmers are employing shade netting and water misters, and coating the fruit with clay.[117]

Prep time 2 passive hours for the dough to rise, plus 45 minutes
Bake time 45 minutes | Makes sixteen 3-inch nests

¼ cup date paste from ½ cup pitted dates, any variety

½ cup unsweetened soy milk, warmed to body temperature

½ teaspoon active dry yeast

½ teaspoon ground vanilla beans or scraped beans from 1 vanilla pod

1¾ cups white whole wheat flour for the dough, plus ¼ cup more for dusting

¼ cup apple glaze from ½ (12-ounce) carton frozen apple juice concentrate

2 pounds sweet red cherries, pitted

4 tablespoons fruit-sweetened strawberry fruit spread

1. To make date paste, barely cover the pitted dates with water in a small bowl and microwave for 2 minutes. Alternatively, heat the dates and water in a small pot for 5 minutes. Cool. Transfer the dates and only as much of their soaking water as required to purée into a smooth, soft paste, using a high-speed blender.

2. Warm the soy milk before pouring in a mixing bowl. Whisk in the yeast, vanilla, and date paste. Wait 10 minutes for the yeast to activate.

3. Add only as much of the white whole wheat flour as needed to create a soft, slightly sticky dough. Add it slowly, mixing it first with a wooden spoon and, as the dough forms, using a clean hand.

4. Knead the dough in the bowl for about 8 minutes or until smooth and soft. Lightly dust the dough with flour, cover the bowl, and allow it to rise for 2 hours. The dough will expand in size but not double.

5. To make the apple glaze, empty half a carton of frozen apple juice concentrate into a small saucepan, bring to a simmer, and reduce the liquid by about half. The reduction is ready when it lightly coats the back of a spoon. The glaze will continue to thicken as it cools. If it becomes too thick to easily apply with a bristle pastry brush, stir in a teaspoon of water. Freeze any extra glaze for future projects.

6. Use a cherry or olive pitter to remove the cherry pits.

7. Preheat the oven to 350°F and place a rack on the middle oven shelf.

8. After the dough has risen, divide it into eight equal pieces, removing one and keeping the remainder well covered.

9. Dust a cutting board with white whole wheat flour. Use a small rolling pin or wooden dowel to roll out the dough ⅛ inch thick. Use a 3-inch cutter or lid to cut out 2 disks. These will be the foundations for the nests.

10. Gather the dough scraps. Divide them into two equal pieces and shape each into a cylinder. Now, using your hands, roll the first against the board to make a long, uniform snake ¼ inch thick and approximately 18 inches long. Fold it in half and pinch the two ends together. Now, holding the folded rope by each end, twist one clockwise and the other counterclockwise, creating a braided rope about 9 inches long. Finally, pinch the ends together once more to form a rope circle. Repeat with the second cylinder of dough.

11. Apply a thick coat of strawberry spread on each of the two disks. Place a rope circle atop each disk, stretching it if needed to hug the disk's perimeter. Press down lightly so that it adheres to the disk. This is your pastry nest.

12. Fill each nest with 5 pitted cherries. Place them on a parchment-lined baking sheet. Cover with plastic wrap. Repeat this process with the remaining seven pieces of dough until all sixteen cherry nests are filled.

13. Use a 1-inch pastry brush to apply a coat of apple glaze to the pastry and the fruit. Bake for 15 minutes. Remove the baking sheet and reapply the apple glaze. Return it to the oven and bake for another 15 minutes.

14. Repeat one more time, applying a third coat of glaze, and bake for a final 15 minutes. The cherry nests are ready when the pastry is golden, and the cherries are slightly wrinkled and juicy.

15. Remove from the oven, apply a final coat of glaze if the fruit or pastry looks opaque. Allow to cool for 10 minutes before transferring to a cooling rack. Serve them warmed.

CIOCCOLATA CALDA

My first introduction to intensely chocolatey, thick Spanish hot chocolate was at the Caffé Rivoire in Florence's glorious Piazza della Signoria during my student days. It was an ideal place to spend an hour sipping this extravagant drink as I watched passersby. Traditionally made with melted chocolate bars and dairy milk or cream, in my remake I ditch the inflammatory fats in cocoa butter and dairy products for flavonoid-rich, low-fat cacao, dates, and vanilla seeds. It is intoxicatingly rich tasting, velvety smooth, and filling, despite being so low in fat and cholesterol-free. A soothing alternative to afternoon tea or an elegant final act after a meal, *Cioccolata Calda* satisfies like dessert and invites praise from all chocolate lovers.

Cacao trees grow in rainforests 10 degrees north and south of the equator in parts of Asia, South America, and West Africa. Sourcing from reputable suppliers is all important for cocoa's environmental impact: Greenhouse gas emissions range from an alarming 400 kg CO_2eq per kg in Suriname (South America), 270 kg CO_2eq per kg in Malaysia (Southeast Asia), and 170 kg CO_2eq per kg in Congo (Africa), all stemming from deforestation first and foremost but also the draining of wetlands. Both practices are very damaging to biodiversity too.

Some countries' farms, happily, have much better climate track records. For example, cocoa GHG emissions levels on Thai farms measure 0.81 kg CO_2eq per kg, 0.74 kg CO_2eq per kg on St. Vincent and the Grenadines' farms, and 0.78 kg CO_2eq per kg on farms in the Dominican Republic. Expect prices to rise with a warming planet, which will put increasing pressure on sustainable growers too. Ground raw cacao powder sold at U.S. retail currently has a climate footprint of 1.13 kg CO_2eq per kg, with 79% of emissions from agriculture, 10% from transportation, 3% from processing, and 8% from packaging.

Sourcing Cacao Is All Important

Certifications from Fairtrade, the Rainforest Alliance, UTZ, Organic, Sustainable Agriculture Network, the European Committee for Standardization (CEN), and the International Organization for Standardization (ISO) try to include only sustainably-grown cacao, with safe working conditions, fair wages, and no child labor. Sadly, child labor and slavery persist in the industry. The Food Empowerment Project's "chocolate list" helps ensure you are purchasing from sources that follow ethical labor standards.[118]

CHOOSING CACAO OR COCOA?

The difference between cacao and cocoa is that the former is unroasted, minimally processed, and fermented at very low temperatures before simply being cold-pressed, then broken into cacao nibs or ground into cacao powder. Cacao retains higher levels of antioxidants. To make cocoa products and chocolate which contain saturated fat-rich cocoa butter, beans are roasted at high temps before undergoing additional processing.

Prep time 5 minutes to make date paste, plus 5 minutes
Cook time 5 minutes   Serves 2

2 to 3 tablespoons date paste from ½ cup pitted dates, or to taste

8 ounces unsweetened soy milk

3 tablespoons low-fat, raw organic cacao powder

¼ teaspoon pure ground vanilla beans or ½ scraped vanilla bean

1. To make date paste, cover the pitted dates with water and microwave for 2 minutes to rehydrate them. Alternatively, simmer the dates with just enough water to cover in a small saucepan for 5 minutes. Place the dates in a high-speed blender with only enough of their soaking water to blend into a super smooth, dense paste. Transfer to a container. Rinse and dry the blender container.

2. Put the soy milk, cacao, vanilla bean seeds, and 2 tablespoons of date paste into the blender. Run on high for 1 minute. Taste to adjust the level of sweetness, chocolate, and vanilla to your taste.

3. Heat in a small saucepan until hot but remove before coming to a boil. Serve hot.

CLAFOUTIS AUX CERISES

Early summer is cherry season, and there's no better time to enjoy *clafoutis*, the traditional baked fruity dessert from Limousin in south-central France. Typically, *clafoutis* features cherries but apricots, peaches, berries, and plums make gorgeous *clafoutis* too. The fruit is baked in a custard, thickened with flour. This gluten-free remake sidesteps the usual eggs, cream, sugar, butter, and white flour that are *clafoutis'* traditional hallmarks, making use instead of whole plant ingredients without shortenings. With a low climate footprint and many anti-inflammatory benefits, what's not to love? This *clafoutis'* sweetness relies principally on the quality of its fruit, so choose fruit at its peak freshness and flavor.

Emissions for cherries grown in French soils are 0.62 kg CO_2eq per kg. Only 5% of the greenhouse gases produced come from fertilizer production, 12% from in-field bacteria producing N_2O from fertilizer, 5% from soil amendments like limestone and urea, which also acts as a nitrogen fertilizer, and 7% from the energy used for pesticides. Seventy percent comes from running farm machinery.

Climate Change in France

France is vulnerable to climate impacts from rising temperatures that cause heat waves, drought, and wildfires, as well as more frequent and violent storms causing flooding, rising sea levels along its coastline, and warmer ocean temperatures. In a 2022 national survey by *Le Monde*, 69% of people said they were willing to significantly modify their lifestyles to help mitigate the effects of climate change. However, in 2024 France dropped from its position of twenty-eighth to thirty-seventh in one year, according to the Climate Change Performance Index, and is now ranked among low climate-performing countries. The assessment is that France's expansion of renewable energy remains inadequate, and that it needs to increase financing to cover adaptation and support to cover losses and damage linked to climate change.

Prep time 20 minutes | Bake time 70–80 minutes | Makes one 10-inch *clafoutis*

⅔ cup dense date paste from 1⅓ cups pitted dates, any variety

A pinch saffron threads, about ⅛ teaspoon and 2 teaspoons very hot water, for steeping

1 cup unsweetened cultured soy or almond yogurt for crème fraîche garnish, plus 3 tablespoons for clafoutis

1 cup gluten-free oat flour

1 cup unsweetened soy milk

1 (16-ounce) package soft tofu, about 2 cups, drained

2 tablespoons arrowroot

½ teaspoon shiro (mild, white) miso paste

1 teaspoon almond extract

3½ cups Rainier or Bing cherries, well washed, air-dried, stems removed

1. Preheat oven to 350°F and place the oven rack on the upper middle shelf.

2. To make date paste, transfer the pitted dates to a microwavable container and cover barely with water. Microwave for two minutes, or simmer on a stovetop for 5 minutes. Allow to cool. Place the rehydrated, softened dates and their soaking water to a high-speed blender. Run for a minute, scraping down the sides as needed, to create a dense, smooth paste.

3. To bloom the saffron pistils, fill a very small bowl with 2 teaspoons of very hot water. Crumble the pistils with your fingers and add them to the water. Steep until use. The saffron will color the custard golden and provide a floral fragrance.

4. To create crème fraîche for your garnish, spoon the cup of soy yogurt onto a 15-inch square of clean unbleached muslin. Tie it up with string and hang the bag to strain over a bowl or the sink. After 2 hours, scrape the thickened yogurt into a small jar or bowl, whip it briefly with a mini whisk or spoon to create a creamy texture like crème fraîche. If it becomes too dense to be soft and creamy, thin with a teaspoon of soy milk and whisk again.

5. Crumble up a piece of parchment paper to soften it, then press it into a 10-inch diameter circular ceramic or glass baking dish to line it to prevent sticking. Choose a dish with sides about 2 inches high to allow for expansion.

6. In a high-speed blender place the oat flour and soy milk. Blend at high speed for 1 minute. Scrape the dense batter into the parchment-lined baking dish and use a rubber spatula to

spread it evenly. Bake it for 10 minutes to set the dough. This dough layer will form the base for the *clafoutis*. Remove the dish from the oven and allow it to cool.

7. Rinse and dry the blender. Combine the drained tofu, 3 tablespoons of yogurt, arrowroot, date paste, saffron and its soaking water, shiro miso paste, and almond extract. Blend on high for a minute or until the batter is very smooth and uniform. Taste and adjust any seasonings as you like. The color should be very pale yellow.

8. Use a rubber spatula to scrape the custard onto the baked dough, spreading it evenly over the surface. Now press each cherry into the thick unbaked custard, submersing them halfway into the custard. Add as many cherries as you can fit.

9. Bake for an hour and begin checking for doneness. The *clafoutis* is ready when the cherries are juicy and soft, and the custard is lightly toasted on top. The very center may still be a little jiggly, but elsewhere, the custard should have set. If it hasn't, return the dish to the oven for an additional 10 minutes or longer, rechecking it frequently for doneness.

10. When it's ready, transfer the *clafoutis* to a cooling rack and allow it time to further congeal as it cools from hot to warm. Then you can cut and plate it. Garnish with a good dollop of the soy crème fraîche and serve immediately.

HINT

Cherry clafoutis *traditionally uses unpitted cherries. The baked pits deepen the dish's almond flavor notes, and the intact cherries prevent the custard from becoming watery. However, if you are serving young children or anyone at risk of swallowing the pits, pit the cherries first or choose different fruit for the* clafoutis.

CRANBERRY PLUM STARS

This very climate-supportive baked dessert for winter features sweet, juicy plums, embedded in cranberry sauce, and wrapped in a tender cookie made from purple corn and kabocha squash. Cranberry Plum Star cups make a splendid, nutritious breakfast, snack, or dessert. Garnish them with a spoonful of soy crème fraîche with a decorative berry or a sprinkle of pomegranate arils. Loaded with fortifying anthocyanins, Cranberry Plum Stars are delicious, whimsical, and healthy—a welcome antidote to winter's gloomy chill.

On U.S. farms, cranberries have a climate footprint of 0.22 kg CO_2eq per kg, with 10% produced by synthetic fertilizers, 42% by in-field bacteria, 10% by bacteria off the field, 5% from draining wetlands for farming, and 30% by the emissions from farm machinery.

Climate Pressures on Cranberries

Cranberries are sensitive to heat stress, which reduces the fruit's yields and increases its susceptibility to disease. Most U.S. cranberries are grown in Massachusetts, New Jersey, Wisconsin, Oregon, and Washington state. While all these areas are experiencing climate change, more rapid warming is occurring in Massachusetts and New Jersey and threatening their cranberry production.[119] Plant scientists are trying to develop viable new varieties of cranberry that can better withstand disease resistance and stress tolerance, but until these are available, the quality and quantity of cranberries will suffer.[120]

Prep time 45 minutes to roast squash and cook cranberries, plus 30 minutes
Bake time 45 minutes | Makes 18 to 20

1 ½ cups cultured, unsweetened soy yogurt for crème fraîche garnish

2 cups date paste from 2½ cups unpitted dates

½ cup apple glaze from ½ (12-ounce) carton of frozen apple juice concentrate

¾ cup kabocha purée from ½ medium roasted kabocha squash or a 15-ounce can of pumpkin purée

2½ to 3 cups cranberry sauce from a (12-ounce) bag fresh organic cranberries or 2 (14-ounce) cans or jars

2 tablespoons golden flaxseed

1 cup purple corn flour (Peruvian *harina morada*)

1 cup buckwheat flour

3 to 3½ pounds red or black plums, pitted, each half sliced in quarters

A spoonful of crème fraîche, a raspberry, blackberry, or ½ teaspoon pomegranate arils, to garnish

1. To make the soy crème fraîche, spoon the soy yogurt onto a square of unbleached muslin. Tie it up with string to make a bag and hang it over the sink or over a bowl. Strain the yogurt for about 2 hours. Open the bag and scrape the thickened yogurt into a bowl. Cover and refrigerate until use. Before serving, use a mini whisk to give the crème fraîche a creamy texture.

2. To make date paste, place dates in a microwavable bowl, cover with water, microwave for 2 minutes. Alternatively, simmer on a stovetop for 5 minutes. Cool and purée the dates in a high-speed blender with as little of their cooking water as needed to create a smooth, dense paste.

3. To make apple glaze, simmer the juice concentrate in a saucepan until it is reduced by half its volume. The reduction is ready when it lightly coats the back of a spoon. It will continue to thicken as it cools. We want to be able to brush it on easily, so if becomes too viscous, thin with a teaspoon of water.

4. To roast the kabocha, preheat oven to 400°F. Cut the squash in half and deseed. Slice each half into 1-inch slabs. Roast on a cookie sheet lined with parchment for 20 to 30 minutes, or until a knife pierces the flesh easily and the cut edges are lightly caramelized. Cool and scrape the flesh off the skin.

5. Place the fresh cranberries in a saucepan, add ⅔ cup water, cover, and simmer for 15 minutes or until tender with some berries intact and some burst. The sauce will congeal and thicken as it cools. Season to taste with date paste, leaving the remaining date paste to sweeten the dough.

6. Use a coffee grinder to grind the golden flaxseed into a powder.

7. In the bowl of a food processor, place the purple corn flour, buckwheat flour, and ground flaxseed. Pulse to combine. Add the roasted kabocha squash and most of the remaining date paste. Run for about 2 minutes. If the dough fails to gather into a ball after 2 minutes, check to see if your mix is too wet (add a little more of one of the flours) or dry (add a spoonful of date paste or water) and reprocess. Taste the dough and sweeten it with more date paste, if desired.

8. Preheat oven to 375°F.

9. Lightly flour a cutting board with purple corn flour. Roll out the dough thinly, to about ⅛ inch thick. Use a 4-inch round cutter or pot lid to cut out dough circles.

10. Use a tulip parchment cupcake liner or a 6-inch square of parchment and center a disk of dough on it. Spoon on 2 heaping teaspoons of cranberries, leaving a ½-inch border around the perimeter. Now gently gather up the parchment with its contents, lightly folding it into the shape of a cup. Gently push it into a muffin tin cavity. Repeat until your tins are filled.

11. Place 5 plum wedges, skin side facing up, into each cup, splaying them to resemble a five-pointed star. Using a pastry brush, apply a coat of apple glaze over the plums, cranberry filling, and exposed edges of the dough cup.

12. Bake the stars on the middle rack for 40 to 45 minutes, checking at 35 minutes for doneness. They are ready when a knife easily pierces the plums and the fruit has lightly caramelized. Transfer to a cooling rack. Gently peel back the parchment paper and brush a coat of apple glaze over the exterior and over the fruit and filling.

13. Serve Cranberry Plum Stars warm, garnishing them with a spoonful of crème fraîche and a berry or a few pomegranate arils on top.

CROSTATINE

Diminutive *crostatas* or mini galettes, whatever you call them, these climate-happy fruit tarts are fun and easy to make. Made from whole grains and fruit, they make a nutritious snack, lovely breakfast, and an elegant dessert. Fold the dough over, empanada style, and they are perfectly leakproof for traveling, kids' lunch boxes, or post-workout snacks. Gluten-free and nutrient dense, *Crostatine* are loaded with flavor, and are far less GHG-emitting than butter-laden pastries.

On average, a mature tree can capture about 48 pounds of CO_2 annually. Pears grown on U.S. farms have a climate footprint of 0.18 kg CO_2eq per kg. Only 5% of these emissions come from fertilizer production, 11% from N_2O-emitted bacteria in the field, 57% of emissions come from the use of farm machinery, and 16% from the production of pesticides.

The Plight of Pear Trees

Over the past thirty years the flowering of pear trees in the U.K. has shifted eleven days earlier than in prior decades. This shift is expected to worsen as the planet continues to warm. Like apples and other fruiting trees, pear trees require a cold dormant period to promote bud burst and flowering. Milder winter temperatures put that at risk. Earlier flowering risks increasing the mismatch in timing between trees and their pollinators, exposes buds to spring frosts, and makes pear trees more susceptible to pest infestations. All these threats negatively impact the quality and quantity of pear yields. Research into more-resistant hybrids and growing strategies is underway to find ways to mitigate pear trees' vulnerabilities.[121]

Prep time 30 minutes | Bake time 25 minutes | Makes about fifteen 4½-inch *crostatine*

1½ cups apricot paste from 2 cups unsulfured apricots

4 tablespoons lemon juice

3 ripe pears, cut in half, seeds removed, cut in ¼-inch slices

1 tablespoon golden flaxseed, freshly ground

¼ teaspoon Ceylon cinnamon, freshly ground

1 cup buckwheat flour

½ cup *besan* (Bengal gram flour) or chickpea flour

⅛ teaspoon freshly grated nutmeg

½ cup medium Japanese sweet potato, pricked with a fork

1 to 2 tablespoons unsweetened applesauce, if needed

3 red plums, cut in half, pits removed, cut in ¼-inch slices

½ cup red or black grapes

½ cup blackberries

½ cup blueberries

½ cup raspberries

¼ cup of pine nuts

¼ cup pistachio nuts, chopped

¼ cup slivered almonds or chopped walnuts

Pine nuts and/or freshly chopped hazelnuts, or pistachio nuts, for garnish

1. Preheat oven to 375°F.

2. In a small heatproof bowl place the apricots and just cover with water. Microwave for 2 minutes. Alternatively, simmer the apricots in a small pot on the stovetop for 5 minutes. Cool. Purée the softened apricots with the soaking water in a high-speed blender for a minute or until uniformly smooth with the consistency of soft jam.

3. Put the lemon juice in a medium mixing bowl. Prep the pears and add them to the bowl, mixing them well with the lemon juice to retard oxidation.

4. Using a coffee grinder, grind the golden flaxseed into a powder.

5. Then grind the Ceylon cinnamon into a powder.

6. In a food processor bowl combine the flours, flaxseed, and Ceylon cinnamon. Use a nutmeg rasp to grate nutmeg. Pulse to mix.

7. Add 4 tablespoons of the apricot paste.

8. Cook the Japanese sweet potato until fork tender, about 4 minutes in a microwave. Alternatively, bake it in a 425°F degree oven for about 40 minutes, checking at 30 minutes for doneness. Do not overcook or the sweet potato will dry out and become tough. Peel while piping hot, quickly mash, measure ½ cup, and add immediately to the food processor. The steam from the hot sweet potato helps to hydrate and soften the dough. Run on high for at least 2 minutes or until the ingredients gather into a soft dough. If the mix is too dry and fails to gather, add applesauce a tablespoon at a time and reprocess. If the mix is too wet to gather, add buckwheat flour, a tablespoon at a time. The consistency of the dough should be soft and pliant, like Play-Doh.

9. Lightly flour a board with buckwheat flour. Gather the dough into a ball, flatten into a disk. Use a light rolling pin or piece of wooden dowel to roll it ⅛ inch thick, flipping it over as you go and sprinkling a bit more flour, if needed, to prevent sticking.

10. Use a 4-inch cutter or lid to cut out disks. Roll the perimeter of each disk to flatten the dough's perimeter slightly more than its center.

11. If using tart pans, fit each dough disk to a nonstick tart pan. Spread apricot paste on the dough's surface. Arrange the pear and plum slices decoratively. Then fill in with grapes, berries, and nuts, cut in half if they are large. Set each composed tart on cookie sheets, lined with parchment paper, spacing them an inch apart.

12. Alternatively, if you pleat the *crostatine* galette-style, lay each dough disk out on a baking sheet lined with parchment paper. Spread apricot paste on the surface, leaving ½ inch along the perimeter. Lay down the pear and/or plum slices, overlapping, as you like. Enfold the dough around the edges of the fruit, folding the dough in small pleats as you go. Use the smaller fruit and nuts to fill in space decoratively.

13. After all the *crostatine* are composed, thin ½ cup of the apricot paste with water, mixing it well. Using a pastry brush, apply a coat of the diluted apricot paste to glaze the dough and its fruit filling.

14. Bake for 15 minutes. Remove the cookie sheets from the oven. Brush on another coat of apricot glaze.

15. Use an additional piece of parchment paper to lightly cover each cookie sheet and return it to the oven to bake for an additional 10 minutes. The *crostatine* are ready when their crusts are golden and toasted on the edges, and the fruit is soft and juicy.

16. Transfer each pastry to a cooling rack. Apply a final coat of apricot glaze. The fruit will release a fair amount of juice during baking but will congeal as the tarts cool.

17. Garnish with a sprinkling of chopped nuts.

18. *Crostatine* will keep for around 5 days, well wrapped, in the fridge. They also freeze beautifully. To reheat, defrost the tarts and then place them in a preheated 200°F oven for 10 minutes or until warm.

HINT

For an elegant presentation, shape the crostatine in 4.5-inch mini fluted nonstick tart pans, with removable bottoms for easy extraction. Or, for a rustic look, fold the dough edges in little pleats to create an edge to hold the fruit filling and its juices.

DORAYAKI

Any cake that uses beans is a winning formula in my book. *Dorayaki* are simple, homey pancakes filled with *anko*, sweetened adzuki bean paste. I tweaked these *dorayaki* to be cleaner and greener by ditching the milk, eggs, honey, and sugar. They may be a little untraditional, but they're delicious and better for the climate and for us too. Petite red adzuki beans are quite health promoting and very low in fat, and with hefty amounts of fiber, protein, potassium, magnesium, iron, vitamin B_6, and calcium. Enjoy them for breakfast or as a snack or dessert.

On Japan farms, dried beans have a climate footprint of 0.79 kg CO_2eq per kg, 8% from fertilizer production, 13% from N_2O emitted by bacteria on and off the field, 20% from draining wetlands for farming, 21% from deforestation, 7% from the production of soil amendments like limestone and urea, 7% from the production of pesticides used, 11% from running farm machinery, and 8% from drying.

Japan's Climate Performance

Global warming has hit Japan with multiple threats: violent storms, floods, heat, droughts, wildfires. Recent and multiple volcanic eruptions exacerbated Japan's environmental challenges by spewing hot ash, smoke, and vapor into the atmosphere. Japan is a biodiversity hot spot with its ecosystems having suffered over the past fifty years from its land-use practices, air pollution, and the worsening climate picture.[122-124]

Global Carbon Atlas ranked Japan the fifth-highest fossil fuel–emitting country in 2022. Its goal is to reduce GHG emissions by 46% of its 2013 levels by 2030 to reach net-zero emissions by 2050. The Climate Action Tracker rates Japan's overall climate mitigation performance as "insufficient." While it adopted a Green Transformation Basic Policy in 2023 as its strategy to decarbonize its economy, it has placed more emphasis on economic growth and economic security than on renewables and has yet to commit to phasing out coal.

Prep time 1 hour to cook the beans, plus 20 minutes
Cook time 15 minutes │ Makes five 3-inch *Dorayaki*

1 cup dried adzuki beans to make 3 cups cooked

2 cups pitted dates to make about 1½ cups date paste

A pinch of saffron pistils, bloomed

2¼ teaspoons shiro (mild, white) miso paste

1 cup A Better Buttermilk (see page 27)

½ teaspoon ground or whole vanilla bean seeds

1 cup white whole wheat flour

½ teaspoon sodium-free baking soda

1 teaspoon sodium-and-aluminum-free baking powder

1. Rinse the adzuki beans. Place in a pot, cover with water by 2 inches, and bring to a boil. Lower to a simmer and cook for 2 minutes. Turn off the heat, cover, and steep the beans for around 30 minutes, or until they swell and sink in the pot. If the beans are old, they may require more time. Drain, refill the pot, and cook on a low simmer until the adzuki beans are tender but intact, for 20 to 30 minutes. Drain and allow to cool but reserve the cooking water.

2. To make the date paste, cover the pitted dates with water and microwave for 2½ minutes. Keep them submerged and soak for 10 minutes to fully soften. Alternatively, simmer them in water on the stovetop for 5 minutes. Transfer the softened dates with only as much of their soaking water as required into a high-speed blender. Blend for 2 minutes at high speed, scraping down the sides of the bowl after a minute. The paste should be very smooth and rather dense. Transfer the date paste to a bowl.

3. Create the saffron "tea" by crumbling the pistils between your thumb and index fingers into a small bowl. Add a teaspoon of very hot water. The tea will steep until we make the *dorayaki* pancake batter in Step 5.

4. In a high-speed blender combine the cooked adzuki beans, 1⅓ cups date paste, and 2 teaspoons shiro miso paste. Blend on high speed for 2 minutes or until the *anko* adzuki paste is smooth and dense. Add a teaspoon or two of the bean soaking water, if needed, to facilitate blending. The *anko* must be quite dense or it will squeeze out of the *dorayaki*. Taste and adjust the seasonings as you prefer. Transfer the *anko* to a bowl. Rinse and dry the blender bowl.

5. Place the A Better Buttermilk, vanilla seeds, saffron tea, ¼ teaspoon shiro miso, and ¼ cup plus 1½ teaspoons of date paste to the blender bowl. Run for 30 seconds to combine. Now add the white whole wheat flour, baking soda, and baking powder. Run at high speed for 2 minutes, scraping down the sides of the bowl as needed. The batter will thicken as the leavening agents are activated, in about 10 minutes. Transfer the batter to a bowl.

6. Heat a large, good-quality nonstick skillet on low for 5 minutes. When a drop of water flicked across its surface sputters and evaporates, the pan is ready. Note: If the pan is too hot, it will darken the pancakes too much; if the pan is too cool, the pancakes will stick. You can adjust your heat level by testing with the first pancake.

7. Using a ¼ cup measuring cup, scoop up batter and pour onto the preheated skillet, forming a 3-inch circle. Bubbles will form on the surface as CO_2 escapes. When the surface has lost its glossiness and is lightly golden on its edges, use a thin silicone or nylon spatula to flip it over. The underside should be golden, neither too light nor dark. Cook for about a minute on the other side, then transfer to a wooden cutting board. Adjust the heat as needed, wait a minute, and proceed to make the pancakes with the remaining batter.

8. When the pancakes are all cooked and have cooled, spoon about a tablespoon of *anko* paste on the underside of one pancake, cover with another, top side up. With your palms cupping the *dorayaki* gently press the pancakes around their perimeters to round their shape. Remove any excess filling that squeezes out. Wrap tightly with plastic wrap and refrigerate until use. The wrap will help retain *dorayaki*'s classic domed shape.

9. Serve *Dorayaki* at room temp or slightly warmed with a delicious hot cup of green tea.

HINT

Cultured A Better Buttermilk makes particularly delicious, moist dorayaki with greater depth of flavor, but if you don't have time to make it, use 1 cup unsweetened soy milk and eliminate the baking soda.

GRAPE DAINTIES

Elegant, light fruit pastries that are as healthy as they are pretty, Grape Dainties are delightful for breakfast, dessert, teatime, or a snack. Cherries and berries make delicious dainties too. It takes a little time for the dough to develop and to roll and fill the pastry, so this recipe is a perfect rainy-day activity when you are in the mood for arts-and-crafts baking. Making Grape Dainties is fun to share with a friend or with kids too. To better manage your time, make the fig paste and grape glaze in advance.

Grape Dainties give us another opportunity to lower our individual climate footprint by reducing food waste. As long as they are not moldy, overripe grapes that have oversoftened and lost their appeal to eat by the bunch are still perfect candidates for Grape Dainties and are all the juicier.

Grown on U.S. farms, grapes carry a climate footprint of 0.32 kg CO_2eq per kg. The key drivers of emissions on U.S. farms are the use of farm machinery (36%), the application of pesticides (19%), the use of synthetic fertilizers (16%), and the N_2O emissions by bacteria in the fields (15%), draining wetlands for farming (5%), and irrigation (4%).

California Grape's Climate Threats

California ranks among the top U.S. states that have suffered the greatest economic damage from climate-caused disasters. The state's extreme weather over recent years includes droughts, floods, tropical storms, high humidity, wildfires, smoke pollution, and mudslides.[125] Like other produce in America's leading agricultural state, table grape yields have been negatively impacted. One example: In August 2023 Tropical Storm Hilary triggered record-breaking rainfall, humidity, and flash flooding in Southern California and the interior of the state. Table grape growers saw a massive loss in yields of 35% of the grapes that had not yet been harvested by the time the storm hit. Some farms lost their entire grape crop that year.[126]

Prep time 2 hours for the dough to rise, plus 1 hour
Bake time 30 to 40 minutes | Makes 16 to 20

1 cup fig paste
from 1½ cups
dried figs, stems
removed

GRAPE GLAZE

1 (12-ounce) carton
100% grape juice
concentrate,
defrosted

DOUGH

½ cup spring
water, warmed to
body temperature

1 teaspoon active
dry yeast

¾ cup silken tofu,
well-drained

3 to 4 cups whole
wheat pastry flour
or white whole
wheat flour

FILLING

2 cups mixed black
and red seedless
grapes

1. Preheat the oven to 375°F.

2. To make fig paste, place figs in a bowl. Barely cover the figs with boiling water or microwave them on high for 2 minutes, or simmer on a stovetop for 5 minutes. Cool. Blend the rehydrated figs with soaking water in a high-speed blender until very smooth and uniform. The fig paste's consistency should resemble a soft marmalade and be easy to spread with a knife. If it is too dense, dilute with a spoonful of water.

3. To make the grape glaze, pour the defrosted juice concentrate into a small pot and bring to a simmer. Reduce the liquid by half. The glaze is ready when it can coat the back of a teaspoon. Remove from the heat. The grape glaze will continue to thicken as it cools. The consistency should be like maple syrup and easily brushed over pastry. If it overthickens, thin with a spoonful of water.

4. To create the dough, put ½ cup warmed spring water in a medium-sized bowl. Sprinkle on yeast and wait 10 minutes for the yeast to activate.

5. In a high-speed blender, place the silken tofu, run on high for a minute or until it is smooth and creamy. Add the blended tofu to the bowl, mixing it well.

6. Incorporate the flour slowly, mixing it with a Danish dough whisk or a wooden spoon, and eventually using a clean hand. Knead the dough in the bowl for 10 minutes, only adding a small amount of flour as needed to form a very soft, slightly moist, and sticky ball of dough.

7. Flour a board and place the dough on it. Flatten, stretch, and fold the dough several times. Reshape it into a ball, dust it with flour, place it back in the bowl, and cover the bowl with a lid or plastic wrap. Allow the dough to rise in a warm draft-free spot for 2 hours, during which it will expand in volume.

8. Gently transfer the dough back to a lightly floured board. Use a bench scraper or chef knife to divide it into quarters. Keep one out and return the other pieces back to the bowl, covering the bowl to prevent drying.

9. Use a small, light rolling pin or a piece of wooden dowel to roll the dough into a ⅛-inch-thick circle.

10. Use a 9-or 9½-inch pot lid to stamp out a circle. Divide the circle in equal quarters with a pizza cutter or sharp paring knife (see Photo 1).

Photo 1

11. Cover three of the quarters with plastic wrap to prevent drying and leave the fourth on the floured board.

12. Use the paring knife to cut 3 slits on each side, spacing them about ¼ inch apart (see Photo 2).

13. Spread a thin layer of fig paste over the surface and center about 8 grapes in a narrow pyramid as shown in Photo 3. Leave a ¼-inch border below the bottom row of grapes. The number of grapes will depend on their size.

Photo 2

14. Fold the right corner over to cover the grapes (Photo 4).

15. Finally, gently stretch the dough on the left to cover the Grape Dainty. It need not reach all the way to the other side. Seal the dough all along the bottom by pressing it firmly (Photo 5).

16. Line a cookie sheet with parchment paper and transfer each composed dainty to it, spacing them an inch or two apart. Repeat Steps 9 through 15 until all the Grape Dainties are filled.

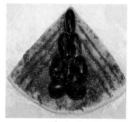

Photo 3

17. Bake for 15 minutes. Remove the baking sheet from the oven. Use a pastry brush to coat the surface of each Dainty with grape glaze. Return the tray to the oven and bake for an additional 20 to 25 minutes, just until the pastry is golden and the grapes have begun to shrivel slightly and release their juices. Do not overbake.

Photo 4

18. Remove the baking tray from the oven. Glaze each Grape Dainty again and transfer them to a cooling rack. As they cool, the grape juices will congeal.

19. Grape Dainties are most delicious when served warm. If you don't serve directly after baking, reheat them in a 200°F oven for 10 minutes, or zap them for 20 seconds in a microwave. Grape Dainties freeze well, but they may be all gone before you need to.

Photo 5

LACY BLACKBERRY CRÊPES

For years Sunday brunch in my family meant whole wheat pancakes with blueberries, but these gorgeous crêpes rewrote that script! The whole gluten-free batter is cooked in the lacelike style of Malaysian roti, roti *jala,* which reveals the jewel-like beauty of the plump blackberry filling. Served in a puddle of blackberry sauce with a glass-like finish, Lacy Blackberry Crêpes look fancy but are very simple to make.

The benchmark climate footprint for fresh berries grown on British farms is 0.20 kg CO_2eq per kg and 0.47 kg CO_2eq per kg in British shops. Berries farmed in Belgium are particularly low emitting at 0.11 kg CO_2eq per kg, and at Belgian retail, frozen berries emit only 0.17 kg CO_2eq per kg in GHG.

Adapting Berry Farming to the Warming Planet

In the past, Oregon was an ideal location to grow strawberries, raspberries, blackberries, marionberries, and boysenberries with its mild, dry early summers. Climate change is altering that calculus, however. Recent heat domes in the Pacific Northwest with triple digit temperatures destroyed half of Oregon's berries in 2021. Grapes in Oregon fared well that year but suffered mightily the year before from the smoke damage from that year's wildfires, which ruined their flavor. With warming trends and smaller snowpack melts from the mountains, adequate water for irrigation has become less reliable. To help them hedge against these climate challenges, some farmers are experimenting with drip irrigation, which better controls the amount of water lost to runoff or evaporation. Others are turning to the traditional Hopi practice of dry farming, whereby different crops that are better adapted to sunny, hot climates are grown together. While yields are smaller, flavors are intensified, and crops can be stored for longer periods after harvest. Others have begun to practice regenerative farming, building soil health to improve water retention and lessen the need for fertilizers. Research is also ongoing to develop heartier berry and other crop variants that are better able to thrive in dryer, hotter environments.[127]

Prep time 30 minutes, plus 2 hours to make soy crème fraîche
Cooking time 20 minutes | Makes about ten 5- to 6-inch crêpes

6 to 8 cups fresh
blackberries

2 cups cultured,
unsweetened soy
yogurt for crème
fraîche garnish

BATTER

1 teaspoon Ceylon
cinnamon, freshly
ground

2 cups mix of your
favorite whole-grain
gluten-free flours, like
buckwheat, oat, teff,
and millet

1 teaspoon ground or
whole vanilla seeds

1 full tablespoon
sodium-and-
aluminum-free baking
powder

¼ teaspoon nutmeg,
freshly grated

1½ cups unsweetened
almond milk or soy milk

PREPARE THE BLACKBERRIES AND SAUCE

1. Rinse the berries and toss them in a saucepan with ⅓ cup of water. Cover and simmer for about 15 minutes, stirring periodically and checking to ensure the fruit isn't dry or overcooked. When ready, the blackberries should be plump, lightened in color from deep purple to magenta, and should have released their juices. Strain the berries and set them aside.

2. Reheat the pot and maintain at a low simmer to reduce the blackberry juice to a thin syrup. The natural pectin in the fruit will thicken the juice and cause it to congeal upon cooling. Remove from the heat when the syrup is dense enough to coat the back of a spoon. Cover and set aside until plating.

MAKE THE CRÈME FRAÎCHE

1. Line a bowl with a square of unbleached muslin. Spoon in the soy yogurt. Tie it up with some string and hang the bag over the sink or over the bowl. Allow it to strain for 2 hours. The longer it drips, the denser your crème fraîche will become. For this dish, 2 hours is sufficient to create a soft tangy mound of crème fraîche for your garnish.

2. Scrape the crème fraîche into a small bowl. Use a mini-whisk and whip it until smooth. Cover and refrigerate the crème fraîche for now.

PREPARE THE BATTER

1. Use a coffee grinder to grind the Ceylon cinnamon into a powder.

2. Combine in a high-speed blender the ground cinnamon, flours, vanilla, and baking powder. Use a nutmeg rasp to grate nutmeg over the blender bowl. Pulse to combine. Now add the milk. Blend for 1 minute until very smooth and entirely lump free.

3. The diameter of your squeeze bottle lid's holes and the density of the batter will determine how well-defined the

crêpes' lacy pattern will be: If the batter is too thin, it will run together and fill in the holes; if it is too dense, you may have trouble squeezing it out of the bottle. Your first crêpe will tell you what you need to know. If it is too thin, add a spoonful of flour and blend it in well. Stir in a spoonful or two of milk if the batter is too thick.

COOK LACY CRÊPES

1. Preheat the oven to 150°F and insert your serving plates to warm.

2. Preheat a nonstick skillet over medium-low heat for 5 minutes. Fill the squeeze bottle with batter.

3. Now the fun begins: You can create all sorts of lacy designs as you gently squeeze the batter into the pan. Small overlapping circles will create a doily-like crêpe, or you can make geometric cross-hatching by adding the batter vertically and then horizontally.

4. Lacy crêpes cook on one side only. Squeeze the bottle into the skillet to design the first crêpe. When the batter loses its sheen and begins to curl up on its edges, pinch an edge of the crêpe to lift it off the pan. Use a thin nylon or silicone spatula if you need help detaching it from the pan.

5. Place the crêpe on a clean kitchen linen or woven mat and cover it immediately with another linen. Covered, the steam released by the hot crêpes will soften them and keep them pliable.

6. Repeat Steps 3 and 4 until all the crêpes are cooked.

FILLING THE CRÊPES AND PLATING

1. Spoon blackberry syrup onto a warm plate to create a shallow puddle.

2. Choose which side of the crêpe to show on its exterior and place that side face down on a cutting board. Spoon on some blackberries and roll the crêpe around them.

3. Transfer to the center of the sauced plate.

4. Garnish with a spoonful of soy crème fraîche. Serve Lacy Blackberry Crêpes warm.

HINT

The traditional tool for making roti jala is a multi-spouted metal funnel. However, I prefer to use a multi-spout squeeze bottle because it allows you to control the flow of batter with precision.

PRETTY APPLE PACKETS

Say goodbye to eco-unfriendly heavy pastry and laminated doughs that are loaded with butter and refined carbs. These delightful apple pastries are simply apples wrapped in a bit of leavened whole-grain dough. Pretty Apple Packets are elegant enough for company, and a green choice for breakfast, brunch, afternoon tea, or dessert. Making these pastries is a playful activity to share with a friend on a rainy day.

Apples grown in U.S. orchards carry a climate footprint of 0.11 kg CO_2eq per kg, with only 6% due to emissions from synthetic fertilizers, 6% from in-field bacteria, and 5% from draining wetlands for farming, 57% from the use of farm machinery, 18% from the application of pesticides, and 5% from irrigation.

Apples' Climate Pressures

Any food that features a carbon-sequestering tree fruit is a boon for the environment. Apples are grown in over half of America, but 63% of the yield comes from Washington State.[128] The Pacific Northwest is facing hotter daytime and nighttime temperatures and more intense heat waves and wildfires, all exacerbated by climate change. Fruit trees like apple trees require cooler evening temperatures to repair and recover. Warmer temperatures negatively affect fruit size, taste, and stability. Like cherry growers, apple growers are employing misters, sunshades, and fruit coatings to mitigate excessive heat.[129]

Prep time 2 hours for dough to rise, plus 40 minutes
Bake time 30 to 40 minutes │ Makes eight to ten 4-inch tarts

½ cup apricot paste from 1 cup unsulfured dried apricots

⅓ cup apple glaze from a 12-ounce carton frozen apple juice concentrate, defrosted

¼ teaspoon Ceylon cinnamon, freshly ground

1 cup unsweetened soy milk, warmed to body temperature

½ teaspoon ground or whole vanilla seeds

1½ teaspoons active dry yeast

2½ to 2¾ cups white whole wheat flour

2 to 3 baking apples (I used pink Lucy Roses for their pretty pink flesh)

Juice from 2 lemons

1. To make the apricot paste, put the dried apricots in a small bowl, cover with water, and microwave for 2 minutes. Alternatively, simmer them in a small saucepan on the stovetop for 5 minutes. Cool. Add the fruit with some of its soaking water to a high-speed blender and purée into a smooth, soft paste with the consistency of jam.

2. To make the apple glaze, empty the contents of a frozen concentrate carton into a small saucepan. Simmer on low until about half the liquid has evaporated. Allow it to cool. The consistency of the apple reduction should be thin enough to easily apply with a pastry brush. If it over-thickens, stir in a teaspoon of water. Any extra glaze can be frozen for up to 3 months.

3. Use a coffee grinder to grind a Ceylon cinnamon quill into a fine powder.

4. Pour the soy milk in a medium ceramic or glass bowl and whisk in 2 tablespoons of apricot paste, vanilla, and ground cinnamon. Microwave the bowl for 30 seconds, or in a small pot on the stovetop, warm slightly to body temperature. Overheating will damage the yeast. Stir in the yeast and wait for 10 minutes for it to activate.

5. Using a Danish dough whisk or a wooden spoon, mix in just enough flour to create a soft, slightly tacky dough. Use a clean hand to knead the dough in the bowl for about 8 minutes. The dough should be smooth. Cover the bowl with a lid or plastic wrap, place it in a warm corner, a proofing box, or in an oven with a proofing setting. Allow the dough to rise for 1½ to 2 hours, during which it will inflate but not double in size.

6. Wash, quarter, core, and cut the apples into ⅛-inch slices.

7. Put lemon juice in a microwaveable bowl and gently stir in the apples. Zap the bowl in a microwave for 2 minutes, or gently simmer on the stovetop for 5 minutes until the apples have softened just enough to become pliant.

8. Preheat the oven to 350°F and position a baking rack on the middle shelf.

9. Divide the dough into nine equal pieces. Keeping the rest well covered to prevent drying, roll the first piece out to ⅛ inch in thickness.

10. Use a sharp paring knife and ruler to cut out a 4-inch square. Wrap the scraps in plastic and reserve them for later.

11. Move your knife ½ inch in from the perimeter and cut right angles at each corner. Each "L" should have "legs" about 1½ inches long (see diagram to the right). Gently lift up each corner to free it from the surrounding dough. Soon we will very gently lift and stretch these thin attached corner strips of dough over the fruit to make pretty dough ribbons to enwrap the apple slices.

12. Spread a thick layer of apricot paste over the dough surface. Lay down about 6 apple slices, staggering them on the dough platform and applying a thin coat of apricot paste between each slice as you overlap them.

13. Pick up two dough corners from opposite sides. Very gently stretch them out, up, and over the fruit and pinch them together to seal the "ribbon." Now pick up the other two opposing dough corners and do the same. Because this dough is whole grain, it is fragile and can tear easily. Don't fret if any of your ribbons break. Just use a little extra dough to patch and smooth the patch.

14. Repeat Steps 9 through 13 until all your dough and apple slices are used. There should be 8 to 10 of them, depending on the dough's thickness.

15. Transfer each apple packet to a baking sheet lined with parchment paper, spacing them an inch apart.

16. Bake them for 10 minutes, then remove the baking sheet and apply a generous amount of apple glaze over the fruit and dough.

17. Return to the oven and bake for 20 minutes. Remove the baking sheet from the oven and apply a second generous coating of apple glaze.

18. Return the tray to the oven for a final 10 minutes of baking. The packets are ready when a knife easily penetrates the apples and the dough is golden. Remove from the oven and brush on the third and final coat of apple glaze.

19. Transfer the pastries to a cooling rack.

20. Pretty Apple Packets are best served warm with your favorite warm beverage.

TORTA DI POLENTA ALL'ARANCIA

Hold the butter, sugar, white flour, and eggs, this is a wholly different approach to Italy's orange-infused polenta cake. Instead, it relies on more eco-friendly, healthier ingredients like puréed orange and an orange juice glaze. The polenta, sweetened with dates and scented with vanilla, Orange Citrus Powder (see page 41), and saffron, is light and moist. This fragrant cake is lovely after a meal, at teatime, and packed in a lunch box. To better manage your time, make the orange paste and glaze in advance.

Oranges grown on U.S. farms have a low climate footprint of 0.11 kg CO_2eq per kg, with 19% of GHG emissions from the production of synthetic fertilizers, 19% produced by in-field bacteria, 6% from off-field bacteria, 11% from the draining of wetlands for farming, 3% from the use of soil amendments like limestone and urea, which release CO_2, 30% from the energy used to run farm power equipment, and 4% from the energy used to irrigate groves.

Florida's Orange Industry's Cautionary Tale

In the United States most oranges are grown today in California and Florida, and to a far lesser extent in Texas and Arizona. Florida's crop has been decimated over the past twenty years due to citrus greening, a bacterial disease spread by the Asian citrus psyllid. Citrus greening turns the fruit green, sour, and inedible. Currently, there is no treatment or cure. This disease, coupled with rising temperatures, droughts, floods, hurricanes, and seawater contamination in irrigation water have damaged 80% of Florida's orange trees.[130, 131]

To put this in perspective, in 2000 Florida produced 233 million boxes of oranges; its 2023 yield was 16.1 million boxes, according to USDA, a drop of 93%. The pathogen is spreading into California, Georgia, Louisiana, Puerto Rico, South Carolina, Texas, and the U.S. Virgin Islands. California, so far, is less impacted although its production has fallen too, from 64 million boxes in 2000 to 45.1 million boxes in 2023, a drop of 30%. The USDA reports that U.S. orange production in 2022–2023 was at an eighty-six-year low. In 2023, the American Farm Bureau Federation stated that all U.S. citrus farmers in general face "an uphill battle to survive."[132, 133]

Prep time 1 hour for orange purée and glaze, plus 30 minutes
Bake time 90 minutes | Makes an 8-inch cake, 6 to 8 servings

1 cup date paste from 1½ cups pitted dates, any variety

1 (12-ounce) carton frozen orange juice concentrate

1 large, ripe, organic orange

1 teaspoon ground or whole vanilla seeds

¼ teaspoon saffron pistils

2 flax eggs, made from 2 tablespoons freshly ground golden flaxseed and 6 tablespoons water

¼ cup aquafaba from the liquid in a (15.5-ounce) can of unsalted chickpeas and a pinch of cream of tartar

Full ¾ cup instant polenta

1 tablespoon sodium-and-aluminum-free baking powder

½ cup white whole wheat flour

1 teaspoon Orange Citrus Powder (see page 41) or zest from 1 large ripe organic orange

½ cup unsweetened almond milk

2 smaller ripe organic oranges, peel and pith removed, cut in ¼-inch slices, to decorate the top

1. To make date paste, place the pitted dates in a small pot, cover with water, simmer for 5 minutes. Alternatively, put them in a small bowl, cover with water, and microwave for 2 minutes. Cool. Use a high-speed blender to purée the dates with some of their soaking water into a smooth, soft paste.

2. To make the orange glaze, empty the carton of frozen orange juice concentrate into a small saucepan. Bring to a gentle simmer. Reduce the liquid by about three-quarters to make orange syrup. It is ready when the syrup lightly coats the back of a spoon. Remove from the heat. The orange reduction will continue to thicken as it cools. Taste. If the glaze is too sour or bitter for your taste, mix in 1 to 2 teaspoons of date paste to balance the flavor.

3. To make orange purée, trim the top and bottom pithy ends of the large, organic orange. Cut in quarters and then cut each quarter in half. Transfer to a pot, just cover with water, add 3 tablespoons of date paste and 1 teaspoon vanilla seeds. Cover and simmer on low, for 45 minutes to 1 hour, stirring occasionally. When ready, the fruit should be extremely soft. Cool slightly. Transfer the cooked orange to a high-speed blender and blend at its highest setting to make a velvety smooth, fragrant purée. Taste and adjust the amount of vanilla and date paste, as needed.

4. To prepare the saffron threads, pulverize them into a powder using a spice grinder or mortar and pestle. Brush the saffron powder into a small bowl with a small bristle brush so you do not waste any. Bloom the saffron into a tea for optimal aroma and flavor by steeping the ground pistils in a few tablespoons of very hot water.

5. To make the flax eggs, combine the freshly ground flaxseed with 6 tablespoons of water in a small bowl, mixing it well. Allow it to thicken, about 10 minutes.

6. To make aquafaba, pour ¼ cup of the viscous liquid from a can of chickpeas into a deep bowl. Using a whisk attachment to an immersion blender or an eggbeater, beat until the liquid becomes foamy. Add a pinch of cream of tartar, about ¹⁄₁₆ teaspoon, and continue whipping the liquid into stiff peaks, about 6 minutes.

7. Preheat the oven to 350°F and place a rack on the middle shelf.

8. Line the bottom and sides of an 8-inch springform cake pan with parchment paper by cutting a disk for the bottom and a 3-inch strip to line the sides of the pan.

9. In a mixing bowl, combine the polenta, baking powder, white whole wheat flour, and Orange Citrus Powder, stirring to combine them well.

10. In another bowl, mix ½ cup date paste, ½ cup orange purée, the flax eggs, almond milk, and saffron tea, stirring well to combine.

11. Pour the wet cake ingredients into the dry ingredients, stirring to combine.

12. Using a silicone spatula, very gently fold the whipped aquafaba into the batter. Then transfer the batter into the lined baking pan.

13. Place the cake pan in the oven on the middle shelf and bake for 30 minutes.

14. Remove the pan and pour a few tablespoons of orange glaze over the top, spreading it evenly with a soft pastry brush. The cake will still be very soft yet, so brush gently. Return the cake to the oven and bake for another 30 minutes before removing the pan to reglaze the cake again.

15. Bake for a final 30 minutes and remove the cake from the oven and reglaze it one final time. Insert a toothpick in the cake's center to test for doneness. When the toothpick comes out clean, the cake is ready. If not, return it to the oven for 5 minutes and retest. When the cake is done, place the baking pan on a cooling rack and cool for 15 to 20 minutes before attempting to release the springform.

16. When the cake is removed from the springform pan, decorate the top with the orange slices.

APPENDIX: RECOMMENDED READING AND RESOURCES

There are so many worthy scientists, climate journalists, and writers working tirelessly to solve the climate crisis and to dispel disinformation that we should learn from and support. Though the following suggestions barely scratch the surface, this list is a good place to start to learn more and join with others.

Books

- Mike Berners-Lee. *There Is No Planet B: A Handbook for the Make or Break Years* (Revised Edition). Cambridge University Press, 2021.
- Christiana Figueres and Tom Rivett-Carnac. *The Future We Choose: Surviving the Climate Crisis.* Vintage, 2020.
- Jeff Goodell. *The Heat Will Kill You First: Life and Death on a Scorched Planet.* Little, Brown and Company, 2023.
- Al Gore. *The Future: Six Drivers of Global Change.* Random House, 2013.
- Paul Hawken (editor). *Drawdown: The Most Comprehensive Plan Ever Proposed to Reverse Global Warming.* Penguin Books, 2017.
- Elizabeth Kolbert. *The Sixth Extinction: An Unnatural History.* Henry Holt and Co., 2014.
- Michael E. Mann. *Our Fragile Moment: How Lessons from Earth's Past Can Help Us Survive the Climate Crisis.* PublicAffairs Books, 2023.
- Bill McKibben. *An Idea Can Go Extinct.* Penguin Books Limited, 2021.
- Hannah Ritchie. *Not the End of the World: How We Can Be the First Generation to Build a Sustainable Planet.* Little, Brown Spark, 2024.
- Mary Robinson. *Climate Justice: Hope, Resilience, and the Fight for a Sustainable Future.* Bloomsbury Publishing, 2018.
- Jonathan Safran Foer. *We Are the Weather: Saving the Planet Begins at Breakfast.* Farrar, Straus and Giroux, 2019.
- David Wallace-Wells. *The Uninhabitable Earth: Life After Warming.* Crown, 2020.
- Bill Weir. *Life as We Know It (Can Be): Stories of People, Climate, and Hope in a Changing World.* Chronicle Prism, 2024.

To Stay Current (many have newsletters that come right to your e-mail inbox)

- Carbon Brief for the latest news and analysis on climate science, energy, and policy— carbonbrief.org

Project Drawdown advances science-based climate solutions by working with businesses and supporting everyday climate grassroots heroes—drawdown.org

Ask NASA Climate for featured articles—climate.nasa.gov/explore/ask-nasa-climate/

NOAA's maps, graphs, and featured articles—climate.gov

Grist for reporting on climate issues, solutions, and equity—grist.org

The Guardian's climate crisis coverage—theguardian.com/environment/climate-crisis

Inside Climate News for reporting on science, politics, and policy—insideclimate-news.org

Climate Desk collates articles from many media outlets—climatedesk.org

World Bank's Development and a Changing Climate blog for news about communities on the front line of the climate crisis—blogs.worldbank.org/climatechange

Union of Concerned Scientists' climate blog, The Equation—blog.ucsusa.org

The UN's Intergovernmental Panel on Climate Change scientific reports—ipcc.ch

World Wildlife Fund's articles on biodiversity, conservation climate crisis, sustainability—worldwildlife.org

The Climate Action Tracker tracks climate actions and policies by governments and measures it against their commitments to the Paris Climate Agreement—climateactiontracker.org

UN's World Meteorological Organization for data, news articles on the climate, economic welfare, and societal security worldwide—wmo.int

Get Involved and Make a Difference

At the September 2023 *New York Times* Climate Forward Event, Al Gore said, "The solutions [to climate change] are gonna come from the grassroots up." Are you wondering what you can do to make a difference? Join with others to learn, share, advocate, and lobby. You can focus internationally, nationally, locally, and in your own backyard as suits your interests and your talents. These organizations are among the most effective and have local chapters.

Citizens' Climate Lobby—globalcitizensclimatelobby.org (trains volunteers to work within their communities and to build relationships with local elected officials)

The Climate Reality Project—climaterealityproject.org (recruits and trains volunteers to work on campaigns to speed the transition to a green economy)

Sunrise Movement—sunrisemovement.org (youth-led)

Third Act—thirdact.org (for those over age 60)

350.org—act350.org (focuses on environmental justice)

NOTES

1. Milman, Oliver. "Global Heating Is Accelerating, Warns Scientist Who Sounded Climate Alarm in the 80s." *The Guardian*, November 2, 2023. https://www.theguardian.com /environment/2023/nov/02/heating-faster-climate-change-greenhouse-james -hansen.

2. Milman, Oliver. "Global Heating Will Pass 1.5C Threshold This Year, Top Ex-NASA Scientist Says." *The Guardian*, January 8, 2024. https://www.theguardian.com/ environment/2024/jan/08/global-temperature-over-1-5-c-climate-change.

3. Carrington, Damian. "World on Brink of Five 'Disastrous' Climate Tipping Points, Study Finds." *The Guardian*, September 8, 2022. https://www.theguardian.com/ environment/2022/sep/08/world-on-brink-five-climate-tipping-points-study-finds.

4. Tandon, Ayesha. "Q&A: Climate Tipping Points Have Put Earth on 'Disastrous Trajectory.' Says New Report." Carbon Brief, December 12, 2023. https://www.carbon brief.org/qa-climate-tipping-points-have-put-earth-on-disastrous-trajectory-says -new-report/.

5. Crippa, M., E. Solazzo, D. Guizzardi, F. Monforti-Ferrario, F. N. Tubiello, and A. Leip. "Food Systems Are Responsible for a Third of Global Anthropogenic GHG Emissions." Nature News, March 8, 2021. https://www.nature.com/articles/s43016-021-00225-9.

6. Climate Nexus. "Animal Agriculture's Impact on Climate Change." November 13, 2019. https://climatenexus.org/climate-issues/food/animal-agricultures-impact-on -climate-change/.

7. Grover, Natalie, and Alex Lawler. "IEA Raises 2024 Oil Demand Forecast but Lags OPEC View." Reuters.com, January 18, 2024. https://www.reuters.com /business/energy/iea-raises-2024-oil-demand-growth-forecast-again-2024-01-18/.

8. Karma, Rogé. "Why the U.S. Is Pumping More Oil Than Any Other Country in History." *The Atlantic*, December 22, 2023. https://www.theatlantic.com/ideas/archive/2023/12 /us-producing-more-oil-climate-change/676893/.

9. Plumer, Brad, and Nadja Popovich. "How the U.S. Became the World's Biggest Gas Supplier." *The New York Times*, February 3, 2024. https://www.nytimes.com/interactive /2024/02/03/climate/us-lng-natural-gas-leader.html.

10. Borst, Ellie. "No, 100 Corporations Do Not Produce 70% of Total Greenhouse Gas Emissions." @politifact, July 22, 2022. https://www.politifact.com/factchecks/2022 /jul/22/instagram-posts/no-100-corporations-do-not-produce-70-total-greenh/.

11. Poore, J., and T. Nemecek. "Reducing Food's Environmental Impacts Through Producers and Consumers." Science.org, June 1, 2018. https://www.science.org/doi/10.1126 /science.aaq0216.

12. Ritchie, Hannah, and Max Roser. "Land Use." Our World in Data, September 2019. https://ourworldindata.org/land-use.

13. Hayek, Matthew N. "The Infectious Disease Trap of Animal Agriculture." *Science Advances*, November 4, 2022. https://pubmed.ncbi.nlm.nih.gov/36322670/.

14. Heredia, Norma, and Santos Garcia. "Animals as Sources of Food-Borne Pathogens: A Review." *Animal Nutrition* [Zhongguo xu mu shou yi xue hui], September 2018. https://pubmed.ncbi.nlm.nih.gov/30175252/.

15. Barnard, Neal D., and Frédéric Leroy. "Children and Adults Should Avoid Consuming Animal Products to Reduce Risk for Chronic Disease: YES." *American Journal of Clinical Nutrition*, October 1, 2020. https://pubmed.ncbi.nlm.nih.gov/32889521/.

16. Gibbs, Joshua, and Francesco P. Cappuccio. "Plant-Based Dietary Patterns for Human and Planetary Health." *Nutrients,* April 13, 2022. https://pubmed.ncbi.nlm.nih.gov/35458176/.

17. Than, Ker. "Could Going Vegan Help Reduce Greenhouse Gas Emissions?" Stanford Doerr School of Sustainability, February 2, 2022. https://sustainability.stanford.edu/news/could-going-vegan-help-reduce-greenhouse-gas-emissions.

18. Yang, John, and Andrew Corkery. "Climate Change Causing a Sense of Despair? Here Are Some Ways to Combat It." PBS, July 30, 2023. https://www.pbs.org/newshour/show/climate-change-causing-a-sense-of-despair-here-are-some-ways-to-combat-it.

19. World Health Organization. "Climate Change." October 12, 2023. https://www.who.int/news-room/fact-sheets/detail/climate-change-and-health.

20. Marchese, David. "You Don't Have to Be Complicit in Our Culture of Destruction." *New York Times*, January 29, 2023. https://www.nytimes.com/interactive/2023/01/30/magazine/robin-wall-kimmerer-interview.html.

21. Foer, Jonathan Safran. *We Are the Weather: Saving the Planet Begins at Breakfast.* New York: Farrar, Straus and Giroux, 2019.

22. Esselstyn, Caldwell B., Jr. "Is Oil Healthy?" *International Journal of Disease Reversal and Prevention* 1, no. 1 (March 19, 2019): 34–36. https://doi.org/10.22230/ijdrp.2019v1n1a35.

23. Ito, Koji. "Review of the Health Benefits of Habitual Consumption of Miso Soup: Focus on the Effects on Sympathetic Nerve Activity, Blood Pressure, and Heart Rate." *Environmental Health and Preventive Medicine*, August 31, 2020. https://pubmed.ncbi.nlm.nih.gov/32867671/.

24. Williams, Jo. "Are Sweeteners Bad for You?" BBC Good Food, June 22, 2023. https://www.bbcgoodfood.com/howto/guide/are-sweeteners-bad-for-you.

25. Arshad, Shiza, Tahniat Rehman, Summaya Saif, Muhammad Shahid Riaz Rajoka, and Muhammad Modassar Ali Nawaz Ranjha. "Replacement of Refined Sugar by Natural

Sweeteners: Focus on Potential Health Benefits." *Heliyon*, September 20, 2022. https://pubmed.ncbi.nlm.nih.gov/36185143/.

26. Hartke, Kristen. "Americans Love Spices. So Why Don't We Grow Them?" NPR, December 26, 2017. https://www.npr.org/sections/thesalt/2017/12/26/572100613/americans-love-spices-so-why-don-t-we-grow-them.

27. Jawad, Ashar. "Top 25 Spice Producing Countries in the World." Yahoo! Finance, September 6, 2023. https://finance.yahoo.com/news/top-25-spice-producing-countries-070939081.html?fr=sycsrp_catchall.

28. Jiang, T. Alan. "Health Benefits of Culinary Herbs and Spices." *Journal of AOAC International*, March 1, 2019. https://pubmed.ncbi.nlm.nih.gov/30651162/.

29. Henriques, Martha. "Spice Trade: How Spices Changed the Ancient World." BBC News, 2019. https://www.bbc.com/future/bespoke/made-on-earth/the-flavours-that-shaped-the-world/.

30. Jampel, Sarah. "Why Some Spices Are So Expensive (& Why You Should Spend the Money)." Food52.com/blog, January 12, 2016. https://food52.com/blog/15514-why-some-spices-are-so-expensive-why-you-should-spend-the-money.

31. Lobo, Christabel. "Why You Should Be Buying Sustainable Spices and Where to Find Them." Allrecipes, March 24, 2021. https://www.allrecipes.com/article/sustainable-spices/.

32. Dordevic, D., H. Butchova, S. Jancikova, B. Macharackova, M. Jarosova, T. Vitez, and I. Kushkevych. "Aluminum Contamination of Food During Culinary Preparation: Case Study with Aluminum Foil and Consumers' Preferences." *Food Science & Nutrition*, September 2019. https://pubmed.ncbi.nlm.nih.gov/31660148/.

33. Hooda, Jagmohan, Ajit Shah, and Li Zhang. "Heme, an Essential Nutrient from Dietary Proteins, Critically Impacts Diverse Physiological and Pathological Processes." *Nutrients* 6, no. 3 (March 13, 2014): 1080–1102. https://doi.org/10.3390/nu6031080.

34. "Protecting Against 'Forever Chemicals.'" News. Harvard T.H. Chan School of Public Health, March 16, 2023. https://www.hsph.harvard.edu/news/hsph-in-the-news/protecting-against-forever-chemicals/#:~:text=Known%20as%20%E2%80%9Cforever%20chemicals%E2%80%9D%20because,%2C%20cosmetics%2C%20and%20toilet%20paper.

35. Loria, Kevin. "You Can't Always Trust Claims on 'Non-Toxic' Cookware." *Consumer Reports*, October 26, 2022. https://www.consumerreports.org/toxic-chemicals-substances/you-cant-always-trust-claims-on-non-toxic-cookware-a4849321487/.

36. CarbonCloud. "The Climate Intelligence Platform." January 24, 2024. https://carbon-cloud.com/.

37. United States Environmental Protection Agency. "What Are the Trends in the Extent and Condition of Wetlands and Their Effects on Human Health and the Environment?" February 27, 2024. https://www.epa.gov/report-environment/wetlands#:~:text=Wetland%20loss%20can%20add%20stress,and%20connectivity%2among%20aquatic%20resources.

38. Ritchie, Hannah, and Max Roser. "Deforestation and Forest Loss." Our World in Data, February 4, 2021. https://ourworldindata.org/deforestation.

39. United States Environmental Protection Agency. "Importance of Methane." EPA, November 1, 2023. https://www.epa.gov/gmi/importance-methane#:~:text=Methane%20is%20the%20second%20most,trapping%20heat%20in%20the%20atmospher.

40. Walhout, Hannah. "When It Comes to Sustainable Spices, 'Single-Origin' Isn't Everything." FoodPrint, September 8, 2023. https://foodprint.org/blog/sustainable-spices/.

41. Vidal, Aurelia. "The Benefits of Using Herbs in Sustainable Landscaping: How Form and Function Can Be Enhanced with Greenery." Coohom.com, July 18, 2023. https://www.coohom.com/article/the-benefits-of-using-herbs-in-sustainable-landscaping.

42. Applequist, W. L., J. A. Brinckmann, A. B. Cunningham, R. E. Hart, M. Heinrich, D. R. Katerere, and T. van Andel. "Scientists' Warning on Climate Change and Medicinal Plants." *Planta Medica*, January 2020. https://pubmed.ncbi.nlm.nih.gov/31731314/.

43. Scott, Michon. "Climate & French Fries." NOAA Climate.gov, November 19, 2020. https://www.climate.gov/news-features/climate-and/climate-french-fries.

44. Desert Research Institute. "Scientists Map Loss of Groundwater Storage Around the World." Phys.org, November 6, 2023. https://phys.org/news/2023-11-scientists-loss-groundwater-storage-world.html.

45. Abnett, Kate. "Explainer: How Climate Change Affects Europe's Farmers." Reuters.com, February 14, 2024. https://www.reuters.com/business/environment/how-climate-change-affects-europes-farmers-2024-02-14/.

46. Walton, Daniel. "A Radical Seed-Breeding Project Could Help Southern Farmers Adapt to Climate Change." Civil Eats, April 18, 2023. https://civileats.com/2023/04/18/a-radical-seed-breeding-project-could-help-southern-farmers-adapt-to-climate-change/.

47. "Nuts about Peanuts." Crop Trust—Securing Our Food, Forever, February 16, 2023. https://www.croptrust.org/news-events/news/nuts-about-peanuts/.

48. Gerretsen, Isabelle. "What Is the Lowest-Carbon Protein?" BBC News, December 15, 2022. https://www.bbc.com/future/article/20221214-what-is-the-lowest-carbon-protein.

49. Harwatt, Helen, Joan Sabaté, Gidon Eshel, Sam Soret, and William Ripple. "Substituting Beans for Beef as a Contribution Toward US Climate Change Targets." *Climatic Change* 143, no. 1–2 (May 11, 2017): 261–270. https://doi.org/10.1007/s10584-017-1969-1.

50. "Climate Expert: Morocco." Sector Project, Sustainable Economic Policy, Deutsche Ge-
sellshaft für Internationale Zusammenarbeit GMBH. Accessed March 7, 2024. https:/
/www.climate-expert.org/en/home/business-adaptation/morocco/.

51. Dwyer, Orla. "Food Waste Makes Up 'half' of Global Food System Emissions." Carbon
Brief, March 13, 2023. https://www.carbonbrief.org/food-waste-makes-up-half
-of-global-food-system-emissions/.

52. Bernstein, Jules. "Black-Eyed Peas Could Help Eliminate Need for Fertilizer." UC
Riverside Center for Plant Cell Biology, January 20, 2022. https://cepceb.ucr.edu
/news/2022/03/18/black-eyed-peas-could-help-eliminate-need-fertilizer.

53. Muzikárová, Soňa. "Eastern Europe Must Not Lag Behind on the Green Transition." Al Jazeera, April 1, 2023. https://www.aljazeera.com/opinions/2023/4/1
/eastern-europe-must-not-lag-behind-on-the-green-transition.

54. Fu, Josie. "The Environmental Controversy Surrounding Heart of Palm." One Green
Planet, August 2023. https://www.onegreenplanet.org/environment/controversy
-heart-of-palm-environmental/.

55. France 24. "Climate Warming Pits Geese Against Farmers in Finland." France 24,
June 17, 2023. https://www.france24.com/en/live-news/20230617-climate-warming
-pits-geese-against-farmers-in-finland.

56. Climate Action Tracker. "Japan." November 30, 2023. https://climateactiontracker.org
/countries/japan/.

57. G20 Climate Risks Atlas. "Japan." G20 Climate Risk Atlas. Accessed March 7, 2024.
https://www.g20climaterisks.org/japan/.

58. Verhoeven, Jos T. A., and Tim L. Setter. "Agricultural Use of Wetlands: Opportunities
and Limitations." *Annals of Botany*, January 2010. https://www.ncbi.nlm.nih.gov
/pmc/articles/PMC2794053/.

59. Wilke, Brook. "Growing Nitrogen with Legume Cover Crops." Michigan State University, W. K. Kellogg Biological Station, KBS Long-Term Agroecosystem Research,
May 10, 2023. https://www.canr.msu.edu/news/growing-nitrogen-with-legume-cover
-crops.

60. "Climate Change in the Indonesian Mind." Yale School of the Environment.
October 11, 2023. https://environment.yale.edu/news/article/climate-change
-indonesian-mind.

61. "Indonesia Climate Change Country Profile: Fact Sheet: Asia." U.S. Agency for
International Development, November 8, 2022. https://www.usaid.gov/climate/
country-profiles/indonesia.

62. Climate Action Tracker. "Indonesia." December 4, 2023. https://climateactiontracker
.org/countries/indonesia/.

63. Fotso, Leslie. "The Sustainability of Superfoods: The Case of Quinoa: Environ-Buzz™ Magazine." EnvironBuzz, June 24, 2022. https://environbuzz.com/the-sustainability-of-superfoods-the-case-of-quinoa/.

64. Schmöckel, Sandra, and Muriel Cozier. "Viewpoint: How Quinoa Exemplifies the Ethical Challenges of Global Agriculture." SCI—Where Science Meets Business, December 11, 2023. https://www.soci.org/news/2023/12/viewpoint-how-quinoa-exemplifies-the-ethical-challenges-of-global-agriculture.

65. Brown, Oli, Antony Froggatt, Natalia Gozak, Nataliya Katser-Buchkovska, and Orysia Lutsevych. "The Consequences of Russia's War on Ukraine for Climate Action, Food Supply and Energy Security, 02 Increasing Ukraine's Vulnerability to Climate Change." Chatham House, September 13, 2023. https://www.chathamhouse.org/2023/09/consequences-russias-war-ukraine-climate-action-food-supply-and-energy-security/02.

66. Bryant, Miranda. "Swedish Government Faces Backlash After Slashing Climate Budget." *The Guardian*, September 21, 2023. https://www.theguardian.com/world/2023/sep/21/swedish-government-faces-backlash-after-slashing-climate-budget.

67. European Investment Bank. "76% of Swedish People in Favour of Stricter Government Measures Imposing Behavioural Changes to Address the Climate Emergency." November 9, 2021. https://www.eib.org/en/press/all/2021-386-76-of-swedish-people-in-favour-of-stricter-government-measures-imposing-behavioural-changes-to-address-the-climate-emergency#:~:text=As%20a%20consequence%2C%20three%2Dquarters,than%20last%20year%2C%2070%25).

68. Arasu, Sibi. "India's Devastating Monsoon Season Is a Sign of Things to Come, as Climate and Poor Planning Combine." AP News, October 1, 2023. https://apnews.com/article/monsoons-climate-change-disasters-india-himalayas-landslides-rains-b1d095811f252ab82268dbefbeef5b3a.

69. Patel, Shivam. "Global Warming Link to Intense Rains in India's Himalayas, Scientists Say." Reuters, August 25, 2023. https://www.reuters.com/business/environment/global-warming-link-intense-rains-indias-himalayas-scientists-2023-08-25/.

70. Nowell, Cecilia. "Diet for a Hotter Climate: Five Plants That Could Help Feed the World." *The Guardian*, August 20, 2022. https://www.theguardian.com/environment/2022/aug/20/ancient-crops-climate-crisis-amaranth-fonio-cowpeas-taro-kernza.

71. British Red Cross. "Flooding in Pakistan: The Latest News." August 30, 2023. https://www.redcross.org.uk/stories/disasters-and-emergencies/world/climate-change-and-pakistan-flooding-affecting-millions#:~:text=More%20than%201%2C700%20people%20lost,are%20being%20hit%20the%20hardest.

72. Baig, Zahid. "Climate Change: Report Says Punjab on List of Most Vulnerable Regions." Business Recorder, July 2, 2023. https://www.brecorder.com/news/40250536#:~

73. Mohan, Vishwa. "Climate Change May Hit Punjab Agri Output by 2050: Study." January 27, 2023. https://timesofindia.indiatimes.com/india/punjab-likely-to-suffer -yield-loss-of-all-major-crops-by-2050-due-to-temp-rise-climate-study/articleshow /97259650.cms.

74. Lo, Joe. "Finland Sets World's Most Ambitious Climate Target in Law." Climate Home News, May 31, 2022. https://www.climatechangenews.com/2022/05/31/finland-sets -worlds-most-ambitious-climate-target-in-law/.

75. Bartholomeusz, Ted. "Rising Sea Levels, Storm Surges and Heavy Rainfall: Outlining the Impacts of Climate Change on Flood Risk in Denmark." PreventionWeb, March 30, 2022. https://www.preventionweb.net/news/rising-sea-levels-storm-surges-and -heavy-rainfall-outlining-impacts-climate-change-flood-risk.

76. Keynoush, Banafsheh. "Iran's Growing Climate Migration Crisis." Middle East Institute, January 30, 2023. https://www.mei.edu/publications/irans-growing -climate-migration-crisis.

77. Esfandiari, Golnaz, and Mohammad Zarghami. "Iran's Climate Migration Crisis Could Turn into National 'Disaster.'" Radio Free Europe / Radio Liberty, December 18, 2023. https://www.rferl.org/a/iran-climate-migrants-crisis/32729538.html.

78. Vaghefi, Saeid Ashraf, Malihe Keykhai, Farshid Jahanbakhshi, Jaleh Sheikholeslami, Azadeh Ahmadi, Hong Yang, and Karim C. Abbaspour. "The Future of Extreme Climate in Iran." Scientific Reports 9, no. 1 (February 6, 2019). https://doi.org/10.1038 /s41598-018-38071-8.

79. Daly, Hannah. "Beef Is Not Sustainable, so Why Are We Subsidising It for Export?" Irish Times, February 2, 2023. https://www.irishtimes.com/science/2023/02/02 /beef-is-not-sustainable-so-why-are-we-subsidising-it-for-export/.

80. Toensmeier, Eric, Rafter Ferguson, and Mamta Mehra. "Perennial Vegetables: A Neglected Resource for Biodiversity, Carbon Sequestration, and Nutrition." PLOS ONE 15, no. 7 (July 10, 2020). https://doi.org/10.1371/journal.pone.0234611.

81. Davis, Alison. "Perennial Grains Could Be the Future of Sustainable Agriculture." Environmental and Energy Study Institute, February 6, 2023. https://www.eesi.org /articles/view/perennial-grains-could-be-the-future-of-sustainable-agriculture.

82. UNESCO World Heritage Centre. "The Sundarbans." Accessed March 8, 2024. https:/ /whc.unesco.org/en/list/798/.

83. Subramanian, Aishwarya, Aditya Mosur Nagarajan, Sruthi Vinod, Samarshi Chakraborty, Krishanasamy Sivagami, Thomas Theodore, Sri Shalini Sathyanarayanan, Perumal Tamizhdurai, and V. L. Mangesh. "Long-Term Impacts of Climate Change on

Coastal and Transitional Eco-Systems in India: An Overview of Its Current Status, Future Projections, Solutions, and Policies." *RSC Advances* 13, no. 18 (April 17, 2023): 12204–28. https://doi.org/10.1039/d2ra07448f.

84. "Winter Chill Brings Summer Fruit: Climate Central." Climate Matters Climate Central, February 15, 2023. https://www.climatecentral.org/graphic/winter -chill-brings-summer-fruit- 2023?graphicSet=Chill%2BMatters&lang=en.

85. University of California Agriculture and Natural Resources. "Almonds." Agricultural Irrigation Water Management. Accessed March 8, 2024. https://ucmanagedrought .ucdavis.edu/Agriculture/Crop_Irrigation_Strategies/Almonds/.

86. California Department of Water Resources. "Major Milestone to Achieving Sustainable Groundwater Management." January 13, 2022. https://water.ca.gov/News/Blog/2022 /January/Major-Milestone-to-Achieving-Sustainable-Groundwater-Management.

87. Sandalow, David, Michael Meidan, Philip Andrews-Speed, Anders Hove, Sally Qiu, and Edmund Downie. "The Guide to Chinese Climate Policy 2022." Oxford Institute for Energy Studies. https://www.oxfordenergy.org/publications/the -guide-to-chinese-climate-policy-2022/.

88. Jara, Mariela. "Peru Faces Challenge of Climate Change-Driven Internal Migration." ReliefWeb, September 28, 2023. https://reliefweb.int/report/peru/peru-faces -challenge-climate-change-driven-internal-migration.

89. MacKenzie, Jill. "Cover Crops and Green Manures in Home Gardens." University of Minnesota Extension, 2018. https://extension.umn.edu/managing-soil-and-nutrients /cover-crops-and-green-manures.

90. "Erosion." U.S. Department of Agriculture Climate Hubs. Accessed March 9, 2024. https://www.climatehubs.usda.gov/climate-impacts/erosion?page=2.

91. "Coastal Erosion in Puglia, Italy." Greenpeace, April 10, 2018. https://media.green -peace.org/archive/Coastal-Erosion-in-Puglia-Italy-27MZIFJWCEE00.html.

92. Climate Adapt. "Protecting Outdoor Agricultural Workers from Extreme Heat in Puglia, Southern Italy." European Climate Adaptation Platform Climate— Adapt, European Commission and European Environment Agency, 2022. https:/ /climate-adapt.eea.europa.eu/en/metadata/case-studies/protecting-outdoor -agricultural-workers-from-extreme-heat-in-puglia.

93. "Squash: The Canary in the Crop Field?" Growing Communities, November 10, 2020. https://growingcommunities.org/blog/2020/11/squash-canary-veg-field.

94. Howarth, Grace. "What Is the Carbon Footprint of Tomatoes? A Life-Cycle Analysis." Impactful Ninja, January 26, 2024. https://impactful.ninja/what-is -the-carbon-footprint-of-tomatoes/.

95. Wells, Caleigh. "Greenhouse Tomatoes Use Less Water. Why Aren't There More?: Greater La." KCRW, September 14, 2022. https://www.kcrw.com/news/shows/greater -la/greenhouse-crops-homeless-mental-health/drought-hydroponic-tomatoes #:~:text=As%20the%20drought%20drags%20on,for%20some%20farmers%20than %20ever.

96. Hossain, Md Saddam, Md Nahidul Islam, Md Mamunur Rahman, Mohammad Golam Mostofa, and Md Arifur Khan. "Sorghum: A Prospective Crop for Climatic Vulnerability, Food and Nutritional Security." *Journal of Agriculture and Food Research* 8 (June 2022): 100300. https://doi.org/10.1016/j.jafr.2022.100300.

97. Cronin, Dana. "An Ancient Grain Made New Again: How Sorghum Could Help U.S. Farms Adapt to Climate Change." Civil Eats, February 7, 2023. https://civileats .com/2023/02/07/an-ancient-grain-made-new-again-how-sorghum-could-help-u -s-farms-adapt-to-climate-change/.

98. Chemtob, Danielle. "Forbes Daily: Pepper Shortage Sends Sriracha Prices Soaring." Forbes, June 27, 2023. https://www.forbes.com/sites/daniellechemtob/2023/06/27 /forbes-daily-pepper-shortage-sends-sriracha-prices-soaring/?sh=5aef5c8a6ba9.

99. Radwin, Maxwell. "Mexico Kills Climate Change Fund, Casting Doubt on Future Environmental Spending." Mongabay Environmental News, April 13, 2023. https:// news.mongabay.com/2023/04/mexico-kills-climate-change-fund-casting-doubt-on -future-environmental-spending/.

100. Rani, Anju, Poonam Devi, Uday Chand Jha, Kamal Dev Sharma, Kadambot H. Siddique, and Harsh Nayyar. "Developing Climate-Resilient Chickpea Involving Physiological and Molecular Approaches with a Focus on Temperature and Drought Stresses." *Frontiers in Plant Science* 10 (February 24, 2020). https://doi.org/10.3389 /fpls.2019.01759.

101. Ramanujan, Krishna. "Broccoli Looks More Like Cauliflower in a Warmer World." *Cornell Chronicle*, Cornell University, January 9, 2023. https://news.cornell.edu/stories /2023/01/broccoli-looks-more-cauliflower-warmer-world.

102. "29 out of 33 Gujarat Districts in the Crosshairs of Extreme Climate Events." Daijiworld.com, August 20, 2023. https://www.daijiworld.com/news/newsDisplay ?newsID=1111875.

103. Sonaiya, Janvi. "Gujarat Confronts Climate Crisis: Alarming Heat Waves, Extreme Weather." *India Tribune*, January 14, 2024. https://indiatribune.com/gujarat -confronts-climate-crisis-alarming-heat-waves-extreme-weather/.

104. Shah, Jumana. "Why Gujarat Farmers Are Staring at Thousands of Crores of Crop Losses." *India Today*, May 4, 2023. https://www.indiatoday.in/india-today -insight/story/why-gujarat-farmers-are-staring-at-thousands-of-crores-of-crop -losses-2368571-2023-05-04.

105. Cohen, Patricia, and Violette Franchi. "In Provence, Winemakers Confront Climate Change." *New York Times*, October 7, 2023. https://www.nytimes .com/2023/10/07/business/economy/wine-climate-change-provence.html #:~:text=Centuries%2Dold%20varieties%20are%20being,a%20winery%20in %20Crestet%2C%20France.

106. Editors of Encyclopaedia Britannica. "Barley." March 5, 2024. https://www .britannica.com/plant/barley-cereal.

107. Waite, Richard, Tim Searchinger, Janet Ranganathan, and Jessica Zionts. "6 Pressing Questions About Beef and Climate Change, Answered." World Resources Institute, March 7, 2022. https://www.wri.org/insights/6-pressing -questions-about-beef-and-climate-change-answered.

108. Bhoyar, Ajay, and Ilinca Anghelescu. "Climate Change in Poultry Production." The Poultry Site, July 24, 2023. https://www.thepoultrysite.com/articles/climate -change-in-poultry-production.

109. Teirstein, Zoya. "As Climate Change Disrupts Ecosystems, a New Outbreak of Bird Flu Spreads to Mammals." Grist, February 10, 2023. https://grist.org/health/as-climate -change-disrupts-ecosystems-a-new-outbreak-of-bird-flu-spreads-to-mammals/.

110. Martínez-Goñi, Xabier Simón, Jon Miranda-Apodaca, and Usue Pérez-López. "Could Buckwheat and Spelt Be Alternatives to Wheat Under Future Environmental Conditions? Study of Their Physiological Response to Drought." *Agricultural Water Management* 278 (March 2023): 108176. https://doi.org/10.1016/j.agwat.2023.108176.

111. Hoplamazian, Mara. "Humans Need New Crops That Can Survive Climate Change. Buckwheat Could Be a Contender." New Hampshire Public Radio, November 1, 2023. https://www.nhpr.org/nh-news/2023-11-01/humans-need-new-food-crops-that -can-survive-climate-change-buckwheat-could-be-a-contender.

112. Stanway, David, and Stephen Coates. "China Vows to Adapt Better to Climate Change as Risks Soar." *Reuters,* June 13, 2022. https://www.reuters.com/world/china /china-vows-adapt-better-climate-change-risks-soar-2022-06-14/.

113. Ghaffari, Bita. "Saffron Supplies Dry Up as Climate Change Shrivels Iran's 'Desert Gold.' Extreme Weather Has Halved Production in the Biggest Supplier of the World's Most Expensive Spice." *Financial Times*, December 26, 2023. https://www.ft.com /content/418a677c-8eaf-4537-9dd6-6ba311cb35ae.

114. Yale Climate Connections Team. "Are Sweet Potatoes a Climate-Resilient Crop of the Future? Yale Center for Environmental Communication, Yale School of the Environment, November 23, 2023. https://yaleclimateconnections.org/2023/11 /are-sweet-potatoes-a-climate-resilient-crop-of-the-future/.

115. Maru, Joyce. "The Prize-Winning Sweet Potato Helping Farmers Respond to Climate Change." Bill & Melinda Gates Foundation, November 15, 2023. https://www.gatesfoundation.org/ideas/articles/sweet-potato-climate-adaptation-cop28.

116. Baumhardt, Alex. "Oregon Cherry Growers Ask Governor for Disaster Declaration After 3rd Bad Season in a Row." Oregon Public Broadcasting, August 7, 2023. https://www.opb.org/article/2023/08/07/oregon-cherry-season-climate-change-farming/.

117. Crowe, Michael. "Climate Change Is Pushing Pacific Northwest Farmers to Protect Crops from Extreme Heat." Civil Eats, December 5, 2022. https://civileats.com/2022/12/05/climate-change-is-pushing-pacific-northwest-farmers-to-protect-crops-from-extreme-heat/.

118. Food Empowerment Project. "F.E.P.'s Chocolate List." March 9, 2024. https://foodispower.org/chocolate-list/.

119. Nazaryan, Alexander. "Climate Change Is Threatening Your Thanksgiving Cranberries." Yahoo! News, November 22, 2023. https://au.news.yahoo.com/climate-change-is-threatening-your-thanksgiving-cranberries-212816791.html.

120. U.S. Department of Agriculture. "USDA Research Seeks to Strengthen Cranberry Resiliency as Climate Change Affects Production." USDA Agricultural Research Service, December 14, 2021. https://www.ars.usda.gov/news-events/news/research-news/2021/usda-research-seeks-to-strengthen-cranberry-resiliency-as-climate-change-affects-production/.

121. Reeves, Laura A., Michael P. D. Garratt, Michelle T. Fountain, and Deepa Senapathi. "Climate-Induced Phenological Shifts in Pears—a Crop of Economic Importance in the UK." *Agriculture, Ecosystems & Environment* 338 (October 15, 2022): 108109. https://doi.org/10.1016/j.agee.2022.108109.

122. G20 Climate Risk Atlas. "Japan." Centro Euro-Mediterraneo sui Cambiamenti Climatici, October 28, 2021. https://www.g20climaterisks.org/japan/.

123. Browning, Oliver. "Japanese Volcano Spews Ash and Smoke in Spectacular Eruption." *Independent*, November 29, 2023. https://www.independent.co.uk/tv/climate/volcano-eruption-japan-niijima-pacific-ocean-b2455440.html.

124. TOKI Team. "Biodiversity in Japan: A Review of Conservation Efforts and Challenges." *TOKI* (blog). September 13, 2023.

125. Lazo, Alejandro. "No Place Is Safe: New National Report on Climate Change Details Sweeping Effects." CalMatters, November 14, 2023. https://calmatters.org/environment/climate-change/2023/11/climate-change-california-national-climate-assessment/.

126. Media, Malcolm. "California Table Grape Growers Report Significant Loss due to Summer Storm." *American Vineyard Magazine*, August 30, 2023. https:/

/americanvineyardmagazine.com/california-table-grape-growers-report-significant
-loss-due-to-summer-storm/.

127. Waldroupe, Amanda. "Hotter, Drier, and Less Predictable, How Oregon Farmers Are
Adapting to Climate Change." Oregon Humanities, December 15, 2021. https://or-
egonhumanities.org/rll/magazine/beyond-fallwinter-2021/hotter-drier-and-less
-predictable/.

128. Edmisten, Mike. "Discover the 10 U.S. States That Grow the Most Apples." A-Z Animals, October 23, 2023. https://a-z-animals.com/blog/discover-the-u-s-states-that
-grow-the-most-apples/.

129. Crowe. "Climate Change Is Pushing Pacific Northwest Farmers to Protect Crops from
Extreme Heat."

130. Smith, Summer. "Citrus Greening Devastates Florida's Orange Crops." WWSB TV,
July 21, 2022. https://www.mysuncoast.com/2022/07/21/citrus-greening-devastates
-floridas-orange-crops/.

131. Blake, Talia. "Florida's Citrus Industry Continues to Struggle Plagued by Disease and
Weather." WMFE, October 24, 2023. https://www.wmfe.org/economy/2023-10-24
/orange-you-glad-i-didnt-say-banana-the-impact-of-citrus-on-the-economy.

132. Munch, Daniel. "U.S. Citrus Production—an Uphill Battle to Survive." American
Farm Bureau Federation, April 25, 2023. https://www.fb.org/market-intel/u-s-citrus
-production-an-uphill-battle-to-survive.

133. Johnson, Lydia. "California Orange Production Predicted to Exceed Florida for the
First Time." AgriPulse Communications, March 5, 2023. https://www.agri-pulse.com
/articles/19345-california-orange-production-predicted-to-exceed-florida-for
-the-first-time.

INDEX

ACKNOWLEDGMENTS

I t takes a village, as they say, and this project would not have seen the light of day if not for the support of many generous people who care deeply about the climate crisis.

I thank my partner in all things, my husband, Giordano, with whom I spent many happy hours cooking, plating, and photographing these recipes. "We eat first with our eyes," Apicius, the ancient Roman gourmand, rightly observed, and Giordano's photographic artistry captures each dish in its most evocative light. His photos are the backbone of this book.

My book agents, Lary Rosenblatt and Barbara Stewart, of 22 MediaWorks enthusiastically believed in my vision for this climate-focused cookbook from the get-go and helped bring it to fruition. They supported the project every step of the way and have gone several extra innings to ensure its success.

It was a propitious day when HCI Books asked to publish this work. I couldn't have asked for a more congenial, productive collaboration with my editor, Darcie Abbene, and art director, Larissa Henoch. This talented duo curated my raw recipes into an enticing and practical guide to save the planet a bite at a time. Thanks to public relations director Lindsey Triebel for arranging the launching of this book and helping it find its way to you.

A special heartfelt thanks to potter Jo Chess for her gorgeous, colorful ceramics and for the sleek Schönwald porcelain provided by Libbey Foodservice, both of which appear throughout the book.

The public would be in even graver danger if not for the dedication of the individuals who keep us informed about the real and urgent dangers of climate change. The tireless, determined efforts of the world's climatologists, climate scientists, economists, writers, and climate journalists inspired me to take on this mantle too but through the lens of sustainable cooking.

Finally, as a chef, I owe a great deal to the countless home cooks worldwide who generation after generation have preserved their rich culinary traditions, creatively using the simplest, humblest fruits of the earth from field, orchard, and woodlands to nourish and sustain their families.

ABOUT THE AUTHOR

Cathy Katin-Grazzini is a sustainable chef and author of *Love the Foods That Love the Planet: Recipes to Cool the Climate and Excite the Senses* (Health Communications, Inc., 2024) and *Love the Foods That Love You Back: Clean, Healthy, Vegan Recipes for Everyone* (Rizzoli International Publications, Inc., 2022). From 2017 to 2022 Cathy was Food Editor for *VEGWORLD Magazine.*

On her blog, cathyskitchenprescription.com, Cathy shares climate-friendly recipes from around the world. She offers guidance on how to eat and cook to lower our individual climate footprints and to improve our health outcomes. Cathy has worked as a culinary teacher, lifestyle coach, and personal chef, and has run corporate employee wellness programs. She is a Climate Reality Leader and supports the initiatives of Third Act, Citizens' Climate Lobby, 350.org, and the Plant Based Treaty.

In 2024 Cathy participated in Climate Reality Leadership Corps training in New York City. In 2015 Cathy was certified in Plant-Based Nutrition from the T. Colin Campbell Center for Nutrition Studies at Cornell and completed professional culinary training at Rouxbe Cooking School. She is a member of the Physicians Committee for Responsible Medicine (PCRM) and trained as a PCRM Food for Life instructor. She and her husband, Giordano Katin-Grazzini, who photographed the cookbook, live in Ridgefield, Connecticut.

http://www.cathyskitchenprescription.com/

https://www.instagram.com/cathyskitchenprescription/

https://www.facebook.com/cathyskitchenprescription/

https://www.linkedin.com/in/cathyskitchenprescription/